THE
DEATH
of
DONNA
WHALEN

ALSO BY
MICHAEL WINTER

Creaking in Their Skins

One Last Good Look

This All Happened

The Big Why

The Architects Are Here

Michael Winter

THE DEATH

of DONNA

WHALEN

HAMISH HAMILTON
CANADA

HAMISH HAMILTON CANADA

Published by the Penguin Group

Penguin Group (Canada), 90 Eglinton Avenue East, Suite 700, Toronto, Ontario, Canada M4P 2Y3
(a division of Pearson Canada Inc.)

Penguin Group (USA) Inc., 375 Hudson Street, New York, New York 10014, U.S.A.
Penguin Books Ltd, 80 Strand, London WC2R 0RL, England
Penguin Ireland, 25 St Stephen's Green, Dublin 2, Ireland (a division of Penguin Books Ltd)
Penguin Group (Australia), 250 Camberwell Road, Camberwell, Victoria 3124, Australia
(a division of Pearson Australia Group Pty Ltd)
Penguin Books India Pvt Ltd, 11 Community Centre, Panchsheel Park, New Delhi – 110 017, India
Penguin Group (NZ), 67 Apollo Drive, Rosedale, North Shore 0745, Auckland, New Zealand
(a division of Pearson New Zealand Ltd)
Penguin Books (South Africa) (Pty) Ltd, 24 Sturdee Avenue, Rosebank,
Johannesburg 2196, South Africa

Penguin Books Ltd, Registered Offices: 80 Strand, London WC2R 0RL, England

First published 2010

1 2 3 4 5 6 7 8 9 10 (RRD)

Copyright © Michael Winter, 2010

Manufactured in the U.S.A.

LIBRARY AND ARCHIVES CANADA CATALOGUING IN PUBLICATION

Winter, Michael, 1965-
The death of Donna Whalen / Michael Winter.

ISBN 978-0-670-06663-6

I. Title.

PS8595.I624D43 2010   C813'.54   C2010-904056-2

Visit the Penguin Group (Canada) website at **www.penguin.ca**

Special and corporate bulk purchase rates available; please see
www.penguin.ca/corporatesales or call 1-800-810-3104, ext. 2477 or 2474

I beseech you, in the bowels of Christ,
think it possible you may be mistaken.

OLIVER CROMWELL

FOREWORD

There was a murder in the city I lived in. Donna Whalen was stabbed thirty-one times in her apartment on Empire Avenue. We all knew about it—it was in the newspapers and on the radio and television for months. I walked the same streets the victim walked, and often passed the house where the murder happened. Her boyfriend, Sheldon Troke, was charged with her murder. I looked up the newspaper reports and talked to people who worked on various aspects of the trial—St John's is a small place. I got my hands on the court transcripts. I received print copies of the wiretaps that were referred to in the trial. It occurred to me that I could write about this murder and conviction in an updated version of Truman Capote's method. I was excited about dramatizing a true event. I was deep into the narrative and then, during times when I was not at work on the story, a cold emotion ambushed me: I didnt like how I felt about what I was writing. The events were disturbing, and I was using someone's tragedy for personal gain. There was a dead, innocent woman at the centre. She had been alive, really alive. The family of Donna Whalen is still around, and who was I to turn their suffering into fiction that, if lauded, was praise to me— who needed that? So I put the manuscript away. I gave up on it and wrote other things. But then some afternoons I'd find the boxes of transcripts on the top shelf of my cupboard and be drawn to them. I'd stand on my toes and flick through photocopied testimony, my face very close to the voices of those who loved Donna Whalen and those who loved Sheldon Troke. There were voices in here that were professional—police, lawyers, forensic experts, medical doctors and the trial judge—and these voices reminded me of Edgar Lee Masters's *Spoon River Anthology*. There were also men and women who were intentionally deceptive, or in one case, losing her mind, and those biased or mistaken opinions put me in mind of Faulkner's characters in *As I Lay Dying*. I needed these previous examples of unconventional storytelling to assure me that there was something accumulating here, a wedge into the human condition that was truer and more vivid than what I could fabricate, some modern story that, while it was in the public domain, wasnt being read by the public.

D.H. Lawrence writes that a book which is not a copy of other books has its own construction, and this suited my treatment of this event—I felt a compulsion to encourage people to read about this trial in a documentary fictional form. I got the boxes down again, and read the preliminary hearings, the voir dire evidence and witness statements, the interviews with police informants, the newspaper reports and search warrants and doctors' notes, the diaries and press releases and private letters, the transcripts of the victim's tape recorder, the police wiretaps and their continuation reports. I spoke pages of it out loud and decided I could not improve on the sheer naked truth of it. There is power in witness testimony, overheard dialogue and private letters, and any intrusion on my part seemed to muddy that power. So, from ten thousand pages of documents, I selected eighty thousand words. I have dramatized scenes by converting testimony into the third person. I have changed the names and locations and merged similar characters.

And so here I present, in as unvarnished a form as possible, what it feels like to have someone murdered in a community that has never known much violence, how the legal system works or doesnt work in conditions that provoke a murder, and what that murder unleashes. I am taking that on because it is important to understand what the repercussions of such an act are once the shock has worn off, as well as capturing the way people speak and the nuances of class and sexism, and how hatred and prejudice and complacency arise. Even portraying the bureaucracy of social services and hospitals and prisons and the intricacies of the law and how the law can double back and bite its own ass. What fear is. A book full of the voices of people who know something tangential to darkness, paragraphs that funnel towards the shock of realizing they are part of a murder trial and will admit to anything, as long as you dont suggest they were an accessory to murder. A succinct snapshot into the life of a neighbourhood, *your* neighbourhood, and how that neighbourhood can be coerced into saying things that satisfy the very forces that are in place to supposedly protect the neighbourhood.

I hope what we have here is a story that is respectful to those who recognize, or had to experience, the true events within this fiction. Readers should judge this book as a work of documentary fiction and not a recreation of fact, though I do hope this selected and rearranged narrative reveals some truths about people and their predicaments without altering the essentials of the events that led up to, and followed, the death of Donna Whalen.

I

FAMILY *and* NEIGHBOURS

Ruth was out hanging clothes and Donna come down and started hanging up clothes. They talked for a minute and Ruth said to her your clothes is awful wet and Donna said the spinner is broke.

I'll take it in the house and spin it out, Ruth said.

No, Donna said, that's okay.

It's only a couple of minutes and it's done.

It would dry quicker on the line because it was kind of late in the afternoon and they just started talking.

That was probably a year and a half before she died. Donna would tell Ruth about Sheldon Troke. A scattered time Ruth saw him around Donna's apartment. He said hello, good day, very casual like, no sitting down and having a big conversation or anything.

That Friday Donna Whalen came out of the house and Ruth Vivian said hello. Donna was a bit excited, she was going to Ontario for a wedding. I bought a new dress and a pair of black shoes, she said. She was to get the purse and the slip the next day. She said, Ruth come up and I'll show it to you. Donna went ahead and Ruth Vivian came up behind her. She seen the dress.

Later on her son, Tom, was out in the back fooling around with a car and Ruth had the door open. She was at the kitchen table. It was hot and she opened two side windows and went over to the sink then she heard the swearing. She came out the door and sung out Tom, come in out of it, because the language if you heard it. She sung out to him and he didnt come in so Ruth stood up in their landing and looked over and Sheldon Troke was on the end of the house and his hand was going—he was hitting the side of the house and he was really mad and Ruth thought he was coming towards the house. You slut, he said, you will never get to the mainland. She called Tom up again and closed the back door. She said Tom, did you hear that? Bastard and cocksuckers and stuff like this. He said Mom, what are talking about. And Ruth said come on we go out to the store. They come out the front door and walked down Empire. Mabel Edicott was on her doorstep and Ruth talked to her about going to bingo that night. Ruth never mentioned what she heard out of Sheldon Troke because she figured it was no one else's business, like you learn to stay out of it. And that is all she thought of it. When you hear rackets in around there, you close your door and hope and pray it will go away. You dont get involved. If anybody shouts, Ruth gets nervous like she got to get away from anybody shouting. When theyre mad they dont even know, theyre just rhyming it out of them. Ruth does it when she's mad.

She went out later to country bingo with Mabel Edicott, on the corner of Rickett's Road and there behind Buckmaster Circle. All you got to do is go straight up over the hill and cut down Aldershot by the Salvation Army and go to the Circle.

She won the letter X. It was a hundred and fifty dollars. They came home right away because Ruth is a real gambler, if she stayed she'd be buying Nevada tickets all night so the minute they sung out the last game, she didnt even wait for them to call back, they were out through the door.

They got a taxi home. If there's anybody going in their way they chip in on a taxi and they get home a lot quicker. It was pretty warm outside and when she opened the door, the heat was on ninety. Ruth said to her husband, Pat, the night like this and the damn heat on ninety and he made a sarcastic remark he said it won't hurt you—this kind of way. Youre home early tonight, he said, you didnt win. Ruth said I won fifty dollars and she said to Mabel Edicott dont tell him the difference. Pat put the silly grin on his face so Ruth went down the store and bought him a few beers. She wasnt gone no more than five minutes, just across the street, pick up a half-dozen beer, but he never had the heat turned off. So they got in a few words. Ruth was just about gone with the heat. She went in the kitchen with Mabel Edicott and they sat down and had a game of queens. The clock is in the kitchen, it didnt dawn on Ruth to look at it and then she said to Mabel, it's one oclock already—I got to get up the morning. Mabel said I wants to get out and get some air. Ruth said oh, Jesus, he got the heat on again. I'm going to kill him in the morning. She was on the pissy side. Most married couples fight over money, Ruth and Pat fight over heat like the devil.

Mabel got ready and she went off and Ruth locked the front door, she went back to her bedroom, got her nightdress out from underneath the pillow and got a wash. Pat was after being up and putting the heat on again, and she let the roar out of her. She opened the front door. She never had on her glasses. The glasses were on top of the entertainment centre in the living room. She could walk right in front of a car because to her everything is far away until she puts her glasses on and then it brings it up to normal.

She was stood up by the door and all of a sudden this voice said you must find it awful hot. It was Donna Whalen.

Ruth said, The son of a bitch got the heat on ninety again tonight.

I'm froze to death, Donna said.

I'm dead with the heat, Ruth said, but I'm starting to get the cold shivers now. And Donna said, I can't wait to go up and put on my jammies and curl up in a blanket on the chesterfield.

Ruth started to shake. I'd better go in, she said, I'm freezing now. And Ruth closed the door and went back to the kitchen and sat down with a puzzle book and then went on to bed. She's terrible with times, especially when she gets into a puzzle. The house could burn down when she gets into them, she dont pay no mind to time.

MABEL EDICOTT

Mabel works up to Holy Heart. She's in the cafeteria. Back then she wasnt working at all. That night she was to her sister's on Rankin Street and she got home around suppertime. Then she went to bingo with Ruth Vivian and played cards with her over at the Vivians'. When she got home her son Keith was there with her two nephews and they were down in the room listening to music and carrying on.

The nephews left a little after one. Mabel straightened up a bit because they had coffee and then she turned on channel 10 and the movie was on and herself and Keith sat down to watch it.

There was this knock on the back door, a soft knock. She went out to the kitchen and answered the door and it was a young fellow asked for Donna. He had blond hair, very nice looking, he was about as tall as Keith, and his hair was cut short to the sides and he was clean shaven except he had a moustache. He had on a jacket.

A soft knock. She had to move the portable dryer out of the way to open the door. That's the only place you could put it in the kitchen. They have no laundry rooms in the apartments theyre in. He asked for Donna and she said she lives next door and she pointed to next door and then she closed the door and locked it and put the dryer back again.

She thought he knocked on the door next door, but she didnt hear any door open or close. Ten or fifteen minutes later, it sounded like if youre changing around the front room and youre moving and youre dragging a table or a heavy chair.

KIM PARROTT

Kim and Donna grew up together, they went to school together, they kind of got married together. Kim's known Donna to take medication but only once that you could tell it had an effect, and that was on the telephone—Donna was home going to bed. She did take pills every day. At first she was telling Kim that it was for back pain and then she told her that if Sheldon was gone the pills would be gone.

That Friday Kim had to take her son, Nicholas, to the doctor. Donna came in, they were talking, and she played a tape recorder. It had one of those small tapes in it. They listened to a few parts of it. The voices on the tape were Donna and Sheldon and they were from the night before. They listened to the tape for about an hour. They werent constantly listening, it was rewinding, fast-forwarding, listening. Donna was trying to find one in particular part, where Sheldon was accusing her of going with Kim every Friday night, calling them sluts. Donna was doing her fingernails. Kim felt Donna used to go home and start something with Sheldon. Kim told her not to be so foolish and Donna said, When you gets a phone call telling you I'm dead, then you'll believe me.

They went down to Donna's in her car. Kim had Nicholas with her. Donna had to pick up a letter for Housing. She went in to her house and Kim stayed out in the car with Nicholas. Kim, where the sun was shining through the kitchen window, she could see Donna's shape stood up and she was gesturing with her hands, talking to someone.

When Donna came out she was yelling and screaming that Kim had told Sheldon she was at Jacob Parrott's going-away party. Jacob is Kim's ex-husband. Donna threatened to haul Kim's head off. Kim said what's wrong with you—she didnt talk to Sheldon, and then Donna couldnt figure out how he found out about it. Sheldon had said he'd figured it out for himself.

They went to Dr Galgay's office on Water Street. Kim brought Nicholas in to get his eyes checked. Donna went in and got some valium. Kim saw the doctor too and got Atasol 30, for Donna. Kim went to doctors with Donna two times a month. Kim didnt use them herself. Some months she didnt go at all. She was supposed to get a special type of pills for back pain and nerves. Kim stopped doing it because she thought she was making a fool of herself going in and asking for things that she didnt need. If Kim did have to explain it, she only had to explain it once and then if you went back to the same doctor, all you got to do is ask for a refill on your pills.

Donna was getting gigantic quantities of pills. She shared them with her neighbours, Ruth and Pat and their son, Tom Vivian. She gave some to Sheldon. If someone asked her for some, she'd give it to them.

Donna dropped the letter off at Housing and then they were on their way to the supermarket. They stopped into a store and Donna got something for her father, Aubrey Whalen, and dropped it off at the graveyard on Blackmarsh Road. An apple flip and a can of Pepsi.

They went to the supermarket on Ropewalk Lane. Donna was shoplifting in there. Kim dont remember what she stole. Food. Then Delta Drugstore. They were there long enough to get the prescription filled. Then to Kim's house. Then Donna had to go home and cook supper.

That night she came over again to do some laundry. Donna had gotten a bed that she bought off Kim's father-in-law and Donna wanted Kim to get in touch with him. Two bureaus and the frame of the bed had been delivered. It was only the boxspring and mattress that wasnt there. Donna wanted it before she left to go to a wedding on the mainland so Sheldon could sleep in a bed instead of on the chesterfield.

This was about eight oclock. Kim had a headache so she asked Donna for an Atasol. She had nothing with her, just her purse. She had the tape recorder in her purse. On the tape Sheldon came out of the bathroom and spoke about a couple of people that Kim couldnt pick out. Then Sheldon asked who Rod's friends were. That's Kim's boyfriend, Rod Tessier. Sheldon said their graves are sunk.

Some parts of the tape were hard to pick out because Donna had the recorder covered over. One part of the tape you hear Donna say what are you doing Sheldon. This is where Sheldon is in the bedroom knocking items off the dresser. He was trying to fix the doily that was on her bureau and he ended up knocking stuff over. He was on something. There was a part about how Sheldon spoke about flowers. Sheldon was thinking about his brother Raymond, Donna said. Sheldon was going to Raymond's grave with flowers.

Sheldon had an extra set of keys to the house and Donna wanted to get away from him because she was afraid of him. She used the excuse to Housing that someone had died in her bathtub.

She told Kim last summer that Sheldon and herself and the kids went to Bowring Park and walked around the park holding hands. This is the only nice thing that Kim knows of that happened between them.

That Friday night they were talking about relationships, boyfriends, daily life. About violence they've been through, and it's nice to be able to talk about it every once in a while. Sheldon had gone into the kitchen and taken a knife and stabbed it into her coffee table saying that he had done it before and he'd do it again. Donna was serious when she spoke about that. She didnt laugh. It was unusual for them to have a serious conversation. Donna was afraid that Sheldon was going to show up at Kim's house looking for her. Every time the cat walked by the window or a bag blew by she would jump up thinking it was Sheldon, and Kim kept telling her calm down Sheldon's gone home, he is gone to bed and sit down relax, have your cup of tea. That didnt help, she kept being jumpy.

Donna told Kim not to mention the tape to anybody. She didnt want nobody to know about it. She was afraid if Sheldon found out he'd think she was going to use it against him. One week Donna wanted to have babies, next week she wanted to get rid of him. Once you get involved with the Trokes you can't get rid of them, Donna said. No way out of the relationship, not just Sheldon, with the whole family, the way she put it.

On Saturday morning Donna's mother phoned and said, Donna's dead. Kim didnt know what she was talking about, if she was dead or if someone wanted to beat up on her. So Kim phoned Donna's house. She left Donna a message. It went along the lines of she was worried about her and asked her to pick up the phone.

Sheldon Troke phoned Kim that Saturday evening. Was Donna seeing anybody or did Kim know of anything that could help him find out what happened and Kim told him no. Sheldon told Kim that Donna's daughter, Sharon, thinks he done it.

Kim has seen Donna with a black eye and a mark over her eyelid and she felt lumps on her head a few times. Donna said Sheldon hit her. She had a black eye, mostly underneath her eye. You wouldnt be able to cover it up. If she put enough foundation on but it would have to be a lot. Donna just said it was a set of keys being flinged at her. Sheldon flung them.

When Donna was leaving that Friday night she said goodbye, take care of yourself. Donna gave Kim a hug and she left. That was unusual. Donna didnt show emotion very well. They used to be really close, past couple of years they havent been. For her to leave giving her a hug take care of yourself is really strange.

SHELDON TROKE

Before Sheldon moved in they used to argue. He was always gone and he used to tell Donna that he done a number of years in jail, and he'd like to get out with his friends and they argued because some mornings he'd leave and didnt come back until three oclock in the morning and some nights he didnt come back at all. He tried to change it and just go to Buckmaster Circle in the daytimes. Everybody comes in the Circle to buy drugs, especially acid. They go downtown to the clubs and to parties. Then Sheldon started going downtown again with his friends and they'd fight over that.

Sheldon drank like a fish. Donna she'd come to the Circle and hear his friends talking. She got along well with his friends. She laughed and she was curious. How much do hash and acid cost and how much do you sell it for and who do you get it off. They used to argue over that too. Sometimes it was just passing comments in a sarcastic way. Sometimes they'd get loud.

When he moved in he moved all his clothes in there. He moved the waterbed in. Everything he had.

One afternoon they were out driving and they hauled into Needs Convenience. They rented a movie for the kids and one for themselves. They got back to the apartment. Donna got a phone call and while she was on the phone she said, Sheldon, there's a girl in Mount Pearl is having a baby shower. You wouldnt mind if I went in? He found out later it wasnt a baby shower. It was a going-away party for Jacob Parrott.

Friday morning he was on the chesterfield at Donna's. Sharon woke him up and said that her grandmother wanted him on the phone. Mrs Whalen asked him was he going to work and Sheldon said yes. I'll call, she said, when Mister leaves. Sheldon lay down on the chesterfield and went back to sleep. The next thing the youngsters were up and the TV was on. Cory was out in the kitchen having breakfast. Donna was sot in the chair watching TV. Donna was telling Cory to hurry up, the school bus would be soon and he was asking her questions like he do every morning and he went on to school and Sharon went on to school and later on Donna's mother showed up. They went out in the kitchen and Mrs Whalen yelled out, she said I thought you were given up drinking and Sheldon said it was just this one last time and she started laughing and her and Donna was laughing, telling her mother about the way he was getting on last night. Then she told her about someone out at the back window. Missus asked was he going to go into work. Sheldon said yes he was going to get Donna to give him a run home to get changed and she said, Aw, forget about it, dont go going in today.

Donna phoned Kim Parrott and she left and went to Kim's. Donna wasnt gone too long and the phone rang. Sheldon thought it was Donna phoning back so he got up and answered the phone and it was Madeline Ryall looking for Donna. She asked would Donna have a pill for her and Sheldon told her he wouldnt know and she explained what she wanted it for and he told her to call Donna back suppertime. He lay down on the chesterfield again. The phone rang again and this time he didnt answer because Donna's phone can ring thirty times a day. It was Jacob Parrott. He said the boat is docked. Not long after that the phone rang for the third time. It's Donna's mother. When he went to answer the phone, Mrs Whalen was after hanging up. He called her back and she told him Sharon phoned her and Donna never dropped the money off for Sharon at school for dinner and so he told Mrs Whalen if Sharon calls back, tell her to come home for dinner. Sharon come home, she got a cheese sandwich, some juice. After having something to eat she was telling him things about school and she went on back to school.

It was going for after one when Donna came home. Kim was out in the car. Donna asked who told him about her going to Jacob Parrott's going-away party and Sheldon said he figured it out for himself. Last night, she said, you told me it was Kim Parrott. Dont mind me when I'm drinking, he said, and Donna said I'm going to go out there and haul the head off her.

It was common for Donna to move her hands. It's not Kim's first time ever seeing her do that.

She left again with Kim. Sharon come home from school about ten after three, she asked him was it all right to go out around the door. Sheldon said yes, but dont go going far. Donna come back again with bottles of Big 8 and she put them in the fridge and left again. Cory come home and then Sharon wasnt there so he went out around the door looking for Sharon.

About suppertime Donna showed up. Then Madeline Ryall opened the door and yelled out and Donna was at the top of the steps and Madeline come up and asked Donna about a purse. Donna said to bring it back when she was finished. Who's going with you, she asked, and Madeline told her and Donna yelled out you'll be into that next and she said into what? and Donna laughed and said homosexual activity—have a cold one for me.

The youngsters come in. Donna got their supper. Cory wanted to go back out and play again and Donna told him he couldnt and he got mad. You can go in Sharon's room and play, she said. Donna was sat down in the living room having a cigarette and then she got Cory ready for bed. Sharon was in her room doing her homework. Around seven-thirty the phone rang. Donna asked Sheldon to answer the phone. If it's Jacob Parrott I'm not here, she said. Sheldon said no, I'm not answering the phone. Sharon answered the phone and it was Jacob and Sharon said something about ten-thirty. Donna said she was going to Kim's. This was about quarter to eight. She left. Around five minutes to nine Sharon come out and asked where her mother was at and Donna was just after hauling up in front of the door. Your mother's downstairs, Sheldon said. Can I go in and watch TV in Mommy's room? He said yes.

Donna asked if Kim phoned. I thought you were into Kim's, he said. I went into Kim's, she said, and Kim wasnt home so I went into her mother-in-law's. That's the Tessiers. Kim was trying to get ahold of Rod's father. He had a pickup and there was a load of gyproc in the pickup and the day before this he could not bring out a boxspring and mattress. Donna was getting upset, this was supposed to be there yesterday and here it is, still not here. Sharon come out of her mother's room and said she was watching the same show they were watching and Donna asked her how she was watching it. In your room, she said, and Donna said I told you not to go in there. Sheldon said, Donna it's my fault, I didnt know.

Sharon went on to bed, it was nine-thirty. Donna phoned Kim again and after she finished she phoned her mother. He and Donna were talking about the show on TV. He'd seen it before. There was a commercial come on at ten to ten and he asked Donna for a run home and she said yes, she was going to suggest that. They were over by the bathroom putting on their sneakers and the phone rings and instead of answering it, Donna lets it ring out and then Kim comes on the line. I still never got ahold of Rod's father, she's saying. Sheldon with his sneakers on. Donna has her sneakers on. They go down over the steps, Sheldon first. Donna locked the door. They got in the car. They sot there for about a minute and let the car warm up. Sheldon can see the outline of one of the Vivians that was sot on the chesterfield. He thought it was Mister. They left there to go into Sheldon's house. On the way in, Donna turned her head. She looked over at the club, First City. Sheldon asked her was she going home. She said she didnt know. Sheldon said what about the youngsters and she said Tom Vivian's going to keep an eye to them. Youre going to lose the youngsters, Sheldon said. And after saying that he realized he shouldnt have said it.

They kept driving in Kenmount Road and got on Farrell Drive. There's a left you take and Donna slowed down but she didnt take the turn. What are you doing, he said. I have to see something, she said. They got down a little farther and she slowed again and she looked at a house and they drove down farther and then there's another turn and she took it and come up around and dropped him off. When he was getting out of the car he said I'll see you tomorrow.

She looked at a house. Sheldon pointed it out to a police officer, on the side of the road going down.

As he was walking in he didnt look back but Donna was driving away. He took off his jacket and sneakers and walked in the hall and looked in the living room and asked his parents what they were doing and they were watching *JFK*. He went in and rolled a cigarette. He was talking about the *JFK*. His father got a phone call and so when Sheldon finished the cigarette he went back out and got a glass of birch beer. He drank that and started walking by the hallway and said good night to his mother and she asked if he had work in the morning and he said yes, and he went up and got in bed and went to sleep. That was Friday night.

KIM PARROTT

Donna and Sheldon had an argument on the way in the road. It started off with Donna slowing down in front of First City, looking for a car, giving some kind of impression that she was going there after she dropped him off. Donna told Kim she had done this to tease him. Sheldon said if she didnt watch out she might lose the children. Donna left them alone a lot, Kim would call there and Sharon might answer and say Mom wasnt home. When Donna was at Kim's house she'd phone home and talk to Sharon. Kim doesnt make no phone calls to anybody's house after ten, she thinks it's very ignorant. But she'd call in the early evening, and Donna was out the majority of times.

Madeline Ryall's a fortune teller. Madeline told Donna she was going to have two more children, but it wasnt with Sheldon Troke. She give Madeline pills. Donna got whacked out on pills herself. Kim warned her a few times dont come to my house in that kind of state, it's not good for the children to see. Donna tried to stay away when she was on too many. Talking to her on the phone it was really hard to understand her. She was afraid of the Trokes. The Trokes make you nervous. Every time Kim would go for a walk, she'd see one of them or she sits on her step and they drive up and down the road. They werent harassing her or anything, they were just going on with their regular lively routine. But constantly seeing the Trokes bothered her.

BERTHA TROKE

A few times when her son was drunk he used to phone Donna and Donna would hang up on him and he'd phone her again and she'd hang up on him again and he'd be mad about that. There'd be no conversation because just as he go and say Donna she'd hang up and she'd keep hanging up on him.

Donna was at court watching a trial and Bertha Troke was there. They had a twenty-minute recess. Donna said to Bertha that her and Sheldon were no longer going out together and Sheldon was a boarder and Bertha was stunned. In order to gain her mother's friendship, Donna said, she had to get Sheldon out of her life because her mother—that's Agnes—thought more about Sheldon than she did of her. Donna was getting on with her life and Bertha said to her sure youre out every night and Sheldon is babysitting. Donna thought about that. I am gone every night aint I. She said that's a sin I'm going to stay home tonight. Then she said well Sheldon dont go out anyway because he goes to work in the morning and when I gets home in the nighttime Sheldon dont ask me where I'm at and if he's asleep the next day he dont ask what time I got home. She looked at Bertha. Youre mad with me now arent you? And Bertha said Donna I'm not mad, why would I be mad with you? But what about the two babies you were going to have?

She mentioned there was a guy at the Health Science and he had a tumour on the brain, Bertha doesnt know his name. She used to go visit him frequent and Sheldon used to babysit for her to go in. She used to go with him. Sheldon even gave Donna money to bring him in stuff.

ALBERT CANNING

Albert had a relationship with Donna Whalen in Grand Falls six years ago. Donna was taking a course at the trade school and staying with her aunt Edie. Albert went out with her for nine months. She was the only lady that he was seeing at the time. They shared both his house and her aunt's house. They were together quite often.

He doesnt know Sheldon Troke. Never met him or spoken to him.

Albert visited Donna in St John's. He didnt come to town very often, once or twice maybe.

The only thing he recalls of Donna using was diet pills.

Albert experienced a grand mal seizure and was at the Grand Falls Hospital for five days. He was transferred by ambulance to the Health Sciences Complex and underwent some tests and was diagnosed with a brain tumour. He was in hospital four and a half months.

Donna visited. Three or four times, five at the most. She told him she was seeing some guy by the name of Sheldon. That was pretty well it. She used to visit Sheldon in jail. Sheldon was aware of her visits to the hospital. The visits were no more than a half-hour, forty-five minutes. Donna's mother was on the next floor. She'd visit her mother Agnes and come up and see Albert or he'd be down visiting her mother and she'd come in.

Just after her mother was discharged the visits stopped. Albert underwent thirty-five treatments of radiotherapy. He lost some of his hair. He was taking steroids and that made him put on a bit of weight.

He visited Donna once at her apartment after that, but she wasnt home. Her aunt Edie was there. He had a cup of tea with Edie. The house was very tidy and clean. Donna was that way. Donna wouldnt be the type to leave a pair of rubber gloves on the kitchen floor. She was a pretty organized lady. She was a smoker when Albert saw her but not a heavy drinker. Occasionally they'd go out to a club, but Donna was not the type of person to get drunk. She was seeing a doctor, a Dr Galgay.

HUBERT GALGAY

Donna Whalen was a patient since she was thirteen. Dr Galgay saw her through her first pregnancy and delivered her first child. She was a healthy person. The last time he saw her she was fairly distraught about some housing problems and things with her kids, but the main reason for her distress was her relationship with Sheldon Troke. The relationship had been on shaky grounds for a number of years and now she was quite worried about her safety. Her mother, Agnes Whalen, seemed to downplay Donna's concerns about the whole issue. Donna was trying to terminate the relationship. Sheldon did not agree. It was the source of a fair number of unpleasant scenes—he was aggressive and menacing, especially when he was drinking. He said the next time she tried to get away from him she wouldnt be leaving under her own steam. She was afraid that he would knock her about.

Donna was a stoic person. She didnt display a lot of emotion. But this time she was worried. Sheldon showed up at her apartment enraged. Voices were raised and Sheldon threatened.

There wasnt a play area for her son at Donna's place, and Cory's a fairly active kid. He tends to wander off at times. A previous occupant of her apartment had died in the bathtub from a seizure and drowned and this spooked her.

In the last going-off she mentioned that her moving house would give her an opportunity to get away from Sheldon and terminate the relationship by that means.

Dr Galgay knew that she had seen other doctors in the city to obtain prescriptions for codeine, valium, cough mixtures, diet pills. She was also using hashish.

Donna was fairly stable. She wasnt weepy but frustrated. Things were in the works as far as the housing authorities, and she was hoping to make a complete break with Sheldon. He had pushed her against the wall during a heated discussion after which he went to his parole officer.

Dr Galgay prescribed a turbuhaler for asthma and some Atasol. These things are not addictive. On that last visit he prescribed nothing. He did a letter for Housing. Donna was aware that he was not going to prescribe her medication. She was using excessive drugs—Lomotil, for instance, is an opiate derivative used to manage bowel disorders, a disorder Donna did not have. Dr Galgay never saw her under the influence of drugs and some of these medications were obtained for the purpose of selling. Herself and friends were involved in obtaining these prescriptions from various doctors and outpatient departments.

SHELDON TROKE

Donna was after buying things. She bought that bedroom suite off Rod Tessier's father, and she also bought a microwave oven from a girl who owed her forty dollars. Donna gave Sheldon no indication that she was going up to Toronto and staying. She asked him to sand the dressers so she could paint them black. Donna asked about certain areas of town. There was apartments across from Kmart on Torbay and right across the street there's a building and she was thinking about moving over there, but it's a highway and cars are just zimming back and forth and when Cory gets older, he can go across a street and get into a car. That's why she wanted to move. They talked about Buckmaster Circle and Sheldon said look you sees what goes on at Buckmaster Circle, and she said well, what about down on the bottom?

Donna used to go to First City. She called it uptown, country and western music. Sheldon wasnt into country music. One time him and Donna were broke up about a month and Donna come over and said that's some friend you got—your friend's trying to slap the make on me. Sheldon said who and she told him and he said do you want to go with me or do you want to go with him? And they got back together that night.

Sheldon got arrested one time for drinking. He was really drunk on Water Street and had a quarter ounce of hash on him. He got picked up and went back to jail for that. Donna told him, If you dont start coming home at a reasonable hour, I'm going to lock you out. He wasnt taking her serious. He come home one night about four in the morning really drunk and he knocked on the door and there was no answer and he knocked again. He booted the door in and went over the steps. He went out in the back hall and booted that door in. Donna wasnt in bed and he figured she was in bed with Cory but she wasnt there, so he assumed they were all in Sharon's room.

The next morning Donna woke him up and asked him why did he boot the doors in. It dawned on him that they'd all been over to her mother's so he felt foolish. I'm a carpenter, he said. I can fix the doors. He hauled his pants on and walked out in the living room and her mother was there. Agnes was shaking her head, laughing at him. He asked Donna, Want to put me on some breakfast? and she looked at him and said when you come home last night you had wings and chips, why dont you put that in the microwave?

He was back in jail and released in September. He come out of the Cotton Club drunk. The police know if he's walking down the road or driving and they sees him, they know who he is and that he's got drinking restrictions.

One night him and Joey Yetman went over to Buckmaster Circle and got really drunk. The next day Donna is there and Sheldon's sister Iris and Sheldon was asking Joey how he got home last night and Joey said he didnt know. There was a girl brought Joey home and later on Sheldon and Donna started arguing about that and Donna thought they were with girls, but it was Iris that give Joey the run home because Iris lives down from Joey.

They went on a tear one weekend up to Joey's house and Donna found out and they were arguing about that. Joey Yetman has a girlfriend and there was a couple of times that Donna come up to

the Circle and there's a Cuban girl talking to Joey and Donna asked
Sheldon if Joey was going out with her and Sheldon said he didnt
know.

When he first started going out with Donna, Rod Tessier used to
go to Donna's house. Rod and Donna had a fight. When Sheldon
was in jail, Donna asked him to ask Rod not to come around the
house any more. So Sheldon asked him and a couple of months later,
Donna said that Tess was going to beat her up. Rod has a sister that
people call Tess but Sheldon thought Donna was talking about Rod
because they call him Tess too. Rod come up in the Circle one day
and he was sot in his car and Sheldon was down in the car having a
few words and he ended up giving Rod a punch in the face, but it was
the wrong Tess.

BERTHA TROKE

Bertha knew Donna Whalen very well. She first met her at Cathy
Furneaux's. Cathy used to go with Bertha's son Raymond. Bertha used
to go back and forth to Cathy's and this day Donna was there. Donna
was a very friendly person and she asked Bertha did she know her
mother Agnes and they got to talking.

While Sheldon was in Springhill Institution, Bertha mentioned
Donna's name and he asked her who she was and Bertha told him
and he said he thought he knew her brother Clifford. Then Donna
was talking to Sheldon on the phone at Cathy Furneaux's. This was
coming close to when Sheldon was getting out and he asked Donna to
go to a movie with him.

It was a couple of days after Sheldon got out that Bertha seen
Donna at Cathy's. Donna had been really nervous about the first time
meeting Sheldon. Shy like. They were going to a movie.

Donna and Sheldon came to the house quite a bit. The first time it would have been not too long after they had gone to the movie. It was in the morning and the two of them were alone. The children came to the house too. Donna used to call Sheldon her old moose. That was a name she had on him.

Donna talked about Vicki Pinhorn. Sheldon used to go steady with Vicki and she asked Bertha did she think Sheldon still cared about Vicki.

He moved in and then they broke up. Bertha can't even call it breaking up because tonight Donna would say we're broke up and tomorrow theyre back together and that was the way it was, broke up tonight and back tomorrow.

Sheldon was sent back a few times towards the penitentiary and Donna visited him. She was afraid she was going to miss his phone call. One day she said that Sheldon didnt love her. Other guys looked at her and Sheldon didnt mind. Bertha said, Sheldon isnt the jealous type.

Most definitely Donna was jealous. Bertha's been there when she've asked people of certain places was Sheldon there, was there any girls there, and even at Bertha's house if Sheldon dropped in Donna asked were there girls there. Donna made no bones about it.

There was a big confusion over a pair of men's underwear, they were black and red and they ended up with Sheldon's clothes and Donna was really mad over them. Bertha said to her why youre mad over a pair of men's underwear, if it was women's I could understand. Donna said theyre not Sheldon's. And Bertha thought about it, they were Paul's. That's Sheldon's brother. Paul had two pairs, blue and red, and so Donna asked how come they would be with Sheldon's clothes and Bertha said the way they are theyre back and forth and they can wear each other's clothes. But she was really mad about it. He could have taken a shower out to Cathy's and maybe he put them on out there. Donna checked it out after. She asked Cathy.

Donna visited Bertha's house a lot, then that pattern changed the last three months before Donna died. She kept out of contact with them all. Bertha give up phoning her and leaving messages. The last time she saw Donna was late in April and she was at the house with Sheldon one afternoon. Sheldon came in to get a loan of a video and Donna kept saying I got to make a run. She said it over and over again and it come to the point that Bertha wanted to call her out in the kitchen and ask her where have you got to go that's so important. She was agitated. Sheldon said, Donna if you wants to go I'll get a way home, and she said no I'll wait for you but she kept walking around and saying it, I got to make a run. She looked worried.

Sheldon telephoned one day wanting to know Dr Galgay's number. Donna was with Sheldon's sister, Iris. Bertha told him Iris wouldnt have been at Dr Galgay's. She mentioned what doctor they could have been to, because Donna had been gone all day and Sheldon was waiting for her to come home to go out. He was babysitting. Iris had to get the kind of pills that Donna wanted and Donna had to get the kind of pills that Iris wanted and they couldnt be seen together in to the hospital. Bertha told them they were crazy. Donna told Iris to say she had a toothache and it was really paining and even if it come to the point that she had to cry, and Iris told Donna to say she had the diarrhea really bad and she couldnt stop going to the bathroom. They could be in there for half the night getting pills.

Bertha only met Kim Parrott once. She used to hear her name all the time but Bertha didnt know any of Donna's friends. Donna told Bertha that Kim Parrott could get diet pills for her until she got too noticeable when she was having Nicholas.

SHELDON TROKE

Sheldon did not know Donna right away. The first one he met in the Whalen family was Clifford. He'd see Donna going back and forth to the store. There was a white store and there was times they used to go down around Pippy Park. That's where Donna was from. Sheldon hung around with a girl Sears and Donna hung around with this girl Sears her younger sister.

The next time he spoke with Donna he was at Westmorland. It's a correctional centre. For a couple of years Sheldon never had much contact with his family because he was away and in there he figured he didnt need that. He was getting released on mandatory supervision at the end of May. He started phoning his family and when he phoned he learned that his brother Raymond was going out with Cathy Furneaux. So he was phoning Cathy's house and talking to Raymond, and Sheldon asked who was there and Donna Whalen was there and Sheldon said, I think I knows her. He spoke with Donna on the phone. He had three or four conversations with her and got her number off her and he phoned her at her house one night.

He was released from Westmorland and he arrived in Newfoundland the same day. He went to Cathy Furneaux's house and that's where he met Donna. It was uncomfortable because they didnt know each other so they just hung around talking and then they left and went to the Avalon Mall and watched a movie. When the movie was over, they went downtown.

They were walking down George Street, there was a girl he used to see, Vicki Pinhorn. He was talking to her for a minute, just saying hello. They went on through a laneway into the La Scala, this was around twelve because the club never opened until one minute after midnight. Sheldon was having a beer. Eugene Driscoll come in and they were talking and then all the regulars. This is Sheldon's first time in this club in a couple of years. Another friend come in and Sheldon got a gram of coke off him. They left, him and Donna, and went into Donna's house. Sheldon spent the night at Donna's. Her children werent there, they were at her mother's.

Sheldon took this gram of coke and cut it up into six lines. He snorted two and gave Donna the bill that's rolled up and she snorted one. Now for the whole two years that he knew Donna, he never seen her have any dealings with cocaine. If he seen Donna drunk twice that would be stretching it.

After that first date they got along good. Donna knew a lot of people that he knew. Joey Yetman was just after getting out of jail, six to eight months before Sheldon did, and he was going back and forth to Donna's house with this blond guy Jacob Parrott.

When Sheldon first met Donna, he cannot say Donna done a lot of prescription pills. When youre in jail, a lot of inmates do valiums. You dont hear tell of people doing Atasols or Tylenols. Sheldon got some off Donna. The first time he took them he got stomach sick. He was drinking beer and got the heaves. So Donna gave him Gravol to stop the upset.

He can't say Donna took any more pills than the rest of them. She took them on a daily basis. Only twice was Donna really buzzed. One time Sheldon come back and there was a glass of Pepsi on the arm of the chesterfield and there was ice cubes still in it. Donna was sot on the chesterfield. She had her feet up on the coffee table and there was a cigarette in her hand and the cigarette was burned down.

KIM PARROTT

Sheldon was always well behaved except for one time. The night they came back from the christening. Donna was Nicholas's godmother, the christening was at Mary Queen of Peace. They went then into Rod's mother's house and Rod wasnt there so Kim walked over to his father's because they live next door to each other, it's not in the same house. There was a big car parked in front. Sheldon was in it. Kim went back over to Mrs Tessier's and Donna was coming out through the door but Sheldon was stood up in front of her. Sheldon asked Donna to wait in the bathroom. So she was in the bathroom and got tired of waiting and when she was coming out one of Rod's brothers was there and they called out to her. She went back to see what they wanted and before she could leave the house everybody came over. Donna was holding on to her chin and she was crying and Kim asked her what was wrong. Sheldon had hit her with the palm of his hand and drove her out the hall a little bit.

Rod came in to get the keys for Sheldon and Donna said to Rod he's going to hit you, dont go out. The two of them were out in the garden and Sheldon hit Rod. Sheldon came back and told Donna to come on so they left and they went home. Rod's ear swelled up. Sheldon came back the next day and apologized to Rod, Kim was even afraid to let him in. Rod's brother yelled out and said he was with him.

The next day Donna told her there was construction on Elizabeth Avenue around Churchill Park and Sheldon was driving crazy. Donna had her feet on the dash and her head between her knees and he was driving through signs and on the wrong side of the road and cars were blowing the horn. He was saying something to Donna about being in the house with five men.

Donna took threats serious. She wouldnt go home. She went up to the hospital where her mother was and her mother phoned and told Sheldon that Donna wasnt coming home so she stayed at Kim's house.

Donna was a bit conceited, yes. If she walked by some men she'd mention to you oh look theyre looking at me. She was a bit paranoid too. She thought Kim was telling people things and it got back to Sheldon. About her and Jacob Parrott and how Donna was robbing food with Rod Tessier for Sheldon's lunches. Sheldon knew that she got caught shoplifting but he never found out about it for two weeks before she died. Sheldon didnt want her getting in trouble, he had a record and she didnt need one.

Donna bought a police scanner from Eugene Driscoll. Donna took the scanner down to Sheldon to see if it was a good buy. Sheldon was home looking after the children. There was a bill of sale with it, it wasnt a stolen police band, it was a bought one. It was late. Donna had run out of gas and got home around two-thirty.

Another time Sheldon had stabbed the coffee table and told her she's lucky she's walking, the next time it'll be a body bag. He tipped the table over and stabbed the bottom of it. With his hands. Like put them underneath and flipped it. The knife was in Donna's kitchen. After Donna died Kim and Rod moved her furniture out. Kim put the coffee table down in the basement. There's a mark in the bottom of it. She put it upstairs and used it, then the police come and took it.

Donna had this tape recorder for two weeks. If she wanted to set up a situation to put on tape, she had time. You could tell by the sound of her voice that she was nervous but she said that she was okay. She said it was a comfortable situation for her. There's situations been worse, she told Kim. A lot of yelling and screaming. The tape was calm as compared to what had happened in the past.

Thursday night before she died Donna was on the phone with her mother and she seen a shadow down by her front door. And when she went to look to try and figure out whose shadow it was, it ran from the door. A few minutes later Sheldon came there and he went out looking.

Donna went to clubs. She went with Tess, that's Rod's sister, Sue Tessier. Kim doesnt know if anybody was there babysitting or if Tom Vivian was watching them from downstairs.

Donna showed Kim a bruise on top of her knee. She said she took and hit Vicki Pinhorn's face off her knee. Donna said she didnt want to fight Vicki, but she wanted to keep up the reputation.

Donna used to call and yell at Sheldon. Kim never knew if he was saying anything back to her. That's how Kim got the impression that Donna instigated arguments with him. Donna was shocking for getting Sheldon on the go. She made out she was talking to a guy on the phone, then she laughed and told him she was talking to Kim. She'd phone and say are we going out tonight, and Kim wouldnt be going out with her or anything, Donna just wanted to get Sheldon on the go.

She stayed with Kim one night that weekend her mom was in the hospital. Kim watched the kids for her to go up to see her mother. Donna slept on the chesterfield.

A couple of months ago Donna was having a cigarette when she got a telephone call from a man who said he could see her in her bedroom and then made a sexual innuendo to her. A few days later Donna was walking up to Kim's house and a man followed her around the old-age home. She'd walk so far and he'd drive ahead and stop and then she'd go and he'd go and when she got upside Kim's door he drove down the road and blew the horn. Kim saw the car. It was a rose colour, a Grand Am, it wasnt brand new. Donna phoned her mother first and then Kim told her to phone Sheldon. Sheldon came and picked her up.

Sometimes Donna was talking to Kim on the phone and she'd lower her voice. She was afraid Tom Vivian was listening. They were talking once in Donna's house and Donna was like shhh he's down there listening. The TV was on downstairs and it was like it was on in Donna's living room. Kim asked why was he listening and Donna said Tom's right infatuated with her.

One time Donna asked her to hide a gun and Kim told her no. Donna was afraid Sheldon would shoot her. Donna hid this gun in the Vivians' basement but the Vivians didnt know about it. Kim never seen it. Donna went through their basement one day to go up to her place. She put the gun up in one of the beams. Then she put it down in a shed in back of her mother's house, in a box of Christmas decorations. Sheldon wanted it back so she took it out of there and gave it back. He wanted to get it cleaned.

EDIE GUZZWELL

Donna called Edie out in Grand Falls, she was just getting ready to milk her cows. Mom's in intensive care, Donna said, at the Grace Hospital. Edie helped raise Donna until she was about twelve years old. Now Agnes was supposed to come out because it was the long weekend. But she went up to have an x-ray on her bowels and whatever they done, she started to have internal bleeding. So Edie and her husband left early the next morning and they got in to the hospital around nine oclock and Donna came up and she had some gifts there for her mom. Her hands were shaking and Edie asked her what was wrong. Agnes was on the phone and Donna got up and lied in the bed. She had on a pair of white jeans with zippers in the legs. She hauled up the zippers and there were bruises on her legs, front and back, and she told Edie that her and Sheldon had been fighting the night before. They had got into a racket over where the car was parked when Donna was in to the hospital. So for that she had red marks on her legs. He must have kicked her because it was from her knees down. She was complaining that her head was paining and she got Edie to feel the bump. Sheldon had put Donna's head through the wall. The bump was the size of an apple and it was soft and spongy.

Donna had this balloon and it had The World's Best Mom on it and she had a little vase there with a rose and she was trying to fix it and her hands were like that. Edie never saw Donna frightened or terrified in all her twenty-six years.

There was a gun in the apartment and Donna was afraid that if she went home that night Sheldon would kill her. Donna had something on Sheldon that could put him away for fifteen years but if she phoned up the police and had him put in jail there was another member of the family she was afraid of.

Donna's father was there and Aubrey said when he went in to work on Monday to the cemetery, he was going to speak to Sheldon. Donna left around four-thirty. The children were at Kim Parrott's so she went home and got clean clothes and a shower and came on back to the hospital. Agnes phoned Sheldon from the hospital and asked him would he move out. Donna seemed to be very relaxed and she made a comment that she was getting on with her life.

SHELDON TROKE

Sheldon kicked the doors in once. That was when no one was home. It seems you do something once and it's brought back to you in ten different ways on ten different occasions. It all depends who gets the story next. That statement about this time you walk, next time it will be a body bag. They were arguing about old bags at the 301 Club.

The gun. Donna never had a gun belonged to Sheldon. They had him under investigation for a bank robbery. That's the only thing he can figure out why Donna would say that.

He was after taking the front off his car. They had it downstairs in the basement, him and Robert Furneaux were working on it. It was dark, about ten at night, and Donna come down. She had a small police scanner. She had the power pack with it and everything. She had a bill of sale and the receipt to show that it was purchased in the store. It wasnt stolen or anything and Eugene Driscoll wanted a hundred dollars for it and Donna asked Sheldon was it a good deal. Sheldon said just see if you can get it for eighty. So she went up and she ended up buying it. That night when he went to bed Sharon woke him up. She asked where Mommy was at and Sheldon said what's wrong? She was sick. So he got her some medicine and phoned Kim's and told Donna that Sharon was sick. She said she was coming down. Half an hour later Sharon came in again and asked where Mommy was at and Sheldon got up and phoned again and Kim told him that Donna was left. Donna come in about ten minutes later and he asked her what took you so long. She said that Rod Tessier was up there and she wanted to make sure everything was all right between Rod and Kim. Rod was after stabbing hisself and Sheldon said to Donna what are you staying up there for, he after stabbing himself. Keeping Kim company, she said.

The next day Donna said it was Kim and Rod and Eugene she give a run down to Kavanagh's and they were in getting some beer and she ran out of gas. She had to get a taxi driver to give her a boost. Sheldon was getting fed up with this because the month before Cory was sick and he phoned into Kim's. Donna wasnt there. That was the night Donna and Kim were going out. Cory was after throwing up and Sheldon told Kim, and Donna phoned and asked was Cory all right and he said he didnt know if he got a temperature. Donna phoned back. She was talking to a nurse at the Janeway and the nurse said to take a glass of ginger ale and beat it with a fork and get all the acid out of it and give him that so his stomach won't get upset.

That day Mrs Whalen had to have day surgery and they snipped her bowel and she started hemorrhaging and she's an elderly woman. Sheldon was in working at the graveyard and waiting for Mr Whalen to come. It was Sheldon's birthday. Mr Whalen was supposed to drop Missus off and then wait and give her a run home again, so he never showed up to the graveyard. About two he sees Donna's car coming down the driveway and Donna and Tom Vivian get out of the car. The way she's walking there was something wrong. She was crying and saying Dad dont understand and Sheldon couldnt pick no sense out of what she was saying. He was holding her and Tom Vivian come over and Sheldon said to Tom what's wrong? Missus took sick, he said, and Donna was saying Dad dont understand, Mom's going to die. Sheldon got Tom to go over and get the car and he helped Donna get in and put the pick and shovel back in the shed and they left and went over to Donna's house to drop Tom off. Sharon was there and Sheldon asked Tom would he keep an eye on her. They went over to the hospital and Mrs Whalen was up in intensive care. They were talking to her and Sheldon left around suppertime. He left to get the youngsters something to eat and when he come back he went up and Donna wasnt there. She was visiting Albert Canning and then she come back in. A few minutes later a nurse told them visiting hours were over.

They went back to Donna's and she put Cory to bed. Sharon was in her room playing Nintendo. Donna went in to lie down and told Sheldon to call her because she wanted to go back over to the hospital again that night. So Sheldon went in and called Donna. Yes, she said, she was getting up. She was a bit cranky with all the stress she was under and Sheldon never said nothing. She stayed in bed asleep. So he went to his grandmother's house just down around the corner from Donna's. His grandmother was there, his father and sister and mother.

This was Sheldon's birthday and they ended up getting a six-pack of beer. Sheldon was talking to them and they gave him socks, shorts and a card.

He went back to Donna's and she said you were at the 301 Club again. Sheldon was telling her that he was at his grandmother's. He was showing her the socks and Donna come up close and said what, were you drinking with your grandmother? Because she smelled the beer off his breath. He pushed her and put the bag down and walked out of the room and picked up the phone to call his mother to verify that he was up there and Donna was roaring you was over at the 301 Club and he roared back he wasnt. Donna roared out dont go getting them involved, you were over to the 301 Club with your old bags and Sheldon threw the phone down and went in and there was a lot of cursing going on. He said if youre going to talk about bags, talk about your own friends and she turned around and told him to go fuck himself and he walked in and grabbed her by the shoulder and hauled her towards him and said what the fuck is your problem? Donna was throwing the socks down and Sheldon was saying every fucking time I moves through the door there's a fight. He was holding her by the shoulder and he turned her and both of them were using the language. They were having words and he walked out and slammed the door. He went in the bedroom. There was a glass on the night table and he was still roaring saying I'm fucking fed up with this. Every time I goes somewhere we got a fucking racket over it, and he was shouting out and picked up the glass and bounced it off a picture. The picture broke. He ended up putting his head through the wall. It wasnt Donna's head, it was his head.

The next morning Donna was gone and Sharon and Cory were gone and he cleaned up the glass and went to his grandmother's. His mother was up there and he asked could he move in with her. His mother said yes. He left there and went to Cathy Furneaux's. After he left Cathy's, he went back to Donna's. And while he was there, he was packing his clothes and the phone rang. It was Donna's mother from hospital. Agnes asked him what was going on. He said I'm fed up with this, I'm moving out. She asked him what happened and he explained it to her. She said youre not going to quit your job, are you? He said no and she asked how he was going to get back and forth to work. My mother and my father, they'll drive me. What about the keys to the shed? He was going to lay them on the stand at the top of the stairs. He got his father to come down. He moved everything out of Donna's. He spent the night at his grandmother's. He slept on her chesterfield. Sunday, that's when he moved in to his mother's. It was the long weekend. Mrs Whalen got out of hospital Monday or Tuesday.

Sheldon's after hearing that Donna had a black eye. His parole officer went to see Donna. There's nothing about a black eye him ever mentioning it. Sheldon spoke with Donna on the phone one day and there was two police officers sot right in the house talking to him and Gary Bemister was one of them. He never heard no references to black eyes then. There was a mark on Donna's eye right here. Donna was having trouble with her station wagon—the battery used to heat up. One time the terminal even melted off and Sheldon brought the battery back to Canadian Tire. He was fixing it one day and he threw the keys up to Donna from the bottom of the steps and Donna caught it. She got it in the eye. It was a point right here when she caught the keys. It was like a scrape.

There was nights Sheldon cried, yes. There was nights he went to Donna, crying, and some nights he'd cry over his brother Raymond. He was going to quit alcohol and she was going to quit pills.

BERTHA TROKE

Sheldon moved out to Cabot Apartments, but that was only for a few days. They werent getting along and they needed to be away from each other for a while. Donna said to Bertha, I got to admit it we do have our arguments but I starts a lot of them.

Bertha was at Sheldon's apartment with Cathy Furneaux and Donna, and Sheldon walked in the door with Vicki Pinhorn. Vicki had an iron in her hand. She was going to iron Sheldon's pants. She went into the bedroom because there was no room out in the living room. When she went in the bedroom Donna went right in on the back of her. She closed the door and you could hear them talking loud and at one point there was a bit of razzing going on. Donna was really mad because Vicki ironed Sheldon's pants and they were broke up. She was furious.

Donna was doing things and she made Bertha promise that, when her and Sheldon were broke up, Bertha wouldnt tell Sheldon that she was shoplifting and doing prescription drugs.

Donna asked Bertha once for a Gravol. She had the flu and she was stomach sick and Bertha laughed and said yes you had a flu too many. She give her a Gravol and Donna said yes the pills had made her sick.

KIM PARROTT

Sheldon smashed an elephant a couple of months before Donna died. Donna was up to Kim's house and it was late. One of the youngsters were after waking up and Sheldon phoned looking for Donna and she answered the phone and told Sheldon she was late because Rod had gotten stabbed. That was a lie. Then Donna hung up and she was still there a few more minutes and he phoned again. Donna asked Kim not to say that she was there. Tell him I just left. So she told him and he said she's nothing but a whore. Kim didnt want to carry no conversation off with him because Donna was there sitting in front of her. And when Donna went home he grabbed her by the face and shoved her and she phoned Kim, it was around three oclock in the morning, and Donna told her what he had done and Kim heard him going with the vacuum cleaner. He was after smashing this glass elephant. He gave Donna money to get a second elephant.

CATHY FURNEAUX

Cathy has known the Trokes for years. She went out with Sheldon's brother Raymond. He's deceased now. She knows Sheldon good this few years. She knows his brother Paul Troke.

Friday night she phoned up the 301 Club to see if Paul or Sheldon was up there. She was talking to the lady that was working the bar. A lady from the Hill had the place rented out because her little girl needed money to go away, so they were from the Hill and that's where Cathy is from so she said I'll go over there.

Cathy's sister-in-law dropped her off. She had a few drinks and talked to a few people. She dont go out to clubs or downtown or nothing. She was mostly sitting down by the people that were playing the music, the Morrells.

It was about two oclock when she left because the club was over, the lights were after coming on. She dropped into the gas station that's up by the club. She went in to pick up a bag of chips. She walked home to Freshwater Road. It's a house with two apartments. Cathy's is the top.

Her son Robert was there, and Sheldon's brother Paul. Robert is sixteen. It had to be around two-thirty. She sat there on the couch, had a cigarette. They were watching TV, she was eating chips. She was talking to them for a few minutes then laid down on the chesterfield and went to sleep. Paul was sitting in the rocking chair and Robert was at the foot of the couch on the floor. You had to go up over another flight for the bedrooms and that.

She woke up on Saturday morning about ten-thirty. The phone rang. It was Bertha Troke. Cathy went up the stairs and woke Paul up. He was up in his bed. Paul stayed at Cathy's place a lot but he did have his own apartment too. When she went in he had the blankets hauled up around him and she just nudged him. She shook him and said Paul and he said what. She said, Have a guess who's dead. She told him Donna. He said why what happened did she OD? No, Cathy said, she slashed up. He said go on, and he just turned in then and went back to sleep.

JOHN MORRELL

John has a sideline, playing music at weddings. Word of mouth. He's familiar with the 301 Club. Fred Riles asked him to play the music at a fundraiser, it was about this sick kid. The second weekend in June. He brought the stereo equipment in and set it up. He went with his wife, Winnie. Cathy Furneaux was there. She was dancing and drinking. She had a flask in her purse and a beer. She said she brought her own booze to save on money. She wanted John to play a song for her. She had it in a purse on a tape. John played the song. He had a couple of dances with her.

They called out last call for the bar and the lights came on about two. Cathy came back and got her tape. She left then. John unhooked his stereo and left about quarter to three. There was two people left besides him and Winnie.

John doesnt know Sheldon Troke or any of the Troke family.

Cathy was feeling good, she wasnt drunk. Whiskey or screech, she poured it in a glass. She wasnt measuring these with any sort of cup, just free pour. He's positive about it because she offered him a drink. She was mixing it with Pepsi because she had a glass of Pepsi.

A lot of people were saying what a consequence that that night he played at the 301, missus got killed.

It was a dark purse, it was about that big and about that high. Cathy laid it on top of his stereo. She had jeans on, John wasnt really sizing her up but she had jeans on and a top and a jacket.

SHARON WHALEN

A truth is something that happened and you say it happened, and a lie is something you made up and it didnt happen.

Sharon heard a big bang and thought it was the coffee table knocked over because her mom might be sleepwalking. Her mom was saying no, Sheldon, no, leave me alone, leave me alone, and she could hear another voice saying be quiet, Donna. A man's voice.

She has two diaries. The one from around the time that her mother died has a teddy bear on the cover. The other has flowers and a sticker. Her mom was cleaning up the water with a cloth and she lifted up the coffee table. It was tipped over. Sheldon was mad, her mom said, and he tipped it over. Her mom was going to see Sharon's nan at the hospital and she was going to drop Sharon and Cory off at Kim's. She didnt tell Sheldon because he doesnt like Kim. They were going to the car and he told her mom to come back into the house. Sharon and Cory waited in the car. She was taking a long time so Sharon told Cory to stay out in the car. She went to the door and peeked in and Sheldon pushed her mom and she grabbed on to the rail and she almost fell down over the stairs. Sheldon hauled her back in and Sharon went up the stairs a bit and looked into her room and he pushed her mom on the bed and

then she got up and was coming towards the door so Sharon ran
back to the car.

Sheldon had his stuff moved into the house and when they were
together he slept there almost every night. But once a week, he'd stay
back. On his birthday he came back from his mom's house. They
were arguing because Sharon's mom was wondering why he was out
so late and he was telling her because it was his birthday and he
wanted to have some fun and she asked him if he was drinking and
he said yeah. Then they started to fight and she came into Sharon's
room and Sheldon came in and he told Sharon that her mom was
bad and she was a devil and he was calling her bad names. He
went out and slammed the door. He called her the B-word and the
S-word. Her mom was crying. In the morning she told Sharon that
he punched her in the eye and he was hitting her on the head. She
had a bruise all around her eye. He was really mad at her. He was
mad because she was asking him a lot of questions. He was yelling
really loud. His voice is really tough.

Another time in the kitchen they were arguing and Sheldon was
drying the dishes and he started to dry a knife and he dug it down in
the table. It didnt stick into the table, it just left a hole in the table.

Christmas Eve Cory wanted to stay up to watch a show. Sheldon
said they could and their mom said they couldnt because they had to
go to bed early. Sharon's mom told the children to go into their room.
Sharon heard a lot of yelling. In the morning her mom told her that
he was hitting her. He was grabbing her and he was kicking her in the
leg and in the stomach.

Another time they were in the living room watching TV and
Sheldon tipped the coffee table over and he broke a glass elephant.
Sharon didnt see this, her mother told her. It was like a round ball
with an elephant inside of it like those things that you shake the snow

in them the sparkles come up. Sharon heard the bang. She went out to see what happened and her mom already cleaned it up and Sharon saw sparkles all over the floor. The coffee table was stood up like normally. Sheldon was gone out then.

Sheldon called her mom the H-word. Whore. The B-word is a female dog. The S-word is spelled s-u-l-t. Her mom used to call Sheldon back bad words. Not the same ones. One night he came home from drinking and they were fighting and then after Sharon's mom went to bed, he was smashing beer bottles. Sharon heard it and when she got up in the morning, she asked what happened. Sheldon was mad, her mom said, and he was breaking the beer bottles. There was pieces of glass on the floor and it smelled. He broke a rocking chair and a phone and the remote control. He smashed the phone on the floor. Sharon heard it and then she saw the phone in the garbage.

He put his fist through the wall. Sharon saw the hole after. He put his fist through the kettle, too. That's what her mom told her. The kettle had a big dent in it. It looked like a handprint. When the phone got broken, her mom got a new phone. He broke that too. The next time that Sheldon ever did anything to her really bad, Sharon asked her mom if she'd phone the police and she said maybe, and then the next time he hit her she wouldnt, and Sharon asked her again and she said maybe the next time. She kept on saying that. She said just before she died, that they were going to move out.

Sheldon hit Cory, but he didnt threaten him. Cory never struck his mother, but he used to say to her, I dont love you any more.

They were fighting about her going away. Sheldon was telling her mom, what are you going to do with the kids. And she asked him if they could stay with him.

SHELDON TROKE

When he loses his temper, he gets really loud. When theyre out, there's people that can hear him out by the door.

Sheldon dont think you need a considerable amount of force to break a wall. Youre talking gyproc. He controls his temper. Sometimes when he was drinking he lost his temper. When he wasnt drinking, he'd go for a walk.

When that elephant broke Sharon wasnt in the living room. It was a talk show that was on and they were porn stars and they got into a conversation about that and Donna was asking would he watch porn flicks and he said he's after watching them and this led to an argument. He had his feet up on the coffee table and gave it a push and he stood the coffee table up and put on his boots and left. He broke an ornament on top, a crystal elephant. He paid for it.

Yes Sharon heard arguments, half the time the whole street did.

They were arguing over the beer, saying that he couldnt get enough. He ended up throwing the beer that was in the box on the floor. He cut his foot. He cleaned it up. Sharon's a smart youngster. Sheldon dont know about lying, but all youngsters are prone to being misled.

He knows the remote control was broke. The back used to fall off. He put an elastic band on it to keep it together.

EDIE GUZZWELL

Edie drove her sister Agnes into the cemetery to talk to Sheldon. Edie and Agnes were supposed to go to Toronto for a wedding, but Edie didnt want to go. She asked Donna would she go in her place. So Agnes was speaking to Sheldon about that. Edie talked to Aubrey and asked him where different people were buried.

Sheldon didnt object to Donna going to Toronto. He was supposed to babysit the children. They would be gone seven days. Agnes said Sheldon was good to the children.

Edie knew that Donna was on prescription drugs. The big thing that Donna was taking was diet pills. She didnt want to be fat.

They were supposed to leave on Tuesday and Donna was killed Saturday. Edie went in and picked up the tickets. She also returned the tickets.

Donna was married at seventeen and divorced at twenty-one. Sharon is a child of that marriage. When they split up, Donna and Sharon went to live with another man and she had Cory. They were together for about three years.

SHARON WHALEN

Her mom went out nights four or five times a week. Sometimes when she came back Sharon was asleep. Tom Vivian looked after her, or Sheldon, though not very much. Her mom went out on her own. When Sheldon was staying at the house, he spent a lot of time with Sharon and Cory. When Cory was bad, he'd get sent to his room or he wouldnt be allowed to have any cookies or he'd get smacked. He was sent to his room for exactly ten minutes. It was explained to Cory what he'd done wrong and why he had to go to his room.

Cory was smacked by Sheldon. Not very often by mom. Cory was bad, like he used to be always bad, but Sheldon didnt hit him all the time when he was bad. When he did smack him, he smacked him on the hands and on his behind. He smacked him hard. It sounded and looked hard. Cory would cry.

Sheldon played a lot with Cory. Not every day but a lot. Sheldon never struck Sharon. She sometimes talked to him about math and spelling. She went to Sheldon with some of her problems. She had a friend, Ashley, who was saying things about her. Sheldon said if someone is really your friend and mad at you, they'll be friends again with you later.

Sharon phoned Sheldon and asked him if he could go to a science fair. He came up to school and saw her science project. Her mom wasnt home then when she called.

When it was her birthday, Sheldon took her out shopping. Her mom had already bought her gifts and she opened them in the morning. They went to the mall to get earrings. Sharon got a bit afraid, she didnt want to get her ears pierced. Sheldon said, You can do it later, because I've got a receipt where it's paid for and you can do it when you feel like having it done. Then they went for something to eat and they talked about ordinary things.

On Mother's Day, Sheldon took her out and gave her money to buy something for her mom. Same thing at Easter. There was perfume he picked up and Sharon helped him wrap it. One Christmas Cory wanted to get a Chicago Bulls hat like Sheldon's, but they couldnt find one his size. He got a hat. It was Sheldon's hat.

BERTHA TROKE

Bertha went to a nightclub with Donna and Cathy Furneaux. It's called Sparky's. Bertha had a drink, and the first song they played Donna jumped up from the table and ran to the bar and she had the phone, it seemed like it was on her shoulder. When she came down she said, I had to let my old moose hear that song. That was Sheldon, and the whole song played out, and she loved that song, and she said Sheldon loved it. Sheldon was babysitting.

When they left Sparky's Bertha wanted to go to Erin's Pub, but they didnt because it was Irish music. So they called a cab. Bertha said Donna you got to call Sheldon and let him know we're going downtown, and she said Sheldon will be asleep when she gets home, he dont ask what time she's going to be home. He'll watch a movie and go to sleep. So they went to this club called the Rob Ryan and when Bertha got home it was going for quarter to three.

When Donna went out there was no time limit on Donna. Donna went home when Donna felt like it but when Sheldon went out and Sheldon said he was going for twenty minutes if Sheldon was five minutes late Donna was upset. Sheldon had to be there right on time. He never went anywhere except for to drop up to his grandmother's or into Cathy Furneaux's. When he was working he never left Donna's. But she've often phoned the house and said is Sheldon there and Bertha would say he just left. Well she had to be able to tell her if he left at twelve or five after, she couldnt say he left ten minutes ago.

There was one conversation that he got very mad at her. He was really drunk that night. He said something like I'm going to kill her, she never answers the phone. It's something Bertha says to her children— she's saying it to them all her life but she never killed any of them.

NORMAN SEVIOUR

Donna was referred because of anxiety and depression. She had recently broken up with her boyfriend. He had attacked her and he was a drinker on mandatory supervision from Springhill because of a stabbing incident. She was fearful of him. Dr Seviour wrote down *attacked* as that is a more sophisticated term than *beat her up*, which is what he wrote in his notes.

He gave her a prescription for valium and a prescription for Atasol 30 which she was taking for headaches. These types of drugs are not regularly given for depression, but for anxiety.

She wanted to move out of her apartment because there had been a death there. She lives in Margaret Anthony's old apartment on Empire Avenue. Margaret was a patient of Dr Seviour's. Donna wanted a letter to give to Housing about the man who had had an epileptic seizure and drowned in the bathtub. This was an incident Dr Seviour knew very well. Margaret Anthony had gotten a letter from him to move out of that apartment for the same reason. Donna was also concerned about the heat and the dust in the apartment, because she was asthmatic.

There were prescriptions that indicate a pattern of abuse of stimulants and analgesics. He did not ask Donna if she was obtaining medication from anyone else. He did ask if she abused medications. These are addictive pills. They can certainly produce a chemical dependency. Atasol 30s are also sold on the street. It is possible a person would go to any lengths.

When he gave her the prescription, he didnt get a call from a drug store. Social Services recipients who have drug cards are not limited to a particular drug store unless a physician raises a flag and says they should be. There's a fair list of doctors seen by Donna Whalen in the last three years of her life, with a hundred and ninety services for that time period.

It's very unusual, even for a person who is quite addicted to diazepam, to take more than 80 to 100 milligrams a day. There is a tendency to increase the dose because of tolerance, but there was no way that Donna could have taken that much in those three days and still have been able to come to his office. He would have noticed the effects.

RUTH VIVIAN

Ruth was in bed with a bad back and Donna brought in a little bit of fruitcake and she sat on the bed talking to Ruth and showed her bruises from here down. Ruth said who done that to you? Sheldon.

Ruth said Donna, honey, you havent got to live like that. You can call the police and have him bonded away. And she said if she ever called the police on him he would kill her or have someone else kill her.

Sharon cut her foot one day. Ruth doesnt know if she turned on the hose or the neighbours turned on the hose. It was a nice day. The kids were out playing and Sharon cut her foot. Ruth ran down and brought Sharon over to her mother and Sheldon made a yell. He was looking for a bandaid. It wasnt a big cut. It was just an ordinary scratch. When he made the yell, Ruth just got up and left. Donna was sot on the chair and she never said one thing or the other.

GARY BEMISTER

Constable Bemister served a subpoena on Jacob Parrott. It was given to him personally. Mr Parrott made a statement. He said, Tell that fucking prosecutor that I will not be there, and I guess that means there'll be a warrant for my arrest.

Constable Bemister read the subpoena to him, explained that a warrant would be issued for his arrest if he failed to appear. Mr Parrott then tore up the subpoena.

KEITH EDICOTT

Keith is twenty-two and lives with his mother. They have a common wall that separates their living room and kitchen from Donna Whalen's apartment. Their two back doors are a foot apart.

Keith got home Friday night around eight-thirty. He went to sleep for a couple of hours and his two cousins came down and they were in his room all night listening to music and talking. They left about one oclock. Sometime around two-thirty in the morning a knock came on the back door. It was a soft knock. Keith was in the living room sitting on the couch with his mother watching a movie. The TV wasnt very loud. His mother was kind of nervous to answer the door that late so she asked him to move up on the other end of the couch where he could see her in the kitchen. She answered the door and engaged in a short conversation with someone.

Keith got a glimpse of the guy. He had blond hair. He didnt hear what was said but when his mother closed the door he asked who it was and she said it was some guy looking for Donna.

After this he heard furniture move. He's not sure which apartment it came from. It could have come from the apartment downstairs or Donna Whalen's. Like a chair being scraped across the floor. He didnt hear a knock on Donna's door.

The movie was over three-thirty and he went to bed ten minutes after. He's a pretty sound sleeper. It was quiet, a few cars going up and down the road. Keith noticed a car earlier on. He looked out the window because he heard it pull up. It was parked at the next apartment down towards the bottom of Suvla Street and it had two headlights on and you could hear the engine running. The window was closed. The car was pointing west, pulled in to the curb.

JEFFREY POPE

The restaurant lobby closes at midnight and the drive-thru area at one. That night they hadn't served a customer for probably twenty minutes or so, it was really slow. Jeffrey Pope was wearing a headset where you can take a drive-thru order and just at the close a car came so he jumped in to take the order. When she got to the window you cash off the order when you take the money and it was exactly one oclock.

You just made it here, Jeffrey said.

Well I love my chicken salad, she said.

And that was the extent of the conversation. It was quick and brief. A brunette, maybe a little bit of a curl in her hair. When he saw the photograph he did realize that was her because of the product that he sold her. They hadn't sold one all night and being the last customer it stood out. No one else was in the car. She was an average customer coming through during your Friday-night business. There was no smell of alcohol. He was face to face with her, maybe two feet away. When they pull up to the drive-thru window, there's a yellow barrier that keeps their car from actually coming into the window so they come along as close to that as they can and when they hand in their money he leans out the window to get the money, he leans out instead of just reaching his hand out, so he came close to her and he has experienced the smell of alcohol from certain cars and has called the police but with her there was no evidence.

At one oclock in the morning you have to realize that she is on the back of the building. So when he leaned out the window it is not lit that well, if there was another person there, you'd see them from probably here down. There was nobody else in the car.

The presentation of a salad is that earlier that day somebody would have prepped up the salads. You have your black salad base and you build your salad from that and your plastic clear see-through Wendy's lid with snap-on top and it's stored in a cooler until ordered along with the dressing so, as it is ordered, it is bagged and presented. The dressing is in a separate pouch.

WILLIS GLOVER

Captain Glover is on the *Flanders*, and one of his crew is Jacob Parrott. A normal shift is Wednesday to Wednesday. They're a week on and a week off. Jacob came to work around nine a.m. He was a bit late. He would get off the same time the following Wednesday.

The last run they left the Cove at six oclock. So shortly after that theyre tied up on Bell Island and that's the end of their shift. They stay there until quarter after seven the next morning.

On Friday night he was talking to Jacob in his room. He was fiddling with a TV. Because of the way he was treating the TV Willis told him he wasnt going to get it to work. After that Willis got washed up and went to his room, did some reading. He was reading until one oclock. That's when he turned off the light. Jacob was still aboard because the door was open and there's no way Jacob Parrott could get upstairs without passing his door. He was in his room because when Willis called him up the next morning he was there. The reason he called him is because he's a hard person to get up. Willis knocked on the door, Jacob didnt answer, so he opened the door and looked in and sung out to him and then he woke. He was covered up in the sleeping bag in the bunk but Willis noticed the clothes that was on the chair and in front him was what he was wearing shortly after when he saw him later on that day.

Anyone that dont belong to Bell Island stays on the boat. Both boats dock on Bell Island for the night because that's where an ambulance would originate from.

There's no generators, theyre hooked up with shore power. You can hear people snoring two rooms back so it's very quiet. If Jacob used a boat that was there he'd have to have a gas tank to fit that boat. They dont leave their gas tanks in the boats, the fishermen dont. It was a pretty good night. The crossing, you could probably do it in ten or fifteen minutes if you had the right boat.

Jacob made a couple of calls that day. Willis is not sure how many but he went ashore a few times to make calls. He was wearing jeans and he had steel-nose sneakers.

He was still on the boat because even to walk along by the washroom you got to tread on a cover that's on a tank top, and that thing is warped and it rattles. You'd have to go a long ways to get a telephone at that hour because there used to be a policy that you closed up everything there at night. One time they had watchmen on there and they used to have it open. Probably up to the Legion or somewhere up in Portugal Cove which is a long ways up the road.

JACOB PARROTT

Jacob would like to apologize. The dates and times were a little bit misunderstood.

His position is a purser deck hand. Right now he's on the *Flanders*. He works eighty-four hours per week, not including overtime. He has a private room aboard the boat.

They'll unload traffic and customers and put the shore power out, take water if needed, tie the boat up in lines, put the ramp up, a gangway on the ramp and then check around. Ask the mate is it free to go, he says yes. If not well there's extra work to do.

That last run on Friday Jacob took off his work clothes, grabbed a shower, caught a movie in his room then read a book. He slept down in his cabin. He did not leave the boat. On Saturday morning they got up about quarter past six to undo the lines, took everything all apart to have the boat ready to sail and bring the people aboard and do their regular runs. The first boat was seven oclock. The second boat is seven-fifteen.

Back then Jacob did not own a vehicle. Usually he'll have a taxi drop him down. He'd go down there on a Tuesday night and relieve the guy who he replaces early, that way he dont have to come down Wednesday morning, he's there ready to work. The police have been down to the boat manys and manys a time when they docked asking for statements. Theyre only doing their job. Captain Glover, he can't account for Jacob's presence from ten-thirty to six-fifteen. Gee great. He got to sleep. He do work twelve hours a day. If you as much as drops a pen on that boat Captain Glover got that door open. You cannot walk up and down those stairs sir. Jacob's been working with the man a lot of years and sailed with the man, very capable, one of the best ship handlers around with the highest endorsement you can get, and when youre responsible for a crew, a multimillion-dollar boat, you tend to be very careful because those boats they dont have security. Anybody could walk aboard and anybody can walk off at any given time.

Jacob could have went over and had a cold beer. Very rarely do he go up on the island itself. He could have been in his room, he could have been down doing the laundry, he could have been watching TV, reading a book. There's a number of things you try to do. Or you go to sleep.

There's barrels of these little what you call punts, skiffs. Flat-bottom boats, not very big, some eighteen feet, some twelve. The local fishermen use them. Theyre not a seaworthy boat that you'd go out in rough weather or nighttime without any navigational aids or lights. It would be suicidal.

You can go down and cut the lines and take the whole lot of them. Anybody can at any given time. If there's a clone of Jacob Parrott and he got Jesus boots to walk across water there's something wrong. He has a truck and camper. Parked in his driveway for the last two years. Just moved last month.

He met Donna about eight years ago when he was dating his ex-wife. Donna dropped in once in a while.

As a result of the marital problems, there was a court order for him to stay away from his wife's place and only contact her through a third party. He was charged of knocking in her door and unlawful entry. He went down to court, pleaded guilty, got a bit of probation and fined. Jacob was hoping for a reconciliation, plus the welfare of his children.

He called Donna three times that Friday. Sharon answered the phone. She said Mom won't be home until about ten. Jacob said very well. He wanted to get ahold of her before she went away to Ontario. Donna was going to Kim's house and Jacob just wanted her to check on the kids. Third party. The message he left—he's not one hundred percent sure he left a message. Plus and minus there. You ask right out what the question is youre getting at about a phone call. This is all phone calls to you. It's against the law to make a phone call? His phone calls to the girl are private. He doesnt have a recorder to record it. He can't remember what was said what time what day when where and what week and what month. Sometimes like yesterday he was answering the telephone maybe three thousand times within an eight-hour period—how can you remember every conversation. The first time his wife walks up in person, those things stick up in the back of your brain. If you broke a leg walking in a manhole, youre not going to forget it because it's a funny thing after your leg is broke and not funny when it's done. When he met Donna at the house he happened to mention to her about the children and she said no problem she'd check. She was pretty straightforward.

He missed his court date because he was down in the woods around Trepassey moose hunting for a couple of days. He never dated Donna Whalen and he never asked Donna to go out in that camper. He did have drinks with Donna. When he was married Donna dropped into the house and he'd be off work having a nice beer on a hot day and she come in and they have a beer. That's common sense of being polite.

SHELDON TROKE

One night Donna and Kim went out. The day after Jacob Parrott
starts phoning. Kim and Rod Tessier had an accident on the way
home. Kim was doing something to Rod when he had an accident
and Jacob starts phoning. How come he's phoning you? Sheldon
asked, and Donna said he wants to get back with Kim. Then the
phone calls kept on. Some days Jacob phoned three times and just
a day ago back you wouldnt hear tell of him. Five times a week
sometimes, two and three times a day. Sheldon went in the house
one day and the answering machine was on. The red light was
blinking and he went over and pushed the button and it rewound
back and it was a message from Jacob. Then the phone rang again.
It was Jacob and he was looking for Donna and Sheldon told him
Donna wasnt there and he said he left a message and Sheldon said
yes, leave another one.

Donna and Kim had a falling-out. Donna was saying things
to Jacob on the phone about Kim. Sheldon doesnt know what
happened. Maybe Kim was giving Rod a blow job and he had the
accident. He heard Donna say to Jacob that if they get back together,
he should ask Kim to get an AIDS test. Jacob said he'd have that
standard anyway.

JACOB PARROTT

Rod Tessier come up and politely wiped his car out on the street so
they had no transportation, Jacob had to go get his truck. Rod and
Kim come up from the club loaded drunk and went over the sidewalk
and kind of took the car with it. Jacob drove them home because Rod
had too much beer. That was the accident.

SHELDON TROKE

Constable Bemister hauled up alongside him one night. Sheldon had two beer. He was talking to Sheldon and he smelled the beer off his breath. He said, Sheldon, you were drinking. Yes, boy, I was. He said, You know, youre not supposed to be drinking, and Sheldon said, I only had the two beer. He said, Sheldon, I got to lock you up anyway. Before he got out of the car, Sheldon was in the back of the police car for him. He was locked up for the weekend.

Next week, he talked to his parole officer. Sheldon, he said, the RCMP are looking for you. What for? You got locked up last weekend. Sheldon said, Yes, I did. The RCMP are saying they found some acid. Sheldon phoned the police and was talking to Charles Stamp and Charles said, Yes, we found acid on you and it's sent away. We're going to have to pick you up, and Sheldon said, All right, I'll be over in about an hour. Charles Stamp said, No, that's all right, we'll see you at two. Sheldon said good enough. He phoned the penitentiary and talked to Mr Brown who works in the clothes room. Sheldon said can I bring some stuff down, radios and clothes and stuff like that and he said yes. Sheldon went over and turned himself in to the police. All this to say he cooperates with the police.

CLIFFORD WHALEN

Clifford is Donna's brother. He used to hang out with Sheldon's brother Raymond. They swam in Kent's Pond when they were seven years old, that's how far back it goes. He might not have seen Raymond for years after that and then just from being around St John's, like running into him.

One summer Clifford was throwing a frisbee around and Sheldon was with some people. This was in Bannerman Park. The frisbee happened to go in their direction and they picked it up and Clifford went over there and said what are you guys up to today and Sheldon said we're going around crushing heads with some pop cans. They had Clifford's frisbee and Sheldon brandished a knife. They might have been rolling around on the ground a little bit and it was broke up and stopped. It was very common to see a knife on Sheldon, even just pinned into his belt. It was like looking at somebody with a pair of shoes on, it was sitting on his side and it was visible.

This murder of his sister, Clifford wakes up with it in the morning, he stays at work with it all day and he comes home with it at night, it's costing Clifford his life. It's devastated his life absolutely.

BERTHA TROKE

When Sheldon was growing up he didnt carry a knife. It was Raymond used to carry a knife in a leather case on his belt.

Sharon used to call Bertha frequent. Sharon was trying to handle Cory, and Bertha told Donna that he's hard to handle. Donna said that Sharon had not mentioned anything to her about it.

When Agnes Whalen was in the hospital, Bertha asked Sheldon about hitting Donna. She's supposed to have a lot of marks on her and he said no she had a little scratch on her face.

Donna did tell Bertha a hundred times over that she had been to a fortune teller and Madeline Ryall told her there was a blond-haired man coming into her life. Donna asked Bertha to go with her to get her fortune told. Bertha said she knew what her fortune is and telling fortunes is a racket. But Donna kept telling her about this blond-haired man and that she was after meeting a lot of new friends when she went to Madeline Ryall's.

CLIFFORD WHALEN

Clifford spoke to Donna on the phone. She was looking forward to coming to Ontario to see them and she felt that if Sheldon didnt kill her before she left for Ontario, he would kill her when she got back.

This past year his phone bills will implicate how many times he called his sister but he would hazard a guess and say seventeen times and before that he hadn't talked to her seventeen times in five or six years. Donna had a nice house and she was happy about the material things she had.

Clifford came back for the funeral. He stayed at his grandparents. The family was doing a lot of grieving and they were all in disbelief. They were expecting to see Donna and she's murdered. There was some fighting about what could have happened. Did Sheldon do it. Everybody had an opinion. Aunt Edie spoke about physical abuse. Donna confided in Edie. But Clifford's mother didnt believe Sheldon killed Donna. He was working with their father at the cemetery and they got along quite well.

She was at a christening and she had kissed somebody there and Sheldon had punched this person in the face and took her and went home and Sheldon pulled in the driveway and jumped out of the car and punched the windshield and broke it and then he came around and grabbed her by the hair and dragged her into the house and told her that if she didnt stop her fucking bullshit she'd be leaving in a body bag.

Sheldon thought she was coming to Ontario to stay. Yes, Sheldon was watching her kids while she was gone, but their mother was coming back to get the children. Sheldon was good with the children. The problems they had were between them.

Sheldon was into cocaine and Donna was into pharmaceutical drugs. They both abused alcohol. The worst violence took place between her and Sheldon when he was on cocaine and drinking. She was having knives held to her, being bullied and pushed around her house, having things in her house broken, getting kicked and punched.

One time they were at a club and Sheldon was quite drunk and he was accusing Donna of flirting with other men. She had left to go home and a short time later Sheldon arrived at her house. He kicked in her door and broke some windows, he was screaming and yelling in a rage, pushing her around and finally he grabbed a knife from her kitchen drawer. He put the knife to her throat and told her if he couldnt have her, nobody could have her and that all the boyfriends' graves are shallow, she wasnt worth doing the forty years over.

Clifford suggested that she call the police on Sheldon and she told him that if Sheldon was sent back to jail to do his parole, he'd have somebody take care of her and if she didnt stop her fucking bullshit, he'd get Iris to punch her out. Clifford said make some tapes when Sheldon starts his bullshit, and she told him that was a good idea.

They'd break up and Sheldon would come to her house, telling her how much he loved her, promising her a better life. And it worked and they'd be together for two weeks and broke up again.

For Donna to sit down and have a conversation on the phone with even a friend of hers, Sheldon would make it out to be a big conspiracy against him for her to be going out to nightclubs with other men. Her jeans were too tight, her top was too low, her dress was too short. When she was talking on the telephone and joking around with her friends, he was screaming at her and quizzing her about things he was hearing her say while not listening to the other party's part of it.

Sheldon's brother Raymond, he went to her house, it was late at night and she let him in. They were talking, Raymond was drunk, and he was putting his arms around her and tried to kiss her. He was coming on to her. She pushed him away and he pinned her down and got a little rough with her and she was really scared and finally he left.

She had fear for Iris too because Sheldon had threatened Iris on her. Donna said theyre fucking nuts, that's the way she put it.

Sheldon would go to the counter where the knives were sitting. He'd take a knife out of the drawer or grab a knife off the counter. She was going through their conversation a little quicker than she normally talked, she wasnt laughing so much and cracking jokes. Her life seemed to be falling apart. Before that, Clifford had talked to her and she was proud of a nice house and happy to be in St John's with her parents. Donna took pride in looking after them as they were getting old, such as they did to Donna and Clifford when they were young. And then it come a point where she was looking for a way out and she would have moved to Ontario.

SHELDON TROKE

Sheldon knows Clifford Whalen. Clifford's got four years on him. When Clifford was seventeen, was he in the habit of going around beating up thirteen-year-olds? Sheldon's been arrested by police on numerous occasions and he do not ever remember being locked up for having a knife.

He never threatened Donna with no knives. He never told Donna that she wasnt allowed to go out or talk on the phone. Sheldon doesnt know what Donna was telling people.

The only time they argued over the phone is if he wouldnt answer the phone and say Donna wasnt there. Sheldon wasnt getting into that. If he starts getting into it, he'll be doing it all the time.

Donna wore what she wanted to wear. She was a nice dresser. Donna wore her clothes tight. She wore tank tops and jean shorts. Donna went out on the front of the house in her bikini getting suntans. In summer she wore nice dresses. Sheldon was at the police station one time and there was pictures there that Donna sent. Just by looking at them pictures, it didnt appear to Sheldon that he had any control over what she wore. She had a bikini top on coming up to Buckmaster Circle.

He never threatened Donna about going to Toronto or that he was going to kill her. She asked him to babysit. He loved Sharon and Cory. There was days that Sharon wanted to go off by herself and play. Sharon knew that Cory was to go with her because he was only young and there was times that Sharon wanted to go off with her girlfriends so Sheldon took Cory to the park. He took the youngsters out on Saturdays and Sundays for drives up to Signal Hill with binoculars to let them see the whales.

Sharon's birthday he took her out to get her ears pierced. They went in the Avalon Mall. She picked out the earrings. Missus was there. The lady that puts the earrings in this gun and clips them in your ear and Sharon sot in the chair. The lady took a marker and put a dot on Sharon's ear and she put the stapler up to her ear and Sharon got nervous and she didnt want to get it done, so the earrings were paid for. Sheldon told her she could keep the earrings and she got her bill. She can come back any time and get her ears pierced. They went down and got something to eat and Sheldon was explaining that it dont hurt and he pinched the back of her elbow. He asked her did she feel that and she said no. That's what it's like, he said. All right I'll get it done, she said, and they went back up again and she sot in the chair and when Missus was getting ready to do it, she wouldnt get it done.

JUDGE RICHARD ADAMS

Clifford Whalen went back to his motel, he ate dinner and went to his room. The telephone was ringing. Whoever was there hung up and Clifford thought maybe he just missed the call.

The phone rang again and he picked it up and said hello and the other end hung up and then eleven-thirty at night, the same thing happened. He talked to two other people that night, his wife twice and his mother once which was a total of six phone calls.

He phoned the police. It was quite late. He explained to them the situation he was involved in and he didnt want to fill out a report but if they were in the area could they make their presence known at the motel. That was the Journey's Inn.

Clifford had made notes during the testimony and the paper he used was stamped on the back JOURNEY'S INN MOTEL and photocopies were received by the Court.

Clifford changed hotels after that. The lady at the desk didnt get those phone calls and the other lady that had been on at that time was on break.

People who had his phone number were family members.

The same day that he completes his testimony here he receives telephone calls at a hotel that he's staying at. The accused had direct access to where he was through the notes to the Court that were given to his lawyer, Mr Lythgoe. There was one time during cross-examination where Mr Lythgoe was referring to the notes and said, I guess this must be where you are staying—he used that notepad from the hotel. So the accused had direct knowledge.

Sheldon Troke is in the Special Handling Unit, separated from all other prisoners, no contact can be made. The phones in Special Handling are turned off at ten at night.

It could be a mistake. Or there may well be people out there who are watching this case and have an interest in what people say in the witness box. To place a call, the caller would have to go through a switchboard of the hotel and ask for Clifford Whalen or for a room number. The chance of a mistake appears to be remote but we dont know who made them. They were probably made from a call box.

CLIFFORD WHALEN

The way Clifford looks at it, before his sister heard of Sheldon Troke, she was a beautiful, kind, caring, loving, honourable, brilliant young lady and Sheldon Troke took her down a path of destruction and walked her right into hell. Donna was never phoning him, telling Clifford about any abuse she went through even if she was going through it, she wanted Clifford to think that she was doing good, her life was good, she was raising her two children. Then when Sheldon Troke came into the picture, the bullshit started.

Clifford's parents liked Sheldon. His father gave this man a job. Sheldon was trying to put the fear of God in Donna, he was infatuated with her, he was jealous, he didnt want her leaving him and Clifford never mutilated his mind into ever seeing his sister dead. He absolutely did not contact his mother and explain to her what was going on and tell her to intervene and tell her to get Donna out of there. His mother is old and her health isnt the best and if Donna wanted her to know something, she was very close to their mother, she could tell her on her own free will.

Donna was doing cocaine. She done it with Sheldon, she told Clifford. She was drinking with the Tessiers. Donna had told Sheldon that when her brother Clifford came down here he wasnt going to stand by and watch the bullshit that was happening in her life. Bullshit was her word.

JUDGE RICHARD ADAMS

What's the problem, Mrs Anstey?

I'm too nervous on this trial.

Youre what?

Very nervous.

That's true and I appreciate and understand that, but I have to say to you, everybody else is nervous too. This is not an easy thing that youre called upon to do but let me say this—we have one of the best systems in the world where citizens decide in very serious cases on the guilt or innocence of the accused person, so it's not just left to lawyers and judges. This is a country that, with all its faults, gives a lot to its citizens by way of peace and security. Bad things happen, yes, but they dont happen here as much as they do in many parts of the world and we have a lot of rights citizens in some parts of the world dont have at all. But sometimes, and properly so, obligations go along with rights and every one of the twelve of you sitting here has the obligation which our country has asked you: to decide this matter under her rules and the manner in which these things are decided. Now I know youre anxious, every person sitting here is, including lawyers, police, everybody. Being anxious and worried can't stand in the way of our duty. If you think about it as a duty, then it is as important as any citizen will ever be called on to do. The Crown is entitled to a jury of twelve. Mr Troke is entitled to a jury of twelve. We can't call in new people now, the trial is under way. The law does say that in case of emergency, I can discharge someone. Someone could have a heart attack and you can go on with eleven. You can go on with ten if you had to but you can't go on with fewer than ten. We'd have to discharge the jury, start all this over again which would be an incredibly expensive and stressful procedure for everyone. So what I'm going to do Mrs Anstey is ask you to stay with it. Your fellow jurors

will support you and your input into this is just as important as any
other juror. All right then, Mr Ash.

KIM PARROTT

Donna told Kim that she and Kim were cousins, that's the way they
looked at each other. Donna took pills every day as she opened her
eyes but she took different amounts at different days. Kim never seen
her walk around not be able to see what she was doing.

Kim seen a hole in Donna's bedroom wall where you turn the light
on. Sheldon did it with his fist. And marks on her wall next to the
kitchen door. Donna said that he kicked her front door in. Kim can't
be certain of the kitchen window. She seen the window broke out, it
was covered with cardboard. He done something to it.

The front door, that happened the night they were coming home
from Mrs Tessier's house, and she had the keys in her hand but she said
something like she never opened the door fast enough, and he kicked
the door in.

The door to Donna's bedroom he took that with his two hands and
hauled it off the hinges and laid it against the wall. Kim seen the door
when it was put back on, there was splinters where the hinges are to.

SHELDON TROKE

While Sheldon was going out with Donna he got an apartment on
Freshwater Road. Cathy Furneaux was right up over him. He went
back to jail again in November. January he got out and he was living
on Empire with Donna. He still had the apartment, though. There
was times that he'd leave Buckmaster Circle and go down to Donna's
and she wouldnt be there. How long she was left he had no idea.

He could haul up there and she'd have left two minutes before. He can't say that Donna was gone all the time. Sure, he wasn't even there himself.

They were broke up again by Regatta. Sheldon moved to his apartment on Freshwater Road. He asked Donna could he take Cory to the Regatta and she said yes. The day it was supposed to go off it didnt. It went off the next day and he took Cory and Cathy Furneaux's young fellow, Robert.

It was in the fall of the year, Donna was looking for a car and she asked Sheldon if you see a cheap car, to let her know about it, and there was times before this when he was in jail he'd be talking to her suppertime and she'd tell him that she's going into Eugene Driscoll's garage that night. A friend of his got a Cougar for sale and he told Donna about it and she told him that she never had the money. This car was in good shape, so Sheldon told her to tell Driscoll about it. He sold cars and Donna said, He's here now. So Sheldon said, Let me talk to him, and he spoke to Eugene about the car. When you give her the gas, instead of having the hand to come up, she had digitals. It was a nice car and Sheldon explained it to him what the car was like and told him who owned it.

Sheldon was sent to a drug addiction program out in Corner Brook. Humberwood. He was straight for two months. He'd go to AA meetings. Donna even come to a couple. But he was drinking a lot. If he dropped into someone's house and they had liquor, he'd have a couple of drinks of it.

One night they were home and Donna phoned Cory's father to see how Cory was doing. Cory was the youngest and got a tendency to get spoiled and Cory's father they were just after having a newborn. Cory wanted to come back and Donna got mad. Sheldon tried to explain to Donna, Cory's feeling that he's not getting the attention with this little youngster. She wanted to drive out over the road and Sheldon said, Donna, you can't go driving out in your car, the ball joints and everything, and she flew right off the handle.

He was rushing into the Avalon Mall picking up some more Christmas presents. Donna was out. He got Sharon to help wrap the gifts. He gave Sharon the gifts that her and Cory were going to give to Donna. There's pictures there of the youngsters, both of them dressing the tree, putting the ornaments on.

Just after Christmas they went down to Mrs Whalen's for supper. They ended up having a fight. They went out after, but not together. Their relationship could be good for two weeks then it was like there was animosity for a couple of days. Donna's mom gave her a half bottle of liquor. Sheldon ended up drinking it and got really drunk. They were arguing. It was like everything would come up and he give Donna a smack in the face and put an ashtray through the kitchen window.

That night Donna called her mother. Mrs Whalen come to the house. She had words to say and asked Donna to come home with her. Donna said no, she wasnt going down. Sheldon shouldnt be drinking liquor, her mother said. He should have more sense.

Sheldon went to sleep. The next morning there was a box there. Cory was after getting a toybox for Christmas and it come in a cardboard box. Sheldon got the box and put it up to the window and cleaned the glass up. They talked about all the arguing and drinking and Donna doing her pills and Sheldon took it upon himself to go out and talk to certain people. He went to Addictions. It's at the Miller Centre across from the penitentiary. He admitted that he had hit Donna. They never had a group themselves for this kind of relationship. The parole service was paying for him to go there so they told him he should have a talk to his parole officer. Sheldon knows what his parole officer is like. You go to see your parole officer, he's locking you up. They said Sheldon youre after telling us this story. Something got to be done. He went to Alan Thorne the next day. He sat there and took some notes and left the office and he come back and said, Sheldon, I was just talking to my boss and he tells me I got to revoke your parole. There's no warrant drawn up right now, but youre aware of it that youre revoking your parole. Sheldon said can I go and come back and he said, if you go now, youre going to be unlawfully at large. Donna's car was out by the door, Sheldon said, and she lives a good ways away. Alan Thorne said, I'll bring the keys over to Donna. Sheldon phoned Donna and told her what was going on and she asked, Why would you go and do a thing like that?

Sheldon sat in the waiting room. He waited for a half-hour, no supervision, just picked up a magazine. The guy from the paddy wagon, he was going to put the handcuffs on him. Sheldon said, Roger I've been waiting half an hour for you. He looked at Sheldon. Alan Thorne come out and Roger asked the parole officer and Alan said he's here a good hour and Sheldon went off with Roger to the lock-up with no cuffs. Alan brought the keys over to Donna and Donna said it never took place and Alan said, Sheldon tells me youre arguing a lot, and Donna asked was his relationship the little white house with the picket fence?

Sheldon was downstairs in the lock-up and a guard come in. It was Donna wanted the keys to the Freshwater apartment. She wanted to close it down. He had to sign a note to consent for Donna to have the keys and he signed it and gave the guard his keys. It was a bed-sitting room with a small kitchen and a bathroom. He had a stereo, a VCR, a TV, bedroom suite, a chesterfield chair, all his clothes. Donna packed everything away in boxes, put the dishes in one box and taped the box and the bedding, the linen from the bathroom in other boxes. She got her father's pickup and she moved everything back in her apartment.

Donna come down to see him with the youngsters. When Sheldon left the visiting room, he went back to the range and a guard told him to get his gear ready, he was going. Sheldon went out by the door and, walking down the road, he got a taxi. He went to Freshwater Road. He got the money off Cathy Furneaux to pay for the taxi. He phoned Donna's. Sharon answered the phone and said Donna just went out. Sharon and Cory were there. Sheldon went down and Donna was coming in so Cory and Sharon put him in the closet in Cory's room. Cory and Sharon were saying come in, Mommy, we got to show you something. And Donna was saying wait now. She was putting some Easter eggs in her room and Cory put his hands up and said shhh dont go saying nothing Sheldon, and Sharon put her hands over Cory's mouth because he kept saying Sheldon Sheldon. So Donna come in and Cory at the closet said look, and it was just a surprise, for the youngsters. They wanted to do it.

Donna wanted him to work with her father into the graveyard and Sheldon told her that he'd go to work and she wanted him to give up selling drugs and give up drinking and give up all his friends. Not that he couldnt talk to them, but go downtown with them all the time. He agreed to do that. He went to work. He give up Buckmaster Circle. He give up selling drugs and give up going downtown.

He started work in April in the Blackmarsh Road cemetery. Just upkeep of the graveyard. There was days they worked four, five, six in the evening. Sheldon was not used to working. He'd come home tired and lie on the chesterfield, go to bed early. For a month he didnt go out at all.

Donna went out just about every night. Sheldon didnt stop her, but they did argue about it. Sheldon started dropping over to the 301

Club. He was getting used to the work. He hadn't worked for years and this is outdoors, youre moving around a lot of topsoil and cleaning up and going with a wheelbarrow and shovel. He'd come home and never had no energy to go out and didnt mind Donna going out. Then he started going over to the 301 Club to have a few beer and they argued about that. He'd say to Donna, What's the difference? You goes out. But it's different, she'd say. I aint doing what youre doing. What am I doing? I'm over having a beer and shooting a game of pool. And then they argued, well, you've got a brother hangs out over there who sells drugs. Next youre going to be selling drugs.

It was weekends he'd go over there. If there was a day it was raining and they didnt work, he'd drop in. One night he got a call. Donna told him she'd be home in an hour. I'm at Kim's house, she said. I'm going and getting a suntan. Sheldon never questioned it. Another time Donna and Sue Tessier and them went out. They went to a club. Donna come home about three in the morning. After the club they went and had Chinese. Sheldon was in bed watching TV when she come home.

Joey Yetman got out of jail and he phoned Sheldon. Drop up, Sheldon said. Joey said, Want to get a few beer? Sheldon said I got to ask Donna first and Joey started ridiculing him. He asked Donna could he get some beer and she said no and Sheldon said come on, Donna, I've got a friend here, I only wants to get a six-pack. And she said well, I dont care if you gets it. So he went down to the store and picked up a six-pack and Joey picked up a six-pack and they come back and it was all tension. He was in the kitchen and the beer was on the counter and Donna was saying, You can't wait to get them all gone, so he bounced the box off the floor and the beer all broke and they put the glass in a bag and Sheldon said to Joey come on, we goes. They got a taxi.

It was a Friday night and they were sat at the 301 Club and three girls come in. At the other end of the club, there was two pool tables. Sheldon's brother Paul was there and his girlfriend Trisha playing pool. Trisha had a miniskirt on. Sheldon was up to the bar. He was talking to the bartender. These three girls come in and he knows one of them and the other one he was just after meeting her about a month before. So Monday Donna and Iris are out going around to doctors and Sheldon wasnt working this Monday. He was babysitting Cory and the phone rang and here it was Donna. She said did you have fun at the 301 Club Friday night? The girls over with the miniskirts and everything on. Sheldon said the only one who had a miniskirt on was Trisha. There was a whole load of them over there, she said, and they started arguing over that and the next minute she hanged up and so Sheldon broke the phone. Cory was sat on the bed alongside. What's wrong, he said, and Sheldon said, Your mom is mad. Cory said, Is she mad at me? and Sheldon said no.

CATHY FURNEAUX

Cathy didnt look at a clock when she left the 301 Club but all clubs closes at two and she didnt leave till the club was closed. It took her twenty minutes to get home. She could have been fast asleep on the sofa by two-twenty in the morning.

She has a long close connection with the Troke family and she thinks of the accused and his brother Paul just like she thinks of her own brother. She'd seen Raymond Troke for about four years. She was in love with the man. Raymond spent a lot of time at her place. He had his own place. They were very close to almost a husband and wife. After his death Cathy stayed close to the rest of his family.

SHELDON TROKE

Donna said he could board there until he got enough money to get an apartment. Mrs Whalen over the phone one day she laughed. What are you, a boarder now? Sheldon wasnt really a boarder. It was just a name put on it. They were still living under the same roof. They werent sleeping together.

He got up for work. He phoned Mrs Whalen. She brought up that she was going to Toronto and she was going to ask Donna if she wanted to go. The topic of the youngsters come up and Sheldon told Mrs Whalen that, if they wanted, he would look after the youngsters.

He went to work and they were in cutting the grass. Sheldon was using the lawnmower and Mr Whalen had the whippersnapper and about eleven in the morning, Donna's mother and her aunt Edie come in and they were driving down. It was talked about then about babysitting the youngsters.

One oclock they were sat in the truck having their dinner and Donna and Tom Vivian come down. Donna come over to the truck and she asked Sheldon could she talk to him and he said yes and there's a monument, a big statue, and they were sot on that and Donna was saying that she was going to get ahold of her brother Clifford and her family on the mainland to see if they could give her fifty dollars each to chip in for some spending money up there. Then she asked him would it be any trouble if, after work, he went to Empire because she was going to her mother's to do some laundry. When they walked back, Donna took the keys off a key ring and she gave Sheldon the keys to the house. Could he fix the hole in the wall. He said give my mother a call because around four she starts to make supper. Donna said she would.

Mr Whalen liked to work overtime. Sheldon told him he couldnt today because Cory was coming home. They left at four. When he got to Donna's, she was just leaving. She had a bag with her. He assumed it was laundry.

Donna come home around eleven that night. She was at her mother's and had laid down. She wasnt feeling well. She was after taking plain Atasols and Atasols with codeine in them.

Sheldon stayed that night at Donna's on the chesterfield. Nothing went on, no kisses or nothing like that. In the graveyard, when she was leaving, he gave her a kiss but that night there was just talk and watching TV. The next morning her father come to pick Sheldon up. And when he was going through the door, Donna asked him what they were going to do tonight. Sheldon said, I dont know, we'll do something and he walked over and gave her a kiss. He went down over the steps, got in the truck and went to work.

After work Sheldon's father come out and picked him up. He went home. He got a shower and phoned Donna. Was she coming in for him. I'll get Tom Vivian to come, she said. He spent the weekend at Donna's and he gave her a hundred dollars to go to Toronto. Donna asked him to buy a pack of cigarettes. All he had on him was twenty dollars. He said give me the money, and she said no, you buy it, and Sheldon said all I got is twenty dollars to get some tobacco for the week and Donna was upset and he said, Donna I was after giving you a hundred, and up to Needs Convenience he'd bought a turnip and some milk and rented out some movies for the youngsters. So that's when he asked Donna for a run home and on the way in the road, they hauled into Stockwood's and he bought two pouches of tobacco and a box of cigarette tubes, just to show that he really had to buy cigarettes.

He worked Monday and Tuesday and Wednesday. That evening they knocked off early. It was raining and it wasnt going to hold up and that night Sheldon had to go to a meeting. It was this new group he was starting and this was the first night. Human resource development.

The parole board set this up. Donna was seeing a counsellor and the counselling that Sheldon was going to was a group. He slept at home.

Thursday he phoned Mrs Whalen and she was telling him down her way it was rainy. He said in our way it's misty, but it's not raining. She said, Mister isnt going to work. Sheldon said, I might take a shot in anyway. She said, Call back and let me know because I'm going into Bidgood's and I'll drop the keys of the shed in to you.

Sheldon phoned her back and told her he wasnt going in, even though he had a lunch ready in the fridge. You wouldnt get a full day's work anyway, she said.

He watched the news. He phoned the Brother Murphy Centre. He was thinking about going to night school. He was talking to the vice-president down there and explained his situation to him and he took Sheldon's name and told him to call back.

He asked his father around dinnertime to give him a run in town. Before that, Sheldon phoned Joey Yetman and asked Joey would he go to a doctor for him. Sheldon's father dropped him off around the school on LeMarchant Road and he walked down over a hill, right in front of it is Cabot Street Apartments. That's where Joey lives. Sheldon knocked on his door and they went to the doctor's office. They were sot down for about ten minutes. Joey went in and come out with a prescription. Sheldon went to the Royal Bank on Freshwater and changed his cheque, crossed the street to Trans Canada Drugs and paid for the prescription and got two bottles of Coke. He left the drug store, went to the police station and signed in. He has to do that once a month. He left there and went to Cathy Furneaux's. There was no one home. The pills that he got were Robaxinal—this doctor wouldnt give Joey Atasols. It's for a muscle spasm. One side is pink. The other side is white. The white side is what has the codeine. Sheldon broke them apart and took the codeine.

He said to Joey, Listen do you want to go over and see this doctor over where Kelly used to be at? They left Cathy's and walked over LeMarchant Road past the hospital. At the fire department they run into Cathy and Paul. Cathy said you won't get nothing off this guy. Sheldon said to Joey give it a shot anyway and Sheldon left then with Cathy and his brother Paul and walked back to Cathy's house.

They come over LeMarchant Road and you go up Monkstown and that'll take you to Cathy's house. Cathy went on to the drug store and Sheldon and Paul picked up a six-pack of Labatt's Blue. They went over to Cathy's. Paul was looking for his drug card. Sheldon told him Cathy would be back in a few minutes and Paul said why dont we take a shot over to the 301 Club?

Sheldon had about three beer gone and they walked over to the club. It was around three-thirty. Cheryl the bartender, she comes on between six and seven, Sheldon was still there when she come to work. They played pool and drank. There was Harvey Rowe and Eugene Driscoll and another guy with Eugene.

About seven-thirty Sheldon and Paul went into their mother's house with Eugene. They were just sitting there. Eugene was telling the stories and everybody was laughing at him. They left there and went back to the 301. Sheldon dont know where they went after that. He dont remember the rest of the evening.

PAUL TROKE

Paul Troke ended up picking up some more time and went back to jail. When he got out Sheldon was after coming home and he was dating Donna. Paul was staying with Cathy Furneaux and he saw Donna at Cathy's. He used to get quite a lot of painkillers off her. He went to

Donna's a few occasions with Sheldon. The neighbours they would see him going in and out there.

Sheldon and Donna they got along okay. Paul had a little bed-sitting room in a boarding house on Victoria Street but he never used it. He wouldnt stay at Cathy's all the time like he used to always be out partying, staying at different friends' houses. He spent a lot of time mostly at the 301 Club but he used to go downtown a lot. He saw Donna downtown. Donna wore really tight jeans and at her house she wore tight spandex workout pants. She was in the habit of wearing sleeveless shirts, like strap shirts.

He's almost six-two with his sneakers on. Right now he weighs 246. Back then he was 180 pounds. He used to do a lot of drinking and he never used to eat that much.

His hair is light brown. That's his natural colour. When the sun gets at it in the summer it lightens a bit but it dont turn red. He gets it cut at Joe's Barber Shop on Merrymeeting Road. Brush cut. One time it was quite busy he went up it was pretty near closing time, she had the door locked. Karen, she's Joe's daughter, she cut his hair. Somebody knocked at the door and Karen answered and Paul heard the person say no I'm not here for a haircut, I'm looking for my brother, and when Paul looked over it was Sheldon.

Sheldon waited out on the step and Paul paid and left. They went down to Cathy's.

KAREN CLANCEY

Karen did a cosmetology course and when she started with the business her father, Joe, taught her how to use the clippers. A spike is cut short around the ears, on the back, off the collar and very close to the head, a rounded shape. So it sticks up on top. It's like a brush cut. She holds her hand tight to your scalp and cuts the hair along the whole way. Paul Troke's hair is short and blond.

Paul was her last customer that day. A knock came on the door, and she usually dont answer unless you keep knocking, so she just opened the curtain and told him they were closed. It was a sunny day. Sheldon said that he wanted to know if his brother Paul was there, and she said yes. And he wanted to know how long he was going to be and she said a couple of minutes.

Paul Troke did come in earlier and they were very busy and he said he would come back later. When he came back he was just simply taking a chance. From what she sees if people need a haircut they sometimes come back a couple of times. It could be three times during that day if they need it done. There are no other barbershops close by on that street. His hair was just a little bit longer than what it was. She basically cleaned it up.

Paul and Sheldon theyre both friendly. Paul's hair is a lighter colour and shorter. Paul specifically asked for sprunch. It's a hairspray. It freezes it in position. Sprunch is applied on a pump bottle. She just sprays it on.

Sometimes people have designs put in the side of their head. Bear claws theyre called. For Paul Troke, she doesnt remember doing them. Without the sprunch it would be flat to the head then. It would look rounder to the shape of the head.

A couple of days after she cut Paul's hair, she saw him on the news and he was arrested for the armed robbery on Water Street. She knows she cut his hair just previous to this because her husband commented on what a good haircut it was.

SHELDON TROKE

Sheldon got dropped off out in town. He went to Cathy Furneaux's to see if Paul was there. Paul's girlfriend Trisha was there and Trisha said that he was gone to get a haircut and Sheldon asked where did he go, was it down to Topcuts or up to the top of Field Street, and Trisha said she thinks at the top of Field Street. So he went there and tried the door. The door was locked. There was curtains or blinds in the window so he knocked on the window and a girl come over and she told him they were closed and he said, I was wondering if Paul Troke was there. She said hang on, and so then she turned around and said yes, and Sheldon said, Tell him I'll be waiting out here. Paul come out and he asked him if he had any Atasols or Tylenols and he said he never had none. He said he might be getting some later and Sheldon told him he was going to a meeting and he said drop back after the meeting. So he left then and walked to the meeting.

Paul had a brush cut. At least once a week Paul's into a fight downtown. He has short hair so when he's fighting, no one can grab his hair.

From going to AA and NA, Sheldon met people that went there for years and they still drank and used drugs but eventually they come off it and they been off it for years. You can go there to a meeting and the people will tell you just because you slip or youre still using, keep coming back. Someday you might get something. There was times he went there using drugs.

CHES HEDDERSON

This is the police's theory: Donna dropped Sheldon off at his mother's that night. Then she went to Kim Parrott's, and on her way home visited the Wendy's restaurant drive-thru. She had a brief discussion with Ruth Vivian on her way into the house. Donna climbed the stairs, changed into her nightgown and ate her chicken salad. Sheldon Troke returned to Donna's, waited in the Empire area for Ms Whalen to return home and an altercation occurred. Contact was made with Paul Troke at Cathy Furneaux's. Paul aided Sheldon in cleaning up and they both left the scene. Sheldon Troke returned home and went to work the next morning.

Ches Hedderson has no idea as to how Sheldon would have gotten back to Donna's. He may have used his mother's red Corsica. Paul Troke didnt have a vehicle. He either walked or got a taxi from Cathy's.

The police recreated what happened at the Edicotts'. Ches Hedderson had Keith Edicott sit at the end of the chesterfield and Ches went outside and knocked on the door and Mabel Edicott opened it. Keith could not see Ches's face because his mother was blocking it. The only part of Ches that he could see was his hair.

This was something that Ches Hedderson took upon himself to do. A spur-of-the-moment thing as he was there speaking with these people. Both Keith and his mother said the person who knocked on the door was no shorter than Inspector Hedderson.

PAUL TROKE

On Thursday, the day before Donna's death, he was up at the 301 Club, this club that he hung out at every single day. Sheldon came in through the back door. There is two doors to the club, a front door and a back door, but the front door to the upstairs is another part of the club and dont be used that often so everybody uses the back door. Eugene Driscoll was there and him and Sheldon went into the bathroom to resolve an argument. Everything got straightened up and they were drinking and playing pool for a few hours. It was after supper when the three of them left. They went into their mother's house. This guy Eugene is a pretty comical guy and they sat around and were laughing and joking for an hour. Eugene was driving so he dropped Paul and Sheldon back at the club and they stayed there until quarter to twelve. It was starting to empty out by then, most of the people were gone and the club closes a little after twelve. They still werent done drinking so they decided to go downtown. They were buzzed or stoned, whatever you want to call it. Sheldon was well on there. They got out of the taxi in front of the Sundance Saloon and there is a hot-dog cart there and Sheldon wanted to get something to eat. Paul walked into Sam Shades to see who was there. He came back out and looked down by the hot-dog stand where he last seen Sheldon and he wasnt there and he looked up the street and couldnt see him anywhere. He saw him no more that night. Paul ended up staying at Cathy's.

Paul can't recall seeing Sheldon on Friday. He went back to the 301. He spent all day right up until it was close to twelve when he left there. Then he went to Field Street and drank some more and went down to Sam Shades and drank with Joey Yetman and his girlfriend. They were staying at a halfway house so they had to be in at twelve, like when Paul got there they were late and when he was going in they were coming out to be back at the halfway house.

He wasnt feeling too good and he was really drunk. He went into the bathroom and this friend had some cocaine. Paul done some in the bathroom but he also got some off him. In one of them stalls on top of the flush box. Then he rolled up a joint and went outside and smoked it. He wanted to get some air, it's only a small club and it was packed. Paul was talking to a couple of people outside and then he went back into the club and he still wasnt feeling good because he was drunk and he was starting to spin around. He was there another half-hour maybe.

He left and started walking towards Gullivers looking for a taxi. He got a cab and went home to Freshwater Road. It was before quarter after two. Robert Furneaux was there. Paul done some more cocaine and Robert was watching a movie on TV. He wasnt really drunk any more because the cocaine was starting to take effect. So he was feeling a bit better and wanted something else to drink, so he left the house. Right across is a club. He walked up there to the top of the sidewalk there by Leo's Restaurant and you got a plain view of the club and it wasnt open, at least there was no lights on, so he went back in the house.

From Cathy's door to Leo's Restaurant is from here to that wall, maybe seven feet. When Paul came back in he went upstairs and put on a pair of jogging pants and the jeans that he had on he flicked them in the washer. He sat down in the chair and then Cathy came home. The door was unlocked. They were talking for a few minutes, he can't remember what they were talking about, it's hard to get any sense out of Cathy when she's drinking. She laid down on the couch and Robert went to bed and Paul went upstairs and ended up going to bed too. He did not get up through the night. He had a key to the house and lost it.

It didnt seem like he was asleep all that long and Cathy woke him up and told him that Donna had committed suicide. There is a lot of stories goes around up there and you never know what to believe and Paul didnt believe it and was still half-asleep. She woke him up again around noon. He got up and went downstairs and got a shower and a shave. He went up to the 301 Club. He was having a few drinks, trying to get rid of his hangover. The bartender called him to the bar—he was wanted on the phone. It was his sister, Iris. The police want to question you. Get ahold of them. He hung up and got the number to the police station off the bartender and called over. He told the woman who answered the phone to connect him with Major Crimes. An officer come on the line and asked Paul if he could come over. He had no transportation so two officers came to pick him up at the back door of the club. They never come in, they stay out there and barmp the horn.

They took photographs of his hands and upper body and face. He was at the station about an hour. Then they dropped him back off at the 301 Club.

A few days later he gave them blood and hair samples. Soon after he bought a vehicle. He paid five hundred dollars for it. It was only a junker, like something to get you from A to B. He drove it out to Glovertown and it broke down. Trisha was with him. Paul dont know much about cars so he didnt even try to find out what was wrong, he just turned the key a few times and it wouldnt go and left it there. He gave the car to George Bennett.

He got back to St John's by stealing a car. Probably a mile down the road from where they left his car at a gas station. The keys were there and that. He and Trisha never went from car to car, there was a car there and they looked in and the keys were in it.

TELEVISION

Donna Whalen was brutally murdered, thirty-one knife wounds to her chest, she was found face down on her living room floor partially covered by a blanket, a pair of underwear twisted around her neck. Police believe at least one of the woman's children saw her being killed. The police also have their suspects. Police first arrived on the scene later that morning after a frantic call to 911 from a child. In fact, they believe two people may have been involved in the young woman's murder. One person that killed Donna Whalen, the other helped wipe the place clean. Police are also looking for a search warrant to comb the second man's car, the car pictured here, for evidence.

AGNES WHALEN AND
PAT VIVIAN WIRETAP

Agnes Whalen: Did you see the news?

Pat Vivian: Yes, my love.

Do you know who owned the car?

That belongs to Paul Troke. Donna was up talking to him. It was just coincident that I happened to know the car and describe the young fellow that was in the car.

They said Sharon seen him. Sharon didnt see him.

They didnt say Sharon.

It was a child.

One of the youngsters. They shouldnt have said that over the news anyway. Because that's putting that girl in danger saying that.

Well they must have something in the car.

They found that car four hundred miles out of town.

They got two suspects and one cleaned up and the other one killed her.

When they told me how many times she was stabbed.

Thirty-one times.

I walked out by the door and my son said youre all shook up about this now and I said yes Tom I am. I hope they skins them alive.

And it's something like Sheldon Troke would do. Is he still under suspicion?

He's still locked up.

They are trying to put it off because if they charges him now his lawyer will get ahold of all the statements.

I was walking over to the doctor and one of the sergeants asked me where I was going and I said to get me vitamin B needle and I said I heard Sheldon was out. He said no and the best of it is he aint getting out no more.

Put the two of them away for life and they'll do a good thing.

When I was at the doctor's I walked upstairs I walked into Sheldon's sister, Iris.

Dont you go talking to them. Theyre all dangerous. I think Iris is dangerouser than any of them.

Iris said there's rumours going around that Sheldon killed her and Paul cleaned up. Now it comes over the news today. So how did Iris know it before the news?

Well theyre going to make an arrest and if you see the car around there. Gary Bemister phoned me and told me that in two weeks' time.

All the furniture got to be moved out.

Pat, that won't be long coming out. I'm going to put that in the basement.

You should sell it and put some money away in a trust for the children.

The children.

How's Sharon.

I'm glad she didnt hear it over the radio. She didnt see nothing only she came out and see her mother on the floor dead. They must have cleaned up because the police said it was cleaned up. They must have given her an awful torturing that night.

KAREN CLANCEY

One day a man, very polite, called up and said, Do you remember Paul Troke. He has a gold ring with a dollar sign on it. Yes, she said, but I dont remember the ring. Paul's been in the shop a few times, she's cut his hair, last time a short spike haircut. Who am I talking to, she said and he said Sheldon Troke. Do you know if it was a Monday or Tuesday and she said well we're closed on Mondays.

Sheldon, on the phone, said that Paul Troke was being accused of something he didnt do, that it was somebody with long hair who done this. A lawyer would be contacting her. When she hung up she was wondering where he was. He concentrated entirely on his brother Paul's involvement in a crime.

As soon as she hung up there was a police officer came in off-duty. She told him all about it.

II
THE
MURDER

Mom said, Let go, no, Sheldon. And she was saying, Leave me alone, and a voice said, Be quiet Donna, be quiet.

Someone who knew her mom's name. Regular talking. Like she was in her dreams. It was not a loud whisper. Sheldon, when he got into an argument he was so loud that people out in the street could hear him. But everything was really quiet. Sharon thought her mom was having a dream, or Sheldon was up, ransacking the house. The fight sounded different. That night it sounded low and other times they were right loud.

Who owned this other voice? Sheldon. I thought Sheldon was up in the house, so probably it was Sheldon.

Sharon has a little clock. You can make it close and it's small and you can put it in your purse or your pocket. It's a digital clock that doesnt light up at night. She's not sure if she saw 30 or two zeros. That bureau been there probably two or three days. She was able to look out into the living room through mirrors. The two bureaus, her old one and the new one that was her mom's, were by each other. She could look out and see things.

The police tried to line these mirrors up, any which way they could to see if they could see from the room out into the living room and they werent able to do it. Is this like a dream or did Sharon actually see things in the mirror? Could have been. The only big lot of noise she heard was the coffee table and the glass break. She didnt fool with her clock, trying to see what time it was, she just went back to sleep, because she thought nothing was wrong. She thought she saw lights going on and off. There's a fan in the living room. It's not the kind that hangs beneath lights. There's a touch light. You have to touch it to make it go brighter and then touch it again to make it go dimmer. She thought her mom might have did it to herself. All the stuff going on, her life she thought it was dull and she thought that she was fat and everybody hated her.

The night before, her mom was wearing tight blue jeans. Sometimes her mom would go in the bathroom and change her clothes and leave some of her dirty clothes on the floor and then come out and go to bed. Sheldon had a baseball top on, it was grey and he had a pair of jeans on. A red and black jacket. He must have come home on Thursday night after Sharon had gone to bed, because when she woke up on Friday morning he was there. At suppertime on Friday her mom was trying to talk to Sheldon but he was playing with Cory. She was saying Sheldon, I wants to tell you what I'm going to get before I goes to the wedding and he didnt answer her, and then she started to get contrary. She had a frown on her face and he said, What's wrong Donna? And then she said, Youre not listening to me. And he said, Yes I am. I just won't answer you. And she said, Well, I dont know. And they started getting into a big fight.

CATHY FURNEAUX

Since Raymond died Cathy slept on the sofa. So when Paul Troke wasnt there that bedroom was open. Her son, Robert, didnt even bother to go in there. Paul wasnt what you call paying any rent. He was only on social assistance hisself and he had his own apartment that they were paying for so the guy wasnt getting any money. If Paul was eating he'd buy bread. If Cathy was going to the supermarket he'd give her twenty-five dollars if he had it.

This other apartment was around Bannerman Park. Cathy even held on the key one time for him. She was never inside of it. Paul said it was awful small, you can put your hands out and touch the walls.

When she got home that night she had a conversation with Paul. He seemed fine to her. He was sat down in the rocking chair. If he was after smoking a draw she could tell. She had seven beer that night, that was tops. She knows if Paul had to come in that front room she would have woke up. Because Paul is a real klutz.

She never hauled the blankets off him. He had the blankets hauled up. Paul always slept like that. He was there probably naked because that's the way he sleeps.

She has a cordless phone that was on the coffee table. The phone was off. She had it turned off because if you leaves it on the battery will go down. That was just a routine. The phone in the front room rings and she picks up the cordless one. That's how she answered the phone when Bertha called the next morning to tell her about Donna.

ROBERT FURNEAUX

That Friday night Paul came home around two and Robert's mom came home shortly after. She locked the door and came up over the stairs and took her coat off and laid it in the kitchen where you puts your coat. Paul was sat in the rocking chair, Robert was on the couch. Him and Paul and Mom were talking and then she laid down on the couch and Robert got on the floor and Paul stayed in the rocking chair and he and Paul watched TV and she fell asleep. Then the two of them went to bed about a half-hour later. They went up over the stairs the same time.

The door has one of those bolt locks on it. You need a key from the inside and the outside and it squeaks when you open up the door. You can hear it up on the top floor. You could jump out through the window. You'd probably break your legs. There was no fire escapes or nothing like that.

Mom woke Robert up and told him Donna Whalen was dead.

Usually Robert hangs out by Leo's, just a couple of doors up from their house on the corner. He has no idea what time he got home other than some time before eleven because he was on probation.

PAUL TROKE AND
CATHY FURNEAUX WIRETAP

Paul: They said me and your statements dont check out. They said that Mom's a liar. They said that I wasnt home in bed and Sheldon wasnt home in bed and they can place me and Sheldon at the scene of the crime. They said to me that you went to bed first.

Cathy: I said I was on the chesterfield.

They said you went to bed first and we stayed up and watched TV.

I said you and Robert were up. I was on the chesterfield.

They fucking lied.

They knew I didnt sleep in the bed.

Me and Sheldon was just out there talking to Jim Lythgoe and he said they must have the DNA testing back and now theyre fucking down trying to fuck us around. Ches Hedderson said I'm a liar. Sheldon's a liar. They got witnesses. I booted the fucking chair across the room. I jumped up. I said now look I got fuck all else to say to ye.

Why dont ye fucking leave me alone. The DNA testing must have come back now because it's a month now right.

It takes six weeks.

Jim Lythgoe said it should be.

Well you know what's wrong. The DNA test came back and everything came back on you and Sheldon all right and theyre just trying to hound ye. Because you know what it is, whatever animal that done that to Donna they can't find the person so they just want someone to pin it on.

He said Mom's a liar. He said Sheldon wasnt home in bed and I wasnt home in bed.

The truth is when I came home, you were sat in the rocking chair, Robert was on the couch, watching TV. I had a big bag of salt-and-fucking-vinegar chips in me hand. I asked ye did you want some and I laid the bag of chips down on the side and I was awake for a while and then I laid on the chesterfield and you and Robert were watching TV and then the two of ye went up to bed.

I'm not sure if I said I went to bed first or fucking you went to sleep first. I said when Cathy wants to go to sleep we turns the TV off and goes to bed which we do. And you know what else he said? He said ever since Donna got murdered you've been getting in nothing but trouble. I said fucking listen here, I've been in trouble all my fucking life. He said you've been taking pills and drinking booze ever since Donna died. Cathy, before Donna died I was into pills and drinking. Like holy fuck.

Jesus Paul I know you always did the fucking pills.

I was hiding it from Trisha but I was still in the fucking pills and the fucking drinking.

There's only once you gave up drinking, you and Joey Yetman had a bet and you gave up for a week and a half.

And then he called Mom a liar and I booted the chair across the room. I'm fucking about to go crazy, boy.

Dont listen to them. Look you knows in your own heart and soul youre innocent and Sheldon knows in his own heart and soul youre innocent and all of us knows youre innocent.

He said to me youre going to get eight to ten years on this armed robbery. I said I'm only fucking on charges. I said I aint found fucking guilty yet.

You dont know nothing. I mean if you knew anything.

I told them. I was getting ready to cooperate with them, Cathy.

That's what I mean.

I got nothing to hide. I was out there trying to help the two fucking bastards and then they called Mom a liar. Then he said your stories dont check. Fuck I was drunk, you were drunk. I dont know who went to bed fucking first.

I wasnt drunk drunk.

I know one thing, fucking I was home.

I wasnt drunk drunk Paul when I came home.

No you werent drunk but you had a buzz going.

I had a buzz going.

I wasnt drunk either. I had a buzz on just the same as yourself.

BERTHA TROKE WIRETAP

That's the way they works it. If they go and tell Paul that you gave a statement and then they'll go to you and say Paul is after rolling over on you, this is the way they works, Cathy. Anyways, as far as I'm concerned about police, I dont give a fuck if my phone is bugged, to be a policeman you got to be streetwise so they'd have to commit crimes theyselves. Or how could they become police, but they'll fucking lie to you and everything else and I knows it because I went through the experience. When Ches Hedderson said to me over there how Sharon said Sheldon done it and I said Sharon also said Jacob Parrott done it and he got in my face about five times and said no she didnt and I said yes she did. I said because Donna's mother told me and Donna's mother did tell me.

CATHY FURNEAUX AND
IRIS TROKE WIRETAP

Cathy: If they comes here any more I'm going to say no. I gave ye everything. Ye searched the house from top to bottom. They done it all to me and I dont want ye around here no more. I got a youngster to look after.

Iris: I'm after looking at it from every angle and I knows in my heart Sheldon didnt do it. But every time I talks to Ruth Vivian she's like—Cathy did you ever get this you can pick out something not being said? It's like that woman almost knew. She knows something, Cathy. The last time I spoke to her she said Donna knew all that week something was going to happen to her.

Cathy: What do they think, I'm fucking nuts or something. That I'll actually let someone in my house that'd be after killing somebody and let them come in here and me be sitting down like nothing ever happened? Sure I'd be fucking frightened to death of the person myself. I mean theyre sick fucking people.

BERTHA TROKE

Bertha Troke didnt know anything about Donna going away until she overheard the conversation Sheldon had with Donna's mother on

the phone. Donna didnt know herself she was going away. Sheldon
had sold his car and he gave her a hundred dollars to put towards her
package. On Thursday before Donna died, Sheldon left to pick up his
cheque because he wasnt working that day. Bertha saw him again that
night around eight-thirty, him and Paul and Eugene Driscoll. They
stayed at Bertha's house and when they were leaving she told Sheldon
he should stay home because he was going to work the next morning
and he said he'd be home.

The next time she heard from Sheldon it was eight on the Friday
night and he phoned. Bertha was watching TV. Did she know that
Joey Yetman's girlfriend won the lotto? Bertha said no, the woman that
won it her picture is in the paper, and Sheldon told her yes she did,
they were halves, and he said well I'll be home around ten oclock. He
was calling from Donna's.

The man that lived next door was after taking off around six-thirty
from the Waterford Hospital and his family were in a panic. He's
fifty-six years old but they were worried about him because he's on
heavy medication and they were looking for him, and Bertha told
them she'd keep a watch out for him and if she heard anyone out into
the house she'd let them know. So she was watching the cars coming
up and down the road. Ten minutes after ten a car pulled up by the
door out towards the curb. Bertha saw the headlights, she couldnt see
the colour of the car. And where her husband Clayton was sitting he
said that's Sheldon, he could see him coming to the steps. She didnt
know if it was Donna or Tom Vivian driving. Agnes Whalen told her
the next morning that Donna drove him home. It was ten after ten
because right by the window there's a gold clock and that's her chair.
Nobody else sits there.

Sheldon came in and walked to the door where that black thing
is hanging over the living room door. He looked in and said what

are ye doing and Bertha told him what was on. He took his coat off, hung it up in the hall and went out in the dining room to roll his cigarette. He got a glass of cream soda and came in. He sat on the end of the chesterfield, smoked the roll and drank his glass of cream soda. It's very quiet there, there's no children and there's just Bertha and Clayton and when youre rolling them cigarettes with the cigarette roller you can hear it clicking.

It was just about over by the time he got in, it started to come up on the screen the names, and Sheldon passed the remark that Lee Harvey Oswald was framed, and got up with the glass and he walked out and put the glass on the cupboard and as he passed the door to go upstairs he said good night. Bertha said are you going to work tomorrow. Now the only reason why she asked him was he didnt always work on Saturdays, and if it had to be any night of the week she wouldnt have asked him. So he continued on and went upstairs. It was close to ten-thirty so there was another story came on and Bertha and Clayton watched that, that was over at twelve-thirty. She went out and started to make Sheldon's lunch and Clayton was still looking at TV. She made the lunch and put it in the refrigerator, and she had his thermos bottle rinsed and took the cover and laid it on the cupboard, took the frying pan out and laid his eggs in it for the next morning. Clayton was after going upstairs ahead of her. It would have been one oclock because Clayton watches *Are You Being Served?* and she's sure he wouldnt have left until it was over because he loves looking at that.

He was up there ahead of her because when she made the lunch she had to turn off the lights and make sure the door was locked.

Sheldon's bedroom. Outside the door it shows where this mat is at the top of the stairs and the washroom and you can see the hamper in Sheldon's bedroom and part of the bed. His bedroom door it could be closed if you had to take the carpet square and fold it back but you couldnt close the door because it wouldnt go over the carpet, you'd have to move the carpet back.

Clayton and Bertha sleep in the same room. That's Bertha's bedroom, her phone and clock, her lamp and teddy bear. That clock, the hands are a sort of lime and it lights up in the nighttime. Do you want to take a loan of it for a night?

When she got to the top of the stairs Sheldon was snoring his head off. There was no light on in his room. There's a white sheer up to the window and it's a long window and it's bright. You could almost go and take a bath without a light on because it was two poles on the outside close to the house. The walls are white, the bedspread is white, the bed is white, the sheer is white.

Bertha got up during the night. Because this complaint that she has you get a feeling that you can't hold, it's not worth going for but still you got to go. It's a common thing with a woman with a large family. The first time she went it was around twenty-five after two. She saw Sheldon in bed and heard him snoring. If he had to have the bedroom door closed she still would have heard him snoring but she wouldnt have been able to see him. The bedroom door wasnt closed. She even told Sheldon that he could close it and how to hoist up the carpet. He said no he didnt need it closed. Not that night but before that.

At three-forty-five Sheldon was in bed. The next time she got up she went downstairs and it was twenty-five after five by her clock but it was six oclock by the clock downstairs. He was still in bed. This clock she got is always losing time.

At six she felt a bit hungry. She got to explain this sickness. This sickness is not something that you can't eat or anything, it's an aggravating feeling. She got a bowl of Special K. After that she went back to bed and started feeling tired because she was awake off and on.

But that's every night for her, that wasnt just that night. That's been going on for years. She got records to prove that.

Now throughout the night it really wasnt sleep, or what she calls sleep is like catnaps. She goes to sleep and wakes up because they have the scanner on too and she listened to that because it was a Friday night and Paul was downtown. She wanted to know where he was at downtown and the scanner lets her know.

Bertha's been getting very little sleep for the past six or seven years. She's under the care of a psychiatrist and this is one of her problems. She dont sleep. She can get her files. She's on the go all night long. She had a few pills left over when she got them from the doctor and she took them. She normally gets up at two oclock in the morning and moves her furniture around and not go to bed at all. A few minutes' sleep is good enough.

You dont get a telegram saying youre going to get like this. This is just something comes over you. Youre not a woman, youre not after having a big family so you got no idea what way this strikes you. Bertha knows what way it strikes her. She's had it over twenty-seven years and it's quite common in a woman after having children. You dont get no warning. It's not something that's going to kill you or youre going to die from it. It's quite tormenting and you didnt have no children so you dont know what youre talking about there. You'll have to talk to a doctor.

Clayton Troke she dont know if he was asleep. Some nights she gets up and she'll say are you awake. Some nights he'll say yes and she'll say do you want to come out and have a bowl of Special K with me. If he dont answer well then she knows he's asleep.

Fifteen minutes' sleep is as good as twenty-four hours to someone else. She's adjusted to this. The proper one for you to talk to would be her doctor or get her file. She's been adjusted to this for years that she dont get to sleep. When you get a bit older you dont require as much sleep. And another thing she's being treated because she's hyper. When youre like that you always got to be on the go. She got out of bed half past two the other morning putting up curtains and cleaning up the house and that. So she was in bed and got up, she can't stay still. If you want she can get her files.

CLAYTON TROKE

Donna was a bad junkie. Every day she was getting the pills. Clayton had run out of the medication he takes for his back and Donna could come up with them. She came in one day, it was just after dinner, and she kicked off her sneakers down at the bottom of the stairs and she ran up over the stairs and asked where was Bertha, and Clayton said she was downstairs putting clothes in the washer. She bumped her leg off the coffee table and said oh fuck. She said now that's going to bruise. And she went downstairs and then her and Bertha come upstairs and she showed them her leg she said look what did I tell you. There was a big bruise on her leg. That's the only time that Clayton ever seen a bruise on her.

On Friday he was home. There was five episodes of *The JFK Story* and he was following it up. He was sitting on the end of the chesterfield close to the window. Sheldon came to the house at ten past ten. Clayton has five clocks in the house. Bertha said there was a car out by the door and Clayton looked. That's Sheldon, he said. He come in through the door and walked into the hall and asked how they were doing. He wasnt drunk. He didnt have anything into him because Sheldon dont usually come home when he's drinking.

Clayton had to phone his brother to see if he could get a truck for to go to pick up some wood. And he couldnt get a pickup for that day.

He could have got one the next evening but he phoned his friend back and told him to forget about the wood.

There was a story coming on that Bertha wanted to look at, Clayton not so much. So she looked at it and that was over. Clayton went to the bathroom. Sheldon was in bed. You couldnt help but notice his room because it's illuminated pretty well.

When Clayton went up over the stairs Bertha was making Sheldon's lunch. He went in the bathroom and got washed. Sheldon was sleeping. After he got washed he got in the bed and shortly after that Bertha come up and she got washed and into bed.

They had a cigarette and Clayton can't sleep, he has a problem with insomnia so he's just lying there in the bed and you can hear Sheldon moving in the bed, you can hear him snore.

Clayton takes an antidepressant and Tylenol 3 for his back. He was just laying in bed awake and Bertha got up and went to the bathroom. Shortly after he went. It would have been about two-thirty. He stayed awake for a half an hour after that. The next thing was he heard Sheldon getting up in the morning. You could smell him cooking downstairs the bacon and eggs. He came upstairs and asked his mother if she could drive him to work and she said are you awake, and Clayton said yes. She said I'm too sick. She was sick for a few days before that.

Clayton drove him to the cemetery and dropped him off down at the bottom. What time should I pick you up, and Sheldon said he'd phone. He might work a couple of hours overtime, he said, because he was after missing work that week. Clayton came on home and went straight back to bed. It was ten minutes to nine because the clock was on the dresser. He was laying there and he heard the scanner. He heard get ahold to Dr Abery, there's a DOA and they said the address and Clayton thought to himself, that's where Donna lives. Then the phone rang. There is nobody calling that early in the morning. Bertha

reached over to answer the phone and before she answered the phone
he said Bertha, Donna is dead. She never heard him. When she hung
up she said, That was Iris. I got to get ahold of Pat Vivian. I wonder
why do I have to get ahold of Pat? And Clayton said Bertha, what
number does Donna live on?

She phoned Pat Vivian and couldnt get no answer. The phone
rang again and it was Iris and she said Donna is dead. Bertha said,
Youre crazy, Donna dead, and she said, Yes, and Bertha asked her what
happened and Iris said that Tom Vivian told her she's sliced up.

Bertha said to Clayton there's no way that Donna is slashed up
because she loved herself too much and she wouldnt harm her body.

The phone rang again and it was Agnes Whalen, Donna's mother.
She told Bertha that Donna was dead. And she wanted to know if
Clayton would go out and pick up her husband, Aubrey. Clayton left
the house right away. He lost no time getting to the graveyard, let's put
it that way. He was thinking how was he going to tell Sheldon about
Donna and he said aloud, Why me.

He drove down through the graveyard and Sheldon was working in
the middle. Aubrey Whalen was up in the Jewish part. Clayton hauled
in and Sheldon came down to the car and said, Clayton, what's wrong,
and he said, Sheldon, I have some bad news for you.

Sheldon's words to him were, Clayton, who is it?

It's Donna, he said, DOA. Clayton was crying at this time because
he didnt know how to tell him. Sheldon sort of screeched, he didnt
bawl right out, he raised his voice and said what and he turned
white. He mistook it for an OD because he said, But Donna never
had no pills last night. And then Clayton said it's a DOA, Donna is
slashed up.

Sheldon started to run up towards Aubrey and then he decided to
walk but he was walking fast up towards him. Clayton dont know

what he said to Aubrey. They got the wheelbarrel and the shovels and put it in the shed and they were hurrying. Both of them came down and Sheldon said you go on right home now, Mr Whalen, and Sheldon got in the car and Clayton said, Did you tell Aubrey, and Sheldon said, How could I tell him that?

They left the graveyard and went out Blackmarsh Road and Sheldon was looking away and he was crying. You could hear him sobbing and going across Pearce Avenue he looked at Clayton and said, What's going to become of poor Sharon and Cory?

Clayton didnt know what to say, he didnt have any words to say to him. They went on and hauled in about two doors down from Donna's and Ches Hedderson came over to the car and he said he wanted to talk to Sheldon. Sheldon was getting out of the car anyway and Clayton said to Ches Hedderson he said how is Sheldon going to get home and Hedderson said we'll look after that.

The squad car was behind them and when Sheldon got out to go back to the car with Ches Hedderson, Agnes Whalen and Tom Vivian come up over the steps and they were saying, Dont tell them nothing, Sheldon, dont tell them nothing, and this is the way they were going with their hands. Dont tell them nothing. Sheldon went back to the car and Clayton drove home.

SHARON WHALEN

The room at the end of the hallway there is Sharon's room. There's a bureau in the middle of the doorway. That was her mom's. She was going to put that bureau in Sharon's room and give Sharon's to Cory. The furniture was being moved around because her mom had gotten new furniture and it had arrived. It was in her mom's room. With the bureau there you arent able to close the door all the way.

The gloves on the floor, her mother never used them and if she ever used them well Sharon wasnt around she'd never leave them on the floor. Because her mom used to like to be clean and tidy.

The top of the garbage can, she never left it on the floor before. The mop and bucket. Mom usually put it in the cupboard. Sharon's seen it out like that in the kitchen before, but not very often. Her mother never cleaned up late at night. The mop and the bucket, the gloves on the floor, the top of the garbage can, they werent there when Sharon went to sleep Friday night.

When she was getting ready for school, Mommy was in the chair by the phone watching TV and Sheldon was sleeping on the couch. This was Friday. Cory was in the kitchen having breakfast. She went to school and her mom was getting Cory ready for daycare up by Tim Hortons. Cory gets to daycare by bus. If he's sick in the morning and better in the afternoon Mom might drive him. The car is white and has rust spots on it. Sharon went home for lunch and had a sandwich. Sheldon was watching TV. He had on jeans and a white and black top. Mom was out shopping. The car was gone, she normally parks on front. Sheldon said bye and Sharon went back and played outside and the bell rang. The subject that afternoon was math corrections. They played a few games and Mrs Grimes read the story. Sharon was skipping and then she and Ashley went up by Mary Brown's on Freshwater Road and played with a couple of friends, Catherine and Nicole. Then they played by the school and then went down by Ashley's house and played for a while. They went to the store and came back and Catherine and Nicole had to go home. Sharon and Ashley skipped and played ball and Mom called her in for supper around six.

After supper, Sharon did her homework and watched *The Simpsons* on TV. She watched half of it in her room and half of it in her mom's room, because Sharon's TV is a little fuzzy. Mom was down at Tom

Vivian's house talking to him and Sheldon was watching TV in the living room. Mom came up from Tom's around nine and she started watching a movie in the living room. Sharon had the same movie on in her mommy's room and it was a movie about a man who left his wife for another lady. The wife came in and started spray-painting things and breaking plates and glasses. Sharon did not go out into the living room because she was afraid Mom would put her to bed. She did go out to look at the *TV Guide* and her mom said your eyes look tired and told her to go to bed. She went to bed and then she could hear them putting their boots on out by the bathroom. Her mom came in and told Sharon that she was dropping Sheldon off. She heard the two of them walking down the stairs. There's no carpet on the stairs going down. While the movie was on and her mom and Sheldon were in the living room, Sharon heard them talking. They were talking and saying what was going to happen next in the movie. When they left Sharon turned her TV on for a few minutes and there was something on about an election and then she turned her radio on and got into bed and fell asleep. It was going on ten p.m. She did not hear her mom come back.

BERTHA TROKE

She phoned Cathy Furneaux and let her know that Donna was dead. She told Cathy that she slashed up. That was what she heard, but she didnt believe it. Donna was the type of a girl that loved life, she loved herself. Iris said she must have OD'd and Bertha said no Donna wouldnt be able to OD.

The police visited their home, two officers. They had no warrant. They said they needed Sheldon's clothes, and Bertha said no problem and she took them upstairs. It was Constable Gary Bemister. This would be the clothes that Sheldon wore home the night before. His jeans were laid across the hamper and his shirt was on the bottom of the bed on the comforter. She couldnt find his shirt. Constable Bemister was the one that found his shirt. She gave his jacket and she wasnt sure of his deck shoes or his sneakers so she told him that he had better take both just to be sure and he said no that's all right, I'll take the sneakers. He didnt want the shoes so he didnt take the shoes. Bertha asked did they know what happened to Donna. Gary Bemister said all they done was sent him to get Sheldon's clothes and to take her statement. He said, If you were found dead here this morning who do you think theyre going to go after? Bertha said what do you mean. He said they'd go after Clayton. Why. Because he's with you, he said. Bertha said so in other words theyre going after Sheldon. He said well it's only routine, they'll question him.

When Sheldon came home Friday evening he never had a spoonful of beer in him. Because if Sheldon had to have a bottle of beer in him he wouldnt have come home because he'd be looking for more. He was perfectly sober. If anything he was tired.

Gary Bemister was in an awful hurry just to write down what she said and get out of there. Do you think the police tell the truth? You got to laugh at that one. Bertha got to laugh too. She just glanced at it like that and threw it to one side. She didnt need to read it because she knew that what she had given was the truth. She could have told Constable Bemister a lot more but he seemed like the piece of wood to her. He wasnt writing down half what she was telling him. Constable Bemister couldnt wait to get out of her house.

GARY BEMISTER

Gary spoke with Bertha Troke and Clayton Troke. He was sat with them in the living room with Constable Charles Stamp as they executed the search warrant. Gary had a quick look into the kitchen and there was a wallet there. He looked through it and it was Sheldon Troke's wallet. There was a card in it, Gullivers Cabs, Car 18 and the name on it was Michael Porter. It was a business card. He did not seize the card, but he did make a note of it.

CATHY FURNEAUX

The phone rings and it's Bertha Troke calling. She said, Cathy have a guess who's dead.

Who.

Donna.

Go on what happened to her, did she OD?

She was slashed up.

Cathy hung up the phone and ran upstairs to Paul's room. She shook him.

I got some bad news, Paul. Have a guess who's dead.

Who?

Donna.

Why what happened to her, what'd she OD?

She slashed her wrists, she slashed up.

Cathy Furneaux went downstairs, she dont know if Paul fell right back to sleep. She was like a hen on a hot rock herself. She couldnt believe that Donna was dead.

Paul didnt get out of bed until quite late that afternoon.

SCOTT LOCKE

Sam Shades is a club between Benders and Pier 17 on a little lane where youre going through George Street. The big club across from it is the Sundance. They have specials on down there, a buck a beer and other specials they sing out during the night.

Scott Locke come in eight oclock Friday night and worked until three. Paul Troke was at the club that night. The club can hold two hundred but it wasnt jammed. Scott used to live over the street from Paul while they were growing up. Paul came in by hisself around ten-thirty. There's a dance floor as soon as you walks in then you go to your left and it's the bar. Around the corner it's the bathrooms and then the stairs to go upstairs.

Scott makes sure nothing gets out of control. He moves through the club. They always check the washrooms. Paul went into the washroom Friday night. He went into a stall. He was with someone in the stall. Scott seen four legs. They might have been having a conversation. Scott went in there to make sure nothing was on the go. No dope or nothing was being smoked. Scott didnt smell nothing. He left the washroom and went back and stood against the wall. Paul came out and he strewed along the side of him, put his head back on the wall and stayed there for a minute and left. He must have had a buzz on. He wasnt drunk, he wasnt loaded. He was half-drunk. Paul Troke is a drinker. He left for fifteen minutes at the most and come back into the club. Not all the way back, back into the hall. He looked like he was whacked out of it.

It's fairly unusual at Sam Shade's that two men go into the washroom and into one stall. Maybe they were talking, Scott didnt want to go in and bang on the door. They could have been up to something. Well if theyre in there and he doesnt smell marijuana he just leaves them, whatever theyre up to theyre up to. Paul was able to walk out of the bar under his own steam. To tell you the truth, Scott is somewhat scared today to say exactly what he thinks.

MICHAEL PORTER

He was driving a taxi downtown. Many people Thursday night. There was one person in particular that stood out. Michael picked this person up at the bottom of Bates Hill. Somewhere close to twelve oclock. Michael was letting people out and this person got in the front seat and asked him to drive.

Where.

I got money drive anywhere, he said.

Well I still got to have a direction.

Take me to a drug store.

The only drug store Michael knew to be open that hour on a Thursday is Shoppers, so that's where they headed. The man asked if he heard tell of the Trokes.

I knew a family of Trokes many years ago, Michael Porter said.

Well I'm Sheldon, he said.

Sheldon said he'd had a fight with his girlfriend and that he didnt know if he was right or she was right.

Everybody has fights, Michael Porter said. Making up is good.

When they got there the fare was about three fifty. Sheldon gave him five dollars and then he thanked him for talking to him. Will you talk to me five years from now?

Michael said, Why not?

I've been in prison.

Well you served your time, you paid your penalty, so why wouldnt I speak to you?

As he was getting out Sheldon Troke reached in his pocket and took out some more money.

No that's okay youre after paying.

It's only money, he said. Where's that going to be five years from now.

He threw it on the dash and got out. It was about eighteen more dollars.

Michael Porter took out a card with the car number on it and gave it to him and told him any time he wants a cab to give him a call.

Sheldon headed east, in that direction of the curling club over there. Michael Porter just backed up the car then and went back to the stand. Sheldon didnt go into the drug store, no he didnt.

TANG MAN

Tang Man operates a Chinese takeout restaurant. She is originally from Hong Kong. She takes orders from customers either in person or by telephone. She also helps out in the kitchen. Her husband, his English is not as good as hers.

She knows a person by the name of Donna Whalen. She usually telephones to place orders for meals. Sometimes she came to the restaurant to place the orders. Tang knows that Donna lived in a house opposite the restaurant but she doesnt know which house.

When Donna called in her orders she asked for Item No. 4 on the menu. That is sweet-and-sour chicken balls, chicken fried noodles, chicken chow mein, chicken fried rice. She asked Tang to place more green onion. It cost five dollars and ninety cents.

When Donna spoke she spoke in a regular tone and also she tends to say words in a long way. To slow down and drag it out.

On Thursday night a man came into the restaurant. It was about twelve-thirty. He asked Tang do you know who I am. He said, Donna Whalen is my girlfriend. He asked for a pack of cigarettes and also a No. 4 from the menu the way Donna likes it, with extra green onions. He appeared to be a little bit drunk. From Tang's experience people who are drunk do not have enough money so she asked him to pay her first. He took his money and other things from his pocket and he counted the money and there was not enough to pay. There was a metal cigarette case, a wallet, some keys. He took a photo card out of his wallet and showed it to Tang. It was of himself. The photo was in the corner, the date. The card was laminated.

He said, Could you let me use a phone.

She handed the telephone set to him and he dialed the number himself. He got through. Donna, he said.

It appeared that the other side hanged up the telephone. So Tang told him maybe she should telephone it for him. He gave her back the telephone set. Tang's husband came out from the kitchen so she asked him to telephone. The customer told her the telephone number and Tang passed it on to her husband in Chinese. Her husband put it through. He listened to the telephone set for a little while.

Oh, he said, the person on the other side makes a lot of noise.

He gave Tang back the telephone set. And she heard a voice from the telephone to the effect that if you call again I will call the police. The person on the other side was very angry, so Tang hanged up the telephone.

The customer said, I will call my sister.

She gave him the telephone and he dialed the telephone himself and then he said oh nobody answer. And he make a gesture with his finger by pointing it to his head. Tang thinks he was trying to think who to telephone. Then he said, I will look for my friend and then he dialed the telephone again. He got through and he asked who are you. It would appear that the other side told him the name, and the customer called the other side by name, Cathy.

The customer said, Yes I also know that I got to sleep too.

Tang walked into the kitchen. He was still speaking. After about two minutes she came out from the kitchen. She heard the customer talk into the telephone. Do you want to talk to her, he said. And then he handed Tang the telephone. She simply hung up the telephone. Then a little gesture like this. Tilt the head. Indicating that he couldnt find the other person. He picked up all the things on the counter. He walked out of the restaurant but he'd left a bunch of keys so after he had passed the first door Tang knocked on the counter and showed him the keys. He came back to take the keys. Then he walked out of the first door and turned back to speak and then pointed his finger at that direction and said, I'm going to look for my girlfriend. Tang went back into the kitchen. She didnt pay attention to where he went. That's what happened.

Tang met Sheldon Troke before this night, more than three times. Normally Donna would telephone in the order and then he came to pick up the order. Other men would come over to pick up orders for Donna. About three different men. One of them came more than once. There was one who was about thirty to forty years of age. He came shortly before this matter arose. One man he had a pot belly. He was well dressed. When Sheldon came to pick up the food he usually was very quiet and he told Tang, Oh I come to pick up the food, and then he read the newspapers.

GARY BEMISTER

Pat Vivian's bedroom was under Donna's and he often used to hear them having sex. It didnt bother him at all about hearing them. He moved from this room, and moved his son Tom in there who would have been able to hear the same thing.

That Thursday night, when Donna thought someone was watching her through the window, she called Pat's house. Pat himself had heard a noise in the back hall. He went to the door and put his ear to the door and listened. Then he saw Sheldon Troke leaving the takeout across the street. Sheldon knocked on Donna's front door. Pat heard the conversation between Donna and Sheldon. Donna said, Dont be so loud, you'll wake up the children. Donna came downstairs and opened up the door and both of them walked up the stairs. They had words for a while and then things settled down.

Pat Vivian had a conversation with Donna Friday afternoon. This is when Donna told him that a person was looking through a window near the back stairs peering into her kitchen window. Ten minutes later Sheldon Troke showed up and stayed the night.

If there was an argument between Donna and Sheldon on Friday night going into Saturday morning, Pat would have heard it because Sheldon has a deep voice.

JOEY YETMAN

He doesnt know why he's here because he dont know nothing. That's why. He wrote down the wrong date though. And when they walked in the first thing they looked at was the calendar. He's employed snow clearing. They landscapes in the summertime so he only started snow clearing two weeks ago. But he's with them now a year.

Before that he had lots of work. Longshore Maritime Data, Le Bar. Le Bar is on George Street. Joey was bartender, sometimes doorman. He worked at Le Bar on Friday and Saturday, other days if they had a bash or something. Like a school bash, he might have worked then.

He knows Sheldon Troke. He's friends with him. He sometimes saw him at Le Bar. Joey had a problem last year. He was hooked on valium but he got off that with the psychiatrist and that.

Gary Bemister says Joey was in the car making a statement? He certainly dont remember none of them ever coming to his door and he'll even bring his family down here—in front of the house writing a statement in a police cruiser, never happened.

GARY BEMISTER

Paul Troke had been attempting to find out who had been with Sheldon on Thursday night and he advised the police that it was Joey Yetman. Gary Bemister interviewed Joey Yetman in a patrol unit outside of his home. Joey Yetman was seated in the rear of the patrol unit, Gary was in the front. They had a conversation and Gary was writing down what he was saying. At one point Gary made a correction which Joey pointed out. At the end of the interview Gary read the statement back to him and Joey indicated that what was on the statement was truthful, however he refused to sign it. He was friends with the Trokes, he knew them, and he didnt want to get involved with the case. This is the statement of Joey Yetman:

> I work at Le Bar on George Street as a doorman and busboy. Thursday night before last I was working eight p.m. to one a.m. I dont know what time Sheldon Troke came into the club but I remember him being there. At midnight I went out by the shooter bar to tell Sheldon to leave because I was getting off. He was asleep and I woke him up. He looked up at me and took out a bottle of pills from his coat pocket. His jacket had red in it and it was black as well. He opened the pill bottle and dumped it on the table. He took about fifteen pills. Some of the pills went on the floor and I picked them up and threw them in the garbage. I was talking to him until about one a.m. and then I left. When I told Sheldon to leave he got upset.

BERTHA TROKE

The last conversation she had with Donna it was Friday afternoon. Sheldon wouldnt be coming home to supper, she said, because he was going in to her house to babysit. She was going to her mother's to go washing. Bertha was just after taking a bit of salmon out of the deep-freeze and Donna said would that be a problem and Bertha said no it's just that she wouldnt have supper too early. And then she said she got Clayton on the other line could you get back and Donna said yeah and she never heard tell of her after.

PAUL TROKE

Paul doesnt remember Cathy waking him up, but it wouldnt be the first time he passed out in bed with a pair of jogging pants and a T-shirt on. Cathy was half out of it herself. If she said she was fine, how she couldnt remember who put the jeans in the washer the next morning. She asked Paul did she wash them. She laid down, she had a bag of chips, she was eating the chips and she was going to sleep because the TV was off and Paul went upstairs.

The very first time when he went to Donna's house, him and Sheldon went there, Sheldon was showing Paul the basement saying we could put some weights here and work out. They used the back door but on all other occasions Paul used the front door.

When Paul did break and enters he wore gloves so he would not leave fingerprints. He knows how important it is not to leave fingerprints or footprints when you are at crimes. Wipe things down, Paul never done it before. Broke into places or whatever and start wiping fingerprints off things no.

He had fifteen to twenty drinks at the 301 Club that Friday. A fair amount, enough to be half-drunk. Some hash. He could have taken painkillers because he used to take them on a regular basis. When youre half-drunk and you do cocaine it levels you out, you dont really be drunk any more because the cocaine takes effect, that's the whole point of taking the cocaine because youre drunk and starting to spin and you want to level out.

CLAYTON TROKE

Sheldon knew Donna was taking pills. He told Clayton that Donna was mad about him drinking and he hawked a couple of bottles off the ceiling. He was sorry for doing it, he didnt mean it, but he was drinking at the time. Donna was in to the house and she said Sheldon was home, he had to patch the wall. They were arguing on the phone and Donna wouldnt talk to him. She used to hang up on him, and she hung up on him three or four times. When he got off the phone, he said, Geez, she gets on my nerves. He said, I'd like to kill her. Well that's in their everyday vocabulary around the house once you rear some children. Clayton says that to his children twenty times a day, but not something that he means.

Bertha and Clayton never discussed their statements because he thought they were going to have to take a lie detector test. It's identical because it's true. Bertha came up halfways over the stairs and she said Clayton, the police are down there and they want to talk to you again. They were after taking a statement from him before, so he said Bertha, tell them to fly to fuck. What I got to say, I'll say it on the stand.

Clayton didnt care really what Gary Bemister wrote down. He had his chance to get on the stand and tell the truth. That's the only thing and he's not sure if he told him that Sheldon got home at ten after ten. Gary Bemister said I only want a short statement, it's not going to take too long—it seemed to Clayton that he shortened the statement up. He just wanted to get out of the house. He didnt ask if it was accurate.

When Bertha gave her statement Clayton was in the house, but not in the same room. He was out talking to Ches Hedderson and Hedderson was making sure that Clayton never heard anything. They were out in the dining room. So, how could he hear.

If Gary Bemister wanted to shorten up this statement, Clayton didnt care. He had to get on the stand to tell the truth and this is what he's doing. There's a few people after getting on the stand and telling the truth and there's a few people not after telling the truth. The police are lying for one thing. And a lot of the witnesses are lying. Forget about telling the police. It's not worthwhile telling the police anything because they won't believe you and they won't be honest about it later. That's the one thing that you got right. The police they are liars, they won't believe the Trokes, they didnt believe the people that got on the stand, neither did you.

Clayton drove Paul down one night to pick up a couple of movies. They came home and watched the movies and the next thing it came over the scanner: Paul Troke is down putting up George Street. He's smashing bottles off of Trapper John's, and Paul looked at his father and his mother. None of the family ever got away with anything. They always disciplined them and Paul said now, Dad, look, if I wasnt here, when I'd come home you'd go off your head. And Clayton said yes, Paul, I would. So another night it come over the scanner—watch Raymond Troke, he's up to no good, he's fighting down on George Street. Raymond was sat down in the living room. Another time Paul was babysitting just down the street a three-minute walk, he was babysitting for Mrs Tucker and it come over again, Paul Troke was fighting. Bertha put on her coat and she said that goddamn nuisance, he told me he was babysitting. She went down to Patsy Tucker's and who should come to the door but

Paul. And then there was another time Sheldon was the only one on the street, the rest of them were away and a taxi driver called in and said the Trokes they won't pay the taxi, and Bertha said aint this ridiculous and Clayton said what can we do about it. They got a vendetta against us. They could hear it on the scanner, all the police cars, they all tried to get in at one time, they were saying, I'll head along there. The next thing another car says I'll be there in a second and a third car, I'll go along too. Because it's Trokes. And when they got to where they were going, the taxi driver—there was about ten cars—it was no Troke at all it was Joey Yetman. And the next thing they said, oh that's all fixed up now, but they never came back and said it wasnt the Trokes. Everybody that had scanners thinks it was Trokes.

It was ten after ten because Paul and Sheldon and Raymond and Iris was after being blamed so many times for doing things that they wasnt doing that Clayton got into the habit of looking at the clock when anything went on down the street.

KIM PARROTT

At first Donna told Kim that she had back pains, but Kim couldnt understand why she needed her to get the pills when she could get them. Kim agreed to do it and it was going on like that for a few months and then she figured Donna was getting hooked to them and Kim was going to stop getting her the pills.

Kim was at her house once and the mop and bucket was out but the gloves were laid over the side of the bucket.

She got caught twice shoplifting. The first time was seven years ago. The second time was with Donna. It was at Woolco into the Avalon Mall. The snow was down. Donna was taking a tummy tucker and Kim pleaded guilty to it. She didnt have no role in it. She tried to avoid her. She was six months pregnant, and she didnt want to keep going back and forth to court.

Donna shoplifted quite a bit. Kim can't say every store she went into or every day but she did shoplift a lot. She took orders from people like Madeline Ryall the palm reader and then go out and shoplift what they ordered. If she was into a store shoplifting she'd go one way and Kim the other way. It's not something Kim wanted to have a part of.

Donna used to go shoplifting with Tom Vivian. She got stuff for everybody. People didnt know where it came from and some people did. They would be done in the day. The items that were stolen were never expensive items. Sneakers, clothes for the kids, Christmas gifts.

Madeline Ryall told Donna's fortune. Someone was going to die and there was going to be lots of blood and police and Sheldon is going to be involved. He was going to be framed or set up, Kim's not sure what it was.

Kim thinks Donna recognized buddy's voice on the phone so she dont know if she was really afraid of it. It upset her but she recognized the voice. Nervous. She got on the floor crawling around.

Donna got the tape machine two weeks before at Kmart. She shoplifted it. Kim told the police at first she didnt let her listen to it. That was a lie. Kim tried to tell them things but she didnt want to say it all, she was afraid, so she tried to tell them in a different way.

Donna never told her about Raymond Troke trying to rape her. Raymond was at her house once or twice and that was with Sheldon. Kim didnt know he was there by himself.

SHELDON TROKE

Your boyfriends' graves are shallow and youre not worth doing forty years over. Sheldon read that in Kim Parrott's statement. Kim heard that on a tape, so Sheldon wonders how Clifford Whalen come to hear that too. Clifford says he wasnt talking to nobody. No one told him no stories but then he goes home one weekend and got a new incident that slipped his mind. Then a month later Kim Parrott comes in talking about the same incident and then Clifford says that he wasnt talking to nobody. No, I knows he wasnt.

SHARON WHALEN

Tom Vivian would come by to get pills, Sharon's not sure about anybody else. He'd spend probably a half-hour there. Mom and Tom would go shopping every day that her mom didnt have a headache. With fights, sometimes Sheldon would start it and sometimes her mom would. It was about even as to who starts it. Donna put the TV on low if there was something coming on the answering machine. When Sharon woke up that night, she didnt hear any noise at the TV.

Sheldon explained to her why he didnt like Kim Parrott and her boyfriend, Rod. Because Rod used to rob stores. Also, Sheldon loaned them things and money and they wouldnt pay him back.

RUTH VIVIAN

One night Ruth was having an argument with her husband, Pat, and Donna was after having an argument with Sheldon and they were out there talking, so you know like women talk. That bitch is always in my back and Donna says, I can't even walk the length of myself but he got to know where I'm at and who I'm with and what time I'm coming home. This was just women talk, you know, like sat down on the doorstep. Ruth never paid no attention to it. She was up there one morning, Donna was getting ready to go see Sheldon—he was down in the pen. She said to Ruth, I'd give anything if he would fly to Jesus and leave me alone. Ruth says that about her husband when theyre mad, wish he would fly to Jesus. She didnt think nothing serious about it. Donna had a visit to see him that day. That was said up in her kitchen. She was sat to her kitchen table. She was pretty upset. Because she asked Ruth did she know a couple of doctors she could call and get some valium and sleeping pills and Ruth said no, she wasnt getting involved in that. She has enough problems with her own husband, she can't handle somebody else's taking the valium. Donna was talking about going away, but she gave Ruth the opinion that once she goes away, she wasnt coming back.

DONNA WHALEN AND SHELDON TROKE ON TAPE RECORDER

I dont even understand anything that youre saying Sheldon—you were downstairs at the bottom, talking up through the window. I never, ever wanted you like that Sheldon. I dont like the arguing and the fighting and the violence and everything else. The way you get on with me. I'm frightened to death to say something to you, I dont know if the table is going to tip over or what.

Sheldon: Sorry, I didnt mean to do it. I guess I know I'm a violent man.

You know yourself the only time you grind your teeth is when youre on the coke.

I know, yes. I'll get you some cocaine now in a few weeks, all right?

Sheldon give it up please. Youre going to leave soon if you dont stop it.

Why?

What are you trying to prove?

I aint trying to prove nothing, here you go.

Sheldon stop it.

No Donna, you stop it.

I'm not doing anything.

I'm not either.

Youre hitting my arm.

Am I? Did you ask for some cocaine tonight, did you ask for it?

No, I asked if you were on it.

Yeah well what the fuck is it your business, I'm trying to help myself all right, where the fuck was Jacob Parrott two weeks ago. Donna, I come here all right because I made an agreement. I love you and I love your friends, I love everything about you all right and I do and I cannot turn around and lie about it because I'd be a two-faced liar right to my eyes, to everybody. I love you more than anything in the fucking world, anything. I would rather turn around and do twenty, twenty-five, thirty, thirty-five, forty, forty-five years in jail because I believe in something and I believe in supporting a cause and that's you, I believe you are worth it, all right. I believe this is fucking lying this is, I dont care what you want to say or what you want to do, I dont care.

ROBERT ASH

Sheldon was the aggressor throughout this conversation. He was the one bringing up the boyfriends. The one suggesting she was cheating on him, indicating how jealous he is, suggesting that Jacob Parrott was coming down to visit. It was constantly Sheldon arguing with Donna about how upset and mad he was at her and he threatened to kill her right there on the tape.

SHELDON TROKE

Sheldon never said anything about boyfriends. He did mention guys'
names. Donna was allowed to have male friends. He never stopped
Donna from having any friends. Now the thing is if Sheldon's
supposed to be home in an hour and he comes back in two hours, it's
an argument. Where were you at? Who were you with? If Donna went
out with her friends—male friends at that—there was no arguing.
He's after babysitting for Donna when she went out with her male
friends. That's what that tape is about. It's about their past. He never
turned around on that tape and threatened to kill Donna. This is
something that she's getting for her mother. You dont hear anything
about sticking a knife into the coffee table. Wouldnt that be a nice
thing to give to your mother? It didnt happen.

Archeologists could turn around and explain dinosaurs that was
twenty million years ago. Sheldon thinks he should be able to explain
his conduct in this tape. He does know one thing. He's doing the
arguing. Donna's not arguing, but when him and Donna argue, Donna
used to argue. Donna was making the tape to give to her mother, to
show that she dont start all the arguments and Sheldon never did say
Donna started all the arguments. The two of them started arguments,
but that's what that tape was for.

From listening to that tape, it appears that tape is stopped. What
was being said that Donna turned the tape off that she didnt want
her mother to hear? When Sheldon was going out with Donna, why
did he have apartments? When they argued, there was lots of times
he left. When he was moving out, Donna asked him, she said, you
can board here.

JACOB PARROTT

Jacob Parrott was up visiting his friend there one time, Cathy Furneaux. Himself and his friend they just dropped in and they were having a few beers and all of a sudden Donna Whalen showed up. She talked to Cathy and they were talking about old times and asking how things were getting on and Jacob was asking her when is she going to talk to Kim and check on the kids and they got into a conversation. Donna was talking about a knife that was stabbed into a table and she stiffened up like a bit frightened. Sheldon and her had an argument, he was sitting at a table and he was stabbing a knife into it saying I did it before and I'd do it again. Jacob figured maybe it could be the coffee or end table in the living room, because usually when people have conversations theyre sitting down in the living room. She mentioned one where they broke up because they had a fight and, in her words, he laid a beating on her. This conversation at Cathy's was maybe about four weeks before Donna was murdered. It came up because of something about her breaking up and he's moving back with his mother.

GARY BEMISTER

On Thursday night Pat Vivian was at Donna's apartment helping her move furniture. He then went back downstairs, had a cigarette and took a sleeping pill and lay down on his bed.

Pat Vivian is known as an individual who sleeps during the day and is up nearly every night, going to bed at six in the morning. That Friday night he says he went to sleep one to one-thirty a.m. One night where he changed his complete pattern and lifestyle, just happened to be the night that Donna Whalen was killed.

His son, Tom Vivian, was involved in shoplifting and obtaining numerous prescription drugs together with Donna Whalen. The police have no concerns that Tom had been harbouring unrequited love towards Donna Whalen. The police knew they were close friends. They were involved in this activity together but there is no indication of any sort of admiration between them. Tom Vivian's room was below Donna's bedroom. He was constantly snooping around and trying to listen in on Donna Whalen.

Gary Bemister was going back and forth to the crime scene a fair bit and he used to drop into the Vivians'. It was quite friendly. He'd ask Ruth how she was today, this sort of thing because she did have failing health.

THE VIVIANS, CHES HEDDERSON AND GARY BEMISTER WIRETAP

Pat Vivian: Just leave the door open.

Ches Hedderson: Like you say it's harassing you.

If I wasnt worrying about that I'd be worrying about the wife. Every time you comes in you upsets us.

You knows yourself it's murder.

Gary Bemister: Did he say anything to you about Sheldon being arrested?

Who, my son? Tom told you he only heard a kick on the door. Dont know who done it. Said he'd take the lie detector.

Is he home?

No.

He said he'd be there for the polygraph tomorrow morning. He can't start folding on us.

Ruth Vivian: I thought that was Tom who was out there. If I had known it was you, I wouldnt come out.

Ches Hedderson: Now dont go speaking the truth. We just wanted to see if there's anything new that you wanted to say at the bail hearing because we dont want any surprises, but you'd be subject to cross-examination if you were called.

Pat: I thought she didnt have to go to court.

You are certainly. I'll check on Mrs Vivian's status but you and Tom.

She aint going to no supreme court.

Ruth: I won't be able to get down there.

Pat: That's why we done the video.

Ruth: If I could get down I would have waited.

Gary Bemister: The thing is that we may call yourself and Pat and Tom, so we dropped by to see if there's anything since Sheldon's arrest you wanted to tell us.

Pat: What you going to be asking me for. I never heard nothing.

You knows we're looking for two.

Yeah I knows that.

That's right. But youre not telling us.

Not telling ye. Jesus.

We'd like to know what youre going to say before youre called.

Pat: I knows what I'm going to say.

Ruth: To go down as a witness and have that tape there. I havent been out of the house.

We just want to make sure that anyone who testifies in court who's under oath theyre saying exactly what they know because if we know different or we learn different we may be coming back to talk to you again. Like you says, we're harassing.

TOM VIVIAN

He went down to the police station with his father Pat and took the polygraph test. He said Donna was a good friend and he often kept an eye on the children. Friday night she came over to say she was driving Sheldon home and asked Tom to be aware of the children. It was around nine-thirty. He was watching TV. He doesnt know when Donna Whalen came home. His father Pat was in the bedroom watching a baseball game. His mother was at bingo. Pat Vivian came out of his bedroom around one a.m. to get a glass of water, but he never spoke to Tom. Sometime between two-thirty and three a.m. he heard a knock at the front door of Donna's apartment but it might have been a kick because when you knock on the door you can hear the glass rattle. He did not hear anyone go up. There was a creaking on the floor upstairs, like someone creeping around. He also heard a noise like a table tip over.

Tom Vivian was taken to another room and for thirty minutes he was alone with Ches Hedderson. Tom repeated that he had told them everything he knew and then he became hyper. Shortly after three p.m. he was advised that he failed the polygraph test and was a suspect in the murder. His father Pat was driven home from the police station and Tom Vivian was charged. He was conveyed to the hospital where vials of blood and other body fluid were taken and then hair samples and pubic hair. He failed some tests that the police had wished him to do and he decided that he wanted to call a lawyer. He was advised to make no further statements.

GARY BEMISTER

Ches Hedderson and Gary Bemister returned to the Vivian residence to reinterview Ruth Vivian and videotape her. She'd had surgery three weeks before for a bowel problem. She spends a great deal of time at home and she goes to bed fairly early now. Friday night she got up around one to get a drink of water to take her medication. It could have been two or three times she gets up. When she came out in the kitchen, her son Tom was in the front room cleaning up the coffee table. She took her pill and then went to the bathroom and back to bed. Her husband Pat was in bed. A little while after Tom came in and opened her bedroom door and asked if she called out to him. She said no and he left the room and she took notice of the time because of the medication she's on. It was about one-fifteen or one-thirty when she heard more than one person going up the stairs to Donna's apartment. She never heard a sound after this and she asked her husband if he heard anything and he said no. The stairs go over the bedroom and she can hear them clearly when they walk up the stairs. Ruth knows it was more than one person that went up because you can hear them take their shoes off. Just as Donna kicked off her heels, Ruth Vivian heard her say Sheldon, dont do that no more. Donna never even had time to get into her bedroom. As soon as her shoes went on that floor, that is when the girl said that. They sounded like pumps. Now it dont take an expert to figure out that something must have went wrong before she got up over the stairs.

TOM VIVIAN

The next day, Saturday, his mother was very upset. The girl upstairs had died. Tom asked his mother if she had heard anything. She turned away. She didnt answer. She knew something but she wasnt saying. The next day she told him. She heard somebody going upstairs and Donna bawling out Sheldon, no more, dont do it no more.

You should tell the police, Tom told her. He was hoping the police would come back that day.

Usually Friday nights they have a game of darts and be down in the basement and if they be talking about something, his mother heard it. If they cursed she'd come out and tell them to knock off cursing.

She was a very caring person, very particular over her appearance and now she doesnt care about none of that. She can't bathe herself. She can't do her hair. She doesnt even know how to pour a cup of tea for herself. They were trying to blame him for it.

RUTH VIVIAN

After bingo Friday night Ruth came home and complained about the heat. She said to Pat your blood is like water and Pat said why dont you go out and run around the block and lose a few pounds and she slammed the door and went out and she was mumbling to herself that son of a bitch, he always got to have his own way, and she walked down towards Mabel Edicott's and she turned in between Mabel's house and Madeline Ryall's. She tried the back door and she couldnt get it open because she has trouble with this arm. A person came around the corner. Ruth froze in her tracks when she saw him. Sheldon Troke. This was around ten-thirty Friday night. They almost banged into one another they were that close. He put his head down and she turned and went around the corner and into Mabel's. Ruth asked her to come over to play cards. She was nervous. Sheldon had a few drinks in to him. It is Donna Whalen's door and then it is Mabel's. Sheldon was wearing a dark leather jacket, jeans, boots. You could tell by the click on the pavement. He walked towards the car. She heard the door close and the car drove off. It drove off too quickly for him to have been driving it. She thinks he got into the back and there was someone else in the car. Ruth kept on walking around the building and did not look back. It was around eleven oclock. Every time she run into Sheldon it is like she used to get a cold feeling, like an afraid feeling, and this is what she got when he passed by. Even though the young fellow never did say nothing to her out of the way, but that is just the way she used to feel every time she used to talk to him or be handy to him.

She went home then and played cards with Mabel Edicott.

JIM LYTHGOE

Now Sheldon is on Empire at ten-thirty Friday night. New information from Ruth Vivian. Ten-thirty gives Sheldon enough time to return to Donna's and wait for her. Or does Ruth have the time and day wrong. The police know there was an argument on Thursday night with similar words being said that Ruth Vivian claims to have heard on Friday night. With regards to the stress that she would be under with her son being a suspect, could there have been confusion that the argument with Sheldon applied to Friday night, to prove that her son was not involved in this matter.

GARY BEMISTER

Tom Vivian declined a further interview. Look, he said, I've already told the police everything I know. And that was his general attitude right up until the last time Gary spoke with him.

When they are on the tape from Thursday night, their voices are quite loud and at no point does Donna trail off. As for the specific comment of No Sheldon dont do it anymore—that comment is not on the audiotape, though Donna does say Sheldon stop it.

PAT VIVIAN

The master bedroom he give it to the young fellow. Ruth was asleep. Pat was fast asleep. Pat never heard a thing until the next morning. He was out in the kitchen doing a few dishes and he heard youngsters crying, but he didnt mind at first. But they kept on crying so he went out to the door and the two children were stood on the doorway crying and he asked them what was wrong and they said, Me mommy is dead, me mommy is dead. Pat got all excited. Come on in the house, he said. It was pouring rain out. They wouldnt come in. He went in and woke Ruth up and woke up his son Tom and when they got back to the door the what's a names was there. He dont know if it was the police or 911 or what. There was a lot of confusion then with the police taking statements.

The night before Pat Vivian called to his son when he was going to bed like he do every night. If he is in his room he says Tom, I am going to bed now. Pat usually goes to bed around nine oclock because he is awake six in the morning on account of his wife.

There was only a dozen beer in the house. Pat had five or six beer over a period of six hours. He can drink beer and he is still alert. He can drink beer and do anything in the house because he dont drink it to get drunk because he is looking after a home.

GARY BEMISTER

After that there was silence. And yet the police know, not based on the evidence of individuals but what the scene itself tells them, that Donna went in, she had food with her because a Wendy's bag was found afterwards in the kitchen. She went into the bathroom, stepped out of her clothes, which were not bloody or anything, and got her nightie and put it on.

JIM LYTHGOE

Tom Vivian was a suspect. He spent hours at the station. Tom's parents had forty minutes to discuss what was going on. Our son is a suspect. Let's call a lawyer. Tom didnt make any further statements. He failed a test. Forty minutes later the police arrive and take a new statement from the Vivians. It is still felt by the police today that Tom Vivian is not telling the truth.

His father Pat was drinking and semi-passed out. And Ruth says the stairs to the upstairs apartment go over her bedroom. Nothing could be further from the truth—her bedroom is as far away as you can get from the stairs. Ruth Vivian said, I could hear them clearly when they walked up the stairs. I knew it was more than one person because I heard them take their shoes off.

Now are we going to suggest that Donna comes home and takes off her clothes and gets on her nightgown and took a pillow from the bedroom, eats her salad and hears a knock on the door and decides to put on her high heels specifically to go down over the steps?

Ruth Vivian heard Donna screaming out, no one else hearing anything. Remarkable. She can hear it over a TV. There is no evidence of anyone else hearing anything that Friday night. But suddenly, after Tom Vivian is a suspect, everything changes within an hour.

ROBERT ASH

Ruth Vivian is describing a time later than what you are describing now. What you are describing would have occurred close to one oclock in the morning and what you are suggesting is that Donna Whalen gets home at one oclock, goes upstairs, takes off her clothes, puts on a nightgown. Mrs Vivian is talking about something later in the morning. Her description is around one-thirty or quarter to two, which gives more than sufficient time for Donna Whalen to have eaten the meal she had bought, time for her to have gotten a pillow if one wasnt on the sofa already. Time enough to do all those things which the physical evidence suggests. Ruth's description of the voice going down, that is something you would expect when you consider that there was a pair of panties wrapped around her neck.

RUTH VIVIAN

She was reluctant to tell the police everything at first because she had a young fellow that was coming up before court and she didnt want him down the pen with anybody that was going to hurt him.

Since the murder, she's tried to move. Ruth has been asking to move now for twenty-five years. She talked to them eight or nine times. She got a doctor's note to help her cause. She talked to a psychiatrist right on LeMarchant Road. She's no good for names.

She had a run-in with Sheldon Troke. He came to the back door one morning and asked her son Tom to stay away from Donna. That was after Tom fixed a flat for her. Just tell him to stay away from Donna is what he said. Ruth never said nothing she just minded her own business, closed the door and came on. She told her son when he came home and that was a long while ago.

SHELDON TROKE

Ruth Vivian is after saying a lot in this courtroom. She's afraid of this and afraid of that. From what Sheldon hears in this courtroom, if Mrs Vivian seen this or Mrs Vivian heard this, Mrs Vivian wouldnt be able to keep it to herself. She runs out and tells a police officer Sheldon phoned her. The next day she runs out and tells another one, and what's on the go? These people are not paying no attention to her. They're just taking some notes. So the next day she runs to a third one. In two days she's after running to three different police officers and in each one of them she's after saying three different things. If Ruth Vivian seen Sheldon Thursday night or she seen him Friday night she would not be able to keep it to herself. She's a liar and she knows it. Power of suggestion. That's what it boils down to.

SHARON WHALEN

She heard a big bang and thought it was the coffee table knocked over. It might be Mom sleep-walking or maybe she rolled off the chesterfield. Sharon heard another voice. She thought she was dreaming it though. The voice whispered be quiet, Donna, be quiet. It sounded like a man's voice. Her mom was saying, No, no, Sheldon! Leave me alone, leave me alone! Sharon went back to sleep. Her bedroom is not far to where the coffee table is. Then Cory woke her up, he was shouting out, Mommy! Mommy! Sharon looked at her clock and it was 8:39 a.m. and she thought it was weird because Mom normally gets up and unlocks Cory's door. Sharon went out to see where Mommy was and the coffee table was tipped over near the kitchen and there was broken glass by the coffee table. Mommy was lying on her stomach and Sharon just thought she was asleep. She went in and opened her brother's door and his room was all a mess. She said okay we got to clean this up for Mom. So that's what she started to do and then she went out and her mother was lying on the floor. There was blood on her shoulder and some blood near her chest dripping down. She took the blanket off and saw some scratches on her legs. Sharon knew that she was dead. She pulled down her mother's nightdress and put the blanket over her so that Cory wouldnt see and then she dialed 911.

I found my mom lying on the floor dead.

What are you saying?

I found my mom lying on the floor and she's dead.

We will send the ambulance.

Ambulance, ambulance. Cory stay away.

We'll send somebody along.

Okay, then.

Then she dialed her nan.

That blanket was kept in her mom's room. If her mom was going to watch TV late at night she had a TV in her room. She didnt sleep out on the couch, but she was sleeping on the couch that night because her new bed wasnt set up in the room. That black blanket was her mom's favourite.

After the phone calls Sharon unlocked two of the doors. First the latch one and then the one downstairs. You pick out the latch part that's right across. There's a push-in lock on the knob. She doesnt remember if that was closed or not. She doesnt even remember going to the back door.

She waited by the front door for the ambulance. Sharon thought her mom had killed herself. She used a knife. She was under a lot of stress. She never had no luck with boyfriends and she always had a lot to do. On the floor near her mom were the cushions on the chesterfield and the coffee table was broken.

III

THE INVESTIGATION

They were about to have coffee when their dispatcher got the call. We've got a hysterical little girl on the phone and she claims her mother is dead. They got into the ambulance and left. Jim Pike and his partner Harold Parsons. Harold was driving. They had their ambulance emergency sirens on. Around four minutes later they arrived just outside the door, walked down over a little embankment and approached the house. They were the first emergency vehicle there. Two kids standing in the doorcasing, a girl and a little boy, dressed in their nightclothes. In the next door there was a man standing in the doorway. An average built person. Just standing there, leaning against the door. He didnt look to be providing any comfort to these two children. The man questioned as to what they were doing and he and Harold ignored him.

The girl said she's up this way. So Jim and Harold followed the two children up the steps. The girl was holding the little boy's hand. She said she woke up and heard her mother call her name but then thought she dreamt it and went back to sleep. The television was on. Whatever channel it was on had finished broadcasting, it was just a snowy screen. There may have been some noise coming from it, but it wasnt enough to bother you. Then the girl pointed, She's over there. The first thing Jim saw was the legs. He could see the blood. The coffee table was tipped over. He approached the head of the patient and at that time he realized the blood was dry.

He moved back the coffee table to get a better look at her face. Her hair was down over her face and there was something there—a black purse. He realized something was wrong. This person was dead—he's seen enough dead people to know—and had been dead for a while. He checked the radial pulse of her arm. There was no pulse and he could feel the temperature of her hand was cold and her fingers were curled and rigid. Harold Parsons was standing there and Jim said turn on a light, Harold. He flicked on a switch which turned on the ceiling fan and so right there and then, Jim just wanted to levitate and get out of there so as not to disturb it any more than what they already done. He checked the legs for rigidity and it was cool to the touch. Jim said to Harold dont touch anything. The blood was dry, so Harold called on his portable radio for the police to come down. All he said was, ASAP.

Jim went out to the ambulance and used their channel 2 frequency which is scrambled—they've got a specialized crystal in the radios. We've got a murder case, he told them, so hurry things up. He went back in and it seemed a long time, but it was probably ten minutes later that the police arrived. The police took their names, got their story, and then Jim and Harold left.

The coffee table was over on the side. It was more or less parallel with the chesterfield. The body was between the coffee table and the chesterfield and the end that was towards the head, Jim moved it back three or four inches to get a better look.

The fire department was coming behind them. They had their lights on, but they werent using the sirens. Jim saw that through the sheers on the living room window. He ran down to the bottom of the stairs to meet them. Two uniformed officers and then another one came after and he was the staff sergeant, Ches Hedderson. Jim was telling them the story as they walked up the stairs, he was giving them basically what they found. He said, This is it. And then Ches Hedderson got on his portable. He said, We need to get Major Crimes at this address.

Hedderson said to one of the police officers to stand at the bottom of the stairs and not let anybody else into the house, not even a policeman.

So there would have been seven people standing around the coffee table three or four feet away from the body.

The fire lieutenant took the two children and brought them across the street and put them in the Rescue to babysit them until the police arrived.

During training there is a lawyer and a police officer come in. They talk about continuity of evidence. Most of it is on-the-job training, you get involved in one situation, and figure out what you should or shouldnt do and just through daily experience and run-ins with the police they tell you what they would like you to do. It is a building of education that way.

The best thing to do is to leave everything, dont touch it and let the police look after it from there. A police car pulled up and Harold and Jim went up with them. They had a police dog. They told the police about the light switch and then asked them would they take over the scene.

In the residence were a couple of street patrol officers and they were noting who was entering and leaving the scene. Dr Philip Abery, he is a forensic pathologist, and Gary Bemister and Charles Stamp, they are identification officers, they were at the scene as well.

CHARLES STAMP

Charles did a walk-through of the house and it was quite neat. A drinking glass on the countertop and a plate, spoon and knife and a fork and a mug and a Pepsi bottle in the sink.

Charles was careful not to walk on anything that might have value and once that's finished you see if there's anything the investigator may need right away. Charles photographs that first then calls in Philip Abery so that he can get the core temperature of the body which has an effect on the investigation.

The house was very clean and Charles didnt see any broom closet that if you went into someone's house and you opened up a closet door you probably see their brooms and mops. He didnt see any place to put her articles so seeing a mop and bucket didnt strike him as being out of the way. The only thing that did strike him were the gloves on the floor. The gloves were examined for fingerprints but he found no friction ridges. What you do is you put your exhibits into a fuming tank, you put cyanoacrylate in a little dish over a light bulb and you also take some hot water and seal the tank off and the krazy glue—that's what they use for cyanoacrylate—the glue will condense into the air and attach itself to the exhibits where there's ridges of a fingerprint. In a fuming tank the friction ridges are white and anywhere else youre using black powder or grey powder or red powder, the ridges appear that colour.

Charles found three fingerprints on the drinking glass in the sink. Two of those fingerprints were identified to Sheldon Troke. The left index and his left thumb.

The water in the bucket is no good for forensic because it's too diluted with cleaning chemicals.

The atmosphere conditions in the room has a big effect on the fingerprint. They will dissipate over a few weeks. If it's nice and warm and the humidity is low, prints can last a long time. There are types of chemicals now that can react to fingerprints that have been there for twenty years. Charles's done three homicide scenes of this nature— you get about six or seven good fingerprints. If he went into his own residence and fingerprinted it he wouldnt get anything. Handle drawers in your kitchen, the doorknobs, anything that's used a lot, medicine cabinets, what youre getting is superimposed fingerprints, one over the other, partial palmprints, the inside ridges of the fingers, and he's after dusting hundreds of doorknobs and it's impossible to get a fingerprint that you can actually take to court and do a chart on because it's very difficult to understand how you can call it a fingerprint when you've got four or five ridges going through the fingerprint from another fingerprint.

You can tell a female's fingerprints. If a female is a housewife their ridges on their fingers are wore from washing dishes and using cleaning chemicals on their hands and the ridges arent out as far. A masonry person, you can usually tell what kind of job they have because of the surface of their fingerprints.

PHILIP ABERY

Dr Abery inserted a thermometer into the abdomen and into the liver. He measured the ambient temperature of the room. Then he took a walk around the entire thing just to get a general picture as to what may have transpired. He viewed the knives in the drawer in the kitchen but did not examine them for fear of interfering with evidence. He cannot say that any of these knives were the knife.

The purpose is to try and give the time interval between death and discovery. They measure alcohol both in the blood and in the vitreous fluid. The vitreous fluid comes from the eye. Both the blood ethanol and the vitreous ethanol were negative.

The body of any suspicious death is secured in the morgue. The body was in a body bag liner inside a locked box. The clothing was one blue nightdress. It was bloodstained on the front and it had slit defects over the left aspect of the front panel. There was a pair of white socks which had blood smearing on the upper aspect but was free of blood on the soles. A pair of white underwear tied in a knot around the individual's neck. He cut at a point distant from the knot to preserve the knot. There are forensic experts who can determine by examining a knot whether the individual was left- or right-handed. He cut the underwear and they came apart. It wasnt a knot at all, but simply firmly twisted into place.

The body was transported by a police van.

There were three sets of earrings in each earlobe, all of which are yellow metal. There were four yellow metal chains around her neck and four yellow metal pendants on the chains and two blue hair buckles.

As the blood settles, if you push on it, you push the fluid out of the way and the skin turns white. With time, the blood clots and it stains the surrounding tissue. At that point, we say lividity is fixed because when you push on it, you cannot push the clot and the staining away. There's no blanching, which occurs within a certain range of hours after death.

The hair was normal, shoulder-length black hair. The scalp was unremarkable with no evidence of any scratches, bruises or lacerations. The ears were unremarkable. Her eyes were brown and partially open. A condition called tache noir, which is French for black line, was noted in the conjunctiva. If an individual dies with their eyes open, the corneas dry and you get this line. There was no evidence of any pinpoint hemorrhages that occur in the eye in cases of strangulation.

There was no evidence of forcible sexual assault.

There were no injuries to the face.

On the right side of the neck there was an area of patent abrasion. If a chain had been pressed hard into the neck. They peeled back the scalp flap and examined the scalp from the inside. There was no evidence of bruising to the scalp. The skull was intact.

They removed the brain and all the organs from the body and performed a neck dissection. This allows blood to drain from the body. If you dont do it in that sequence you may cause artificial hemorrhaging to the neck. There was no evidence of injury to the neck.

One cannot date wounds with accuracy. On a recent abrasion, healing starts to occur and you see peaked-up edges. That occurs after several days.

In terms of the panties being used as a ligature, it's fairly soft material and you may see a ligature mark, but you may not. So the panties themselves may not leave any injury. However, the underwear would push on the chain.

They put the wound edges back together with scotch tape and measured them. There are elastic fibres that run in the skin. If you cut a wound parallel to those fibres, it stays like a slit. If you cut across the fibres, the wound gapes open. A wound in its natural state may not be the correct size because of the cutting of these elastic fibres.

The heart has been cut. The pulmonary vein and the vena cava have been cut. The lungs tend to collapse. In order for the lungs to stay inflated, we have a negative pressure in the chest. It's like a vacuum in our chest. Once a stab wound occurs, there are two potential sources of air to enter the chest cavity—one from the lung itself because, as you breathe in, the air will escape from the lung into the pleural cavity. And then there's the wound to the outside. A sucking chest wound forms a flap that allows air to get in, but doesnt allow air out, so pressure can build up in the chest cavity and this can compromise an individual's ability to breathe and vocalize.

There are reports of people who have had fairly extensive injuries, their hearts blown completely out and have still been able to run twenty or forty feet. So it's impossible to say that it would absolutely prevent her from being able to move around.

Any of the wounds to the lung could cause death, although death may not be very rapid. The wound that cuts the pulmonary artery on its own would be capable of causing death. The wound that penetrates the left ventricle of the heart. The wound to the vena cava.

If youre going to be stabbed in the chest, there are several things youre going to do. One of them is defend with your arms or legs to try and knock the knife away. If you know the knife is coming towards the heart, there may be a tendency to move the body to protect it. You end up with wounds on the lateral side of the chest.

Defensive wounds are attempts to ward off blows or thrusts of a weapon with your hands. Dr Abery sees injuries to the backs of the hands where you might put your arm up. In the case of an edged weapon, the individual will grab at the knife to remove it from the assailant and when the assailant draws the knife back, you can't hold the blade so it cuts into the hand. It's the location of the wounds rather than their configuration which suggests these are defensive wounds.

The majority of knives are single-edged weapons. The back of the knife is flat and the face of the knife has a cutting edge. When that is inserted, you get one edge to the wound that's sharp and the other edge is slightly blunted.

They examine the organs for injury as they are in the body. Then they remove the organs and look underneath, so the continuity of the track of the wound is not maintained. You can't measure accurately the depth of a wound track. A four-inch knife could cause a six-inch wound if, on penetration, there is indentation of the wall. When a knife is thrust fully into the body and with sufficient force to indent a chest cavity, the hilt of the knife impacts against the skin, and you have a hilt injury to the wound. When you look at the stab wound, instead of nice sharp margins, you see bruising. That would indicate that the hilt of the knife has caused a bruise at the time of stabbing. Here, all of the wounds have clean margins and no evidence of hilt injury.

In the photograph the stomach is quite full. She had eaten a meal that extended her stomach and the contents have not yet passed to the small bowel. However, you can't use stomach contents to determine the time of death. Dr Abery has had cases where the individual has been in the intensive care unit on a respirator and he knows they haven't eaten, but at autopsy you find gastric contents.

The body was thirty-one degrees at about ten a.m. You would lose that much temperature in six to eight hours, so you might be looking at between two and four oclock in the morning.

GARY BEMISTER

Gary Bemister looked around the living room: a remote control was underneath a chair, the television was on. There were two lights on, one in each corner. Dr Abery was examining the body and pronounced the lady dead. Gary noticed several stab wounds in the left breast area. He did not touch the body. There was a large amount of blood at the scene. It was quite difficult to see what wounds. There was a pair of panties around the lady's neck, and they were bunched in the front. There was a sanitary pad alongside of the body. Paper bags were over her head and hands. He did a preliminary look for any outstanding physical evidence, to determine if a break and entry had occurred. There was some blood around the handle on the kitchen utility drawer and inside, on the cutlery tray. All of the doors at one time or another had been forced or broken into. The windows seemed secure. He took some photographs of the deceased and arranged transportation to the Health Sciences Centre. He also used an industrial-grade camcorder with a video light. Him and Charles Stamp started on the outside of the scene and did a walk-through to show as much detail as possible.

There's a heavy rain when they are walking on back of the swings. You seem to hear it. They went in through the front door and started upstairs, they scanned through some children's toys. There appears to be a white material on the first three or four stairs going up. There was a red lego block there. That's the top of the stairs and a pair of sneakers. Those shots of the body are graphic because the scene is a fresh complaint and you have to cover off all areas. Those shots are looking for injuries that suggest a sexual assault. The stain in the carpet, especially when the body of the deceased was removed, was extremely noticeable in colour from the rest of the carpet.

There is a photograph on the fridge, a gentleman with a beard and moustache. That's Sheldon Troke. A tea bag right on top of the garbage. There's a bucket with dirty water but there's no colour of red in it. In on the bathroom floor there's jeans, a bra and a blouse. The master bedroom, a police scanner is on top of the television.

Gary Bemister took responsibility for seizing all of these exhibits. The kitchen table and the coffee table, a paper bag that was over the hand, a left hand nail clipping and scraping from Dr Abery, a piece of fibre that was seized on the outside of the right hand. It's very small you can't really see it. They use a portable light source called the luma light.

There's a pubic hair combing, a vaginal smear, a rectal smear, a plucked hair from the head of the deceased, a plucked eyebrow hair. A pair of lady's underwear twisted around the neck area were allowed to dry overnight and put in a bag the next morning. They were bloodstained. A paper bag over the right hand, a paper bag on the head, four chains and pendants, three sets of earrings, two blue plastic buckles. They would have been on her hair. A pair of white socks. A bedsheet that the deceased was wrapped in from her home. A nightdress that the deceased had on at the time, you can see it's bloodstained. There are cuts in the nightdress around the chest area. The body bag liner is just something the deceased was wrapped in. The police van normally carries clean body bags. She was placed in the sheet first and the liner, then the bag. The liner is transparent, it's not as strong. The body bag itself has handles. A blond hair on the nightdress. A sanitary napkin found under the right leg. Some paint samples taken from the doorknob area as a control sample.

Alongside the coffee table was a Wendy's bag with a plate and cover and a receipt. Somebody had obviously finished their lunch. The bag looks like it's almost sitting up on the floor. Donna Whalen had some sort of salad to eat that night.

The two children were now in the back of Agnes Whalen's car. Mrs Whalen is their grandmother. Ches Hedderson leaned in on the passenger side. The children were in their pyjamas. Sharon had a housecoat on. Cory said that Sheldon killed his mother. He stabbed her. Mrs Whalen stopped him from saying anything more. Ches Hedderson told her to be quiet. He asked Sharon what happened and she said, Sheldon killed Mom. He asked if she saw what happened and she said no. Mrs Whalen said the children dont know what happened. They only think that's what happened because Donna told them about Sheldon being in jail for stabbing someone before. Sharon said Sheldon stabbed her mother. During the next minute or so Ches Hedderson had difficulty getting the children to say what happened as Mrs Whalen was interfering. He told her not to speak to the children again.

CHARLES STAMP

That's right they didnt find pumps they found sneakers. You walk in a hallway and the first room on your right is the little boy's room. Over here is a bureau and his bed and a closet. You walk down to the end of the hall and this is Sharon's room. In the middle there is a dresser. It's kind of out of place, but that's the way it was.

The kitchen looks very dark. What happens is the flash strikes the wall that's closer and reflects that light back to the camera. The kitchen wasnt dark at the time.

You can see a bible opened up on the carpet. There's a religious poem. This one is a welcome to the Salvation Army, the door is open to you, if youre searching for a life. It says Donna Whalen, 14 years old, single, grade nine. This one is a search for God.

Some cigarette butts, an ashtray next to the coffee table. There are pamphlets, a writing pad, an alcohol and drug dependency fax sheet, power stepper exercise, a valium pamphlet, information for family of offenders and a daycare subsidy cancellation notice. This was in the storage area of the coffee table.

A large black handbag was in the living room on the carpet in front of the chesterfield next to the coffee table. There's cosmetics and a container full of pills and a notebook of doctors' names and some money owed, some airplane flight information. There is a wallet and a driver's licence, credit cards, health cards, nine dollars and seventy-eight cents and a small battery. Part of the handbag is on her head.

A blood-soaked pillow was on the carpet in the living room between the coffee table and the chesterfield. A beige doily was partly under the coffee table on the living room carpet.

Charles looked for footprints on the linoleum floor, the kitchen floor, the bathroom floor and the hardwood floors. Then he took the photographs. Gary Bemister used oblique light, Charles did not. There was a footprint found.

You see a wooden rocking chair and there is a mat underneath the rear leg of the rocking chair and a brown mat underneath a table. The blood impression that he got was right between the mat underneath the rocking chair going towards the brown mat. Someone had walked in blood and then walked out in that direction. A heel print.

GARY BEMISTER

The next day Gary went with Charles Stamp to the crime scene to find photo albums or address books. Constable Stamp removed a photo album and two address books. They were there twenty minutes. They concentrated on the living room and the master bedroom. There's two end tables. Gary Bemister was dressed like he is today, shirt and tie. He was wearing a pair of shoes, the same pair he has on right now. He was sitting in the office and Charles Stamp noticed the print on his shoe. Gary took his shoe off and they used a small bit of margarine and rubbed it on the heel and Gary walked on a piece of paper. When you walk, the pattern from the heel is embedded in the paper and then they use some black powder and go over the margarine on the paper and the pattern type will come up. Charles Stamp made a photocopy of it on a transparent sheet and that enables him to lay it directly on top of any photographic impression they have to see if it matches. They couldnt positively identify it as Gary Bemister's because they couldnt locate any accidental characteristics—when you own a pair of shoes you accumulate nicks. You have to actually compare these marks to positively say that an impression was made by this shoe. They put the sheet directly over a photograph that was enlarged to actual size of the blood impression on the floor. You have to put a known item in the photograph, in this case, it was a six-inch ruler, and you can enlarge a photograph until the six-inch ruler is actually six inches. So you know that everything in that photograph is actual size and Charles Stamp laid it directly over the impression. He gave Gary back the shoe immediately. It was his heel print.

CHARLES STAMP

He lifted some friction ridges from the hot water tap on the sink in the bathroom. You can see the H. It's not a pattern by your end joints. If you grab a hot water tap, you dont grab it by your finger. You grab it around what's termed the delta. It's a fingerprint pattern like the mouth of a river, ridges going this way and all of a sudden, the ridges diverge. Most of these ridges run side to side or slightly slanted, if you want to look at your own fingers. But around this area here in everybody's finger, there is a delta. Charles searched it against prints that he had and he also sent it to Ottawa and they searched it and it was negative. Charles strongly suspects it was not made by a finger.

PHILIP ABERY

Most people assume that forensic pathologists spend all of their time with dead people. They do, but their area of expertise is in injury analysis and you dont have to be dead for them to give an opinion on an injury.

There was a sanitary napkin under the body, but Dr Abery didnt see any evidence of bleeding to suggest she was on her period. He took sections of the uterus, but the uterus lining tends to dissolve and it's very difficult to say by examining under the microscope whether or not at what stage in the menstrual cycle she was in.

Dr Abery can't speak to the habits of the deceased as to whether she wore her makeup or her chains to bed. His only experience is with his wife and he knows she wears her chains to bed and occasionally wears her makeup to bed.

He does know that Donna Whalen must have been bleeding predominantly outside rather than inside her body because inside the body he only found five hundred millilitres of blood, and that's only a little more than you'd donate when you went to the Red Cross.

She may have voluntarily removed her panties for purposes of a sexual relationship with someone.

With regards to consensual sexual activity without ejaculation, there's no way to tell whether that occurred or not.

The fingernail is well manicured there. That was before he did a finger clipping because when he does finger clippings, he clips right down.

There is a series of prick marks around the stab wounds. When youre stabbing an individual, it's difficult to say how far into the body youre going to go with each stab, because youre into a situation where youre not using the same degree of force all the time. Youre not hitting the same body area. The person may be turning and all type of things. So stab wounds vary greatly. These superficial wounds could have been caused by the victim trying to move away from the knife as the knife came toward her. Perhaps she moved back so the forward thrust reached its maximum. Or she partly blocked a thrust so the knife didnt go as far as the person had intended. Or she grabbed the individual's hand.

If the assailant was at his full reach when he was poking, then that would inhibit the penetration of the wound. If there was torture-type prodding with a knife and the assailant's motive was not at that point to inflict a deep wound, that could also be responsible for it. Have sexual intercourse with me or I'm going to do something to you and you prick a person with a knife.

Dr Abery's own view is there's a message here with the underwear being wrapped around the neck and these intimidating wounds. There's a message that there's something between the assailant and the victim.

Death is not an event. It is a process. It's very unusual for a person to be alive one minute and dead the next. It takes a little bit of time, even with massive gunshot wounds to the head and things like that, people do not die immediately.

Once a person dies, the stomach starts to digest itself. This is a process called autolysis and this happens to some extent in all organs. It's not a physiological function of the stomach. It's just that the stomach enzymes, as the cells die they release enzymes and these enzymes break down the organs. But the stomach stops functioning at death, it will not pulse food down into the small bowel or into the colon once death has occurred.

As a body decomposes, bacteria in the colon start to break down the body. Because the digestive organs such as the stomach and the pancreas no longer have a blood supply and can no longer protect themselves, cells die and release these enzymes, it breaks itself down.

You've got the heart that's cut. You've got the main vein in the body cut. You've got the main vessel coming from the lungs that is cut. All of these carry a substantial volume of blood. In addition, you've got the lungs bleeding. If those wounds are in quick repetition, death is fairly rapid.

Her bleeding is outside the body rather than inside. If she had been sitting on the chesterfield and got up, blood would start to run down. There's a demarcation point at the chest upwards, so she didnt get up. If she did get up and hold a pillow close to her, that might prevent blood from draining downwards. But she probably died so quickly that she didnt have the strength or the time. These wounds occurred bang, bang, bang, one after the other.

If you sat the deceased upright, the wounds are lateral. If you lay the deceased on her side, then theyre vertical. She wasnt strangled. What would the reason be for moving the body? Either to confuse the crime scene or to check that the individual is alive. There are cases where assailants have tried doing CPR on people that they've just killed.

LOUISE MOTTY

Louise Motty interviewed Sharon a couple of times. She took her to her mother's wake at the funeral home and she spoke with her quite often at Presentation House as well as at her grandmother's house. Presentation House is a shelter for children that have either been apprehended by Social Services or children such as Sharon who need a safe house.

Sharon had all these dreams. She was afraid that whoever killed her mother was going to Presentation House to get her. She was terrified at that thought. When they went to the wake, she wanted to know if Sheldon was going to be there. She was terrified of him. She had written some things in her diary, things she had witnessed between her mother and Sheldon Troke. Sheldon hit her mother or there was loud arguments or he'd beat up furniture. Louise, she said, I wrote in my diary that if Sheldon killed my mom, I would like to die too. And so they had to talk about this. But her biggest fear was that Sheldon would come after her and Louise had to reassure her that herself and Constable Bemister would take care of her and they'd let nobody at her and at Presentation House, the doors were locked and nobody could get in there and that reassured her somewhat. But every day it was always: Is Sheldon in jail now? Can he get out? Are the bars strong enough? Does he know? When she went down to her grandmother's, it turned to does he know that I'm down here? Will he come down here and get me? She talked about a van that she had seen on the road and she wondered who was in that van, it was constant.

That was another comment too: I wonder if he knew that I was in the house that night. Would he come after me because I was in the house? It was an extreme fear and a lot of it was being home and finding her mom's body that morning. Louise has never seen fear in a child like she saw in Sharon, of any child witness that she's had to bring through the court before the accused person.

EDIE GUZZWELL

Constable Motty phoned her and said that the children were ready to come home. So Edie Guzzwell and Agnes Whalen went up to the station and Edie went in ahead and they had some kind of a little play area set up, and Cory came out and he wrapped his arms around her knees and said Aunt Edie, Mommy is dead and Sheldon killed her. He was trying to tell her something about his mom's legs had blood on them or they had bruises. Sharon was inside talking to Constable Motty. They let Sharon come out and Sharon told her that Sheldon had killed her mother. She'd heard Sheldon's voice and her mother say stop it Sheldon.

RUTH VIVIAN

Saturday night Ruth played darts at the Piccadilly Club and they had a dinner and dance and Ruth knew Pat was going to have a few beers so she picked up a half-dozen for him so he wouldnt get sick the next day. That Sunday afternoon he was sat at the kitchen table and Ruth had a lay on the chesterfield. Tom said, Mom, youre wanted on the phone. Ruth said, hang on a minute, and she went and answered the telephone. This person started asking her questions about what time was it Donna came home Friday night, who was she with, was she by herself, things like this, and Ruth took it for granted it was a police officer. Then he mentioned his name, that it was Sheldon Troke, and she couldnt figure out how he got her number because theyre not in the phone book under her name or Pat's.

Sheldon told her to make sure—like the way he said it made her afraid—make sure you say it was nine-thirty I left Donna's and he made that clear and it didnt sound like to be nice and say it. It frightened Ruth. She didnt say nothing to her husband because she knows what her husband is like when he gets mad so she stayed at the kitchen for a second and came out to the living room and out front, went around the side of the house—there was a police officer out in the back and she told him. She said, Sheldon Troke just called here.

KIM PARROTT

Her friend had been stabbed to death, so that put a damper on her situation. She was nervous at the time she gave her statement. If something like that could happen to Donna, it could happen to her.

The police turned up at Kim's home. They spoke to her out in the car. She was shown a drawing, but it was a copy. She did not know anyone who resembled that person. She was talking to Donna on Friday, and Donna had a tape recorder. If anything ever happened to her make sure this tape recorder is found, is what she said.

Kim told the police she didnt hear the tape. And then she told them she did. She was afraid of the Trokes and the Troke reputation—that's basically her whole problem through all this. You dont have to be threatened to be nervous. You just got to know the reputation. Things that Donna said to Kim alone were enough to make you nervous. Hearing the tape made her nervous. She didnt know what she was dealing with. Sheldon's been in jail before for stabbing.

MABEL EDICOTT AND THE VIVIANS WIRETAP

Mabel: I'll read it to you if you can hear me. Keith will you go out in the kitchen and pass me in the paper on the table?

Ruth: Now it's impossible not to hear you. That's his brother.

No they got Paul in for armed robbery. They havent got him in for that reason.

The light-haired guy?

He's in for armed robbery.

But he's in on the murder too.

You dont know that. Youre only going on hearsay.

Pat Vivian: I can picture that little youngster that morning screeching out.

Mabel: Thirty-one knife wounds. That's not counting the beating up she took.

Ruth: Her jaws and everything were broke.

Mabel: And he must have strangled her with her underwear. Dirty rotten bastard. God forgive me.

She knows who killed her mommy. You knows it was Sheldon.

The only Troke that's blond is Paul. All the rest got dark hair.

I won't doubt but that Sheldon was in on the robbery too.

That happened afterwards. There was more people in on it but they were with Paul Troke.

Buddy upstairs walking over the room.

Police still over there?

They just walked over the room.

Theyre up there listening to you. Well youre not saying anything wrong anyway.

I'm only talking to you and you werent prepped.

I'm not intending to be.

I hope they puts him away in a little fucking icy cold room.

They say everywhere they went the only cooperation they got was from down to Mrs Vivian's.

If you knows something you got to tell it.

She's never out of my mind.

What happened is he ended up breaking her jaw, that way she couldnt scream.

Then he raped her.

I heard them. But the last going-off she could barely sing that way.

You heard her singing out?

I only wish I had to stay up longer.

I only wish you had to get it in your head to call the police.

How could I have called the police?

If I heard a big argument next door.

There wasnt no big argument. Who said that?

But she was saying Sheldon stop dont do it no more.

That's right.

That's enough to phone the police on.

They were always into it. That was nothing new.

That's true.

I hope he rots, the bastards whoever done it.

You knows now whoever.

Like you said to Pat, if they only had to put the knife in and get it over.

He was after strangling her I'd say. She was probably dead before he stabbed her.

It could have started down the hall because I heard her taking off her pumps. And I knew exactly because I told the police. I dont know if theyre up listening to me. What odds.

Well this is the start, it's out in the papers.

GARY BEMISTER

Ruth Vivian was having a lot of back pain and she spent a good deal of time lying on her bed. She had a television in her bedroom. Gary was seated on the side of her bed. There were police officers upstairs constantly, between the guards that they had at the scene and the identification personnel who were up there. They were moving furniture around, seizing exhibits, taking pictures. Ruth Vivian's bedroom door was open and Gary had no problem hearing the officers upstairs. One day he heard the cameras, they had the automatic wind and you could hear the film advancing in their cameras. They still had their police boots on and as Gary was speaking with Ruth Vivian there was a police officer upstairs tapping his foot on the floor and you could hear that very easily. That was in the middle of the day so you can imagine what it would be like there in the early-morning hours.

When Ruth got to the details regarding her son Tom she changed her mind. At first Tom went to bed at nine-thirty and then she said she got the nights confused. Her son cleaned up the coffee table and end tables in the living room. This was later on that Friday evening after Mabel Edicott left. What happened here was she got the sequence of events within Friday night confused, not Friday night as opposed to Thursday night.

There was somebody possibly waiting outside for Donna. She came home with a bag of Wendy's and that food was all eaten so there was a time period between when she got home and when someone came to visit her.

It is clear that she went in alone shortly after one. And went upstairs and stepped right out of her clothes in the bathroom. Got her nightie on and lay down. Up to that point no one else is around.

Mabel Edicott and her son Keith, they heard the soft knock on their own kitchen door and Mabel Edicott heard the knock on Donna's door and yet they didnt hear any sounds coming from that apartment that evening. Until the sound like dragging furniture.

There was a violent act that took place in a fairly small area. And it is quite easy to hear from apartments on all sides. The only sign of any type of bloodletting was in the living room area. A great portion of blood was spilled on the couch and then a large soaking on the floor when Donna went to the floor. The initial attack was on the sofa when she was dressed.

She had on a pair of socks.

About the pumps. When you are going upstairs, whether you are a woman in high heels or a man, it is only the ball of your foot that touches the stairway.

SHELDON TROKE

Sheldon got up at seven and went in the bathroom. He got washed. He went downstairs. There was two eggs in the frying pan. He cooked his breakfast and phoned Mrs Whalen. Mister was up and Agnes told Sheldon that she'd call back when Mister was leaving for work.

He ate his breakfast. He went in the living room and had a cup of coffee, a cigarette, watched the news—five after eight, the phone rang.

Mister was after leaving and he had to go to the dump to drop off
the garbage that was in the truck. Actually, it was the grass that they
mowed in the graveyard. Agnes told him to leave in about a half an
hour and Sheldon looked at the clock and said I'll leave at eight-thirty.
How'd you and Donna get along last night, she asked. Sheldon said all
right. She said, Did Donna go home? I dont know, he said. She might
have went over to Kim's. They said goodbye. Sheldon went upstairs and
called his parents and asked for a run to work. His father come down.

He got aboard the car and Clayton dropped him to work and Mr
Whalen wasnt there. Sheldon walked around the graveyard to see how
much grass was left and what else needed to be done and Mr Whalen
come and Sheldon walked down and met him and they walked back
up towards the shed. Mr Whalen opened the shed and got the tools
out. He told Sheldon he had some more work to do in the Jewish
Cemetery, which is a small cemetery at the top of the graveyard.
Sheldon was going to start Mr Abbott's son's grave, Gil Abbott. He
sells cars or he used to. His son was there and his grave over the years
was after sinking and Sheldon told Mr Whalen that he'd start that and
take the sods off and fill it in. So he got Mister to give him a hand
to line up the grave where he was going to cut the sods off. They
were talking and got everything lined up. They had the wheelbarrows
and everything. Mr Whalen went back up to the Jewish Cemetery.
Sheldon had something like a pick but it cuts the sods off the ground
with a side. It's flat on one side and they got a handle on it like a
pickaxe. He was using that and he noticed a car driving back down the
road again and he looked and it was his father. Sheldon walked down
towards where Mr Whalen's pickup is at and when he got down, he
could see that there was something wrong, the way his father was sot
in the car. Sheldon walked over and opened the door. What's wrong,
Dad? and he said Sheldon, I've got some bad news.

How can you explain it? Sheldon was in jail one time and there was a guard Lewis Tulk come on the range and got him. Sheldon could tell just by the way he approached him and the way he was talking that there was something wrong. He told Sheldon that the chaplain wanted to see him and as he was walking up to the chapel with the guard, and he said Lewis, who is it? His brother Raymond was after passing away.

He said to his father, What's wrong? and he says, Donna. What about Donna? DOA. Now he thought he'd said OD'd. Sheldon said oh Jesus, and he started to run and he was heading towards Mr Whalen and he didnt want to run up to him and say it to him so he went up and said Mr Whalen we got to go, and Aubrey said, What? You got to go? and Sheldon said no, *we* got to go, and Aubrey got his wheelbarrow and started putting it away, like Mr Whalen puts everything in order, and Sheldon was saying Mr Whalen, we got to go, we can put this away later. And he asked Sheldon what was wrong and he didnt want to tell him. He said Donna's sick, and he asked was she in hospital and Sheldon said he didnt know. They got down to the car and the truck and Mr Whalen said he was going to go home and Sheldon said yes and they left and Sheldon remembers when they left the graveyard, they were driving down the road and they were turning and he wanted to get down to Donna's and there was a dog walking across the street and the dog it was just taking its time and where his father was stopped to turn he had to wait for the dog and Sheldon was saying to his father, Donna wasnt on nothing last night. Donna wasnt on nothing.

They got to Donna's and pulled up on the right-hand side. There was a lot of vehicles there. Sheldon got out of the car and was going to Mrs Whalen. Pat Vivian and Mrs Whalen were coming across the street and Ches Hedderson come over and he said, Youre Sheldon? He said yes. He asked would he get in the car and Sheldon got in the car and he started to write things down and then when he see Mrs Whalen he got out of the car and started to go across the street and never got across the street. Missus and Pat Vivian come across the street and Sheldon was going to ask Mrs Whalen where were the youngsters and her and Pat were saying, Dont go saying nothing, and Ches Hedderson come over and he got in between them and Sheldon was trying to talk to Mrs Whalen and Ches Hedderson was moving her back away from Sheldon and they had a few words with each other and Sheldon told Ches Hedderson to leave her alone, she was seventy years old. And Sheldon started asking what was on the go and Hedderson told him to get back in the car we're dealing with a possible homicide, and Sheldon just stopped and went and got in the car and then Hedderson asked another officer to get in the car with him.

He asked Sheldon would he go to the police station with him. Sheldon said I got to talk to my father, and he said, No, that's all right, I'll tell him. And he got out and went up and told Sheldon's father whatever he told him.

They went to the police station. They come in through the back. They were getting off the elevator and Ches Hedderson stopped him and asked him to stay down by the elevator. It's off a hallway. He said I got to see where the youngsters are at. Sheldon asked him how the youngsters were and he said theyre all right, and he walked over and looked and he said to the other officer, Okay, come on, and they brought him down the hallway to an interrogation room.

Ches Hedderson asked Sheldon for his coat. He took his coat off and gave it to him and he put the coat in another room. They were in the interrogation room. Hedderson come in and the other officer there read a caution. They asked Sheldon if he wanted a lawyer, if he wanted to give a statement, then started firing all these questions at him. It was about nine-thirty in the morning. Asking him what happened last night, what time he got home, did anybody see him leave Donna's, who was home at his house when he got home, did he have sex with Donna, did he kill Donna, did he know who would have killed Donna. Hedderson asked him would he give a DNA test and to give blood at the Health Sciences Centre and let them take photographs. They did that at the Health Sciences Centre. Sheldon was asking them questions and they wouldnt answer them. He asked them in the afternoon can he talk to a lawyer and they said yes and he called Jim Lythgoe and explained what was going on and that he was going to do everything they asked him.

It came around suppertime and Sheldon was after doing everything and him and another officer were sot in the interrogation room and the officer was staring at Sheldon. He kept staring and a half an hour went by and Sheldon asked him do you need anything else. He didnt answer. So Sheldon said do you want to give me a run home? And they did. He went home. He phoned the Whalens' residence. He was talking to Agnes and asked her how the kids were doing and she told him that Clifford had them out for ice cream that day. After that he phoned Kim, asking her do she know of anyone that would do this to Donna and do she know if Donna was seeing anyone and anything she know, tell to the police.

Sheldon never threatened no one. Nobody throughout this whole investigation was never threatened. Excuse me, so-called investigation.

CHARLES STAMP

The first one is a facial view. The next is an overall shot showing the clothing Sheldon Troke was wearing. Photograph three is from the centre of the chest down to the floor including the legs and the boots and pants. The right hand, then the left hand. The palm side of the hands. Photograph seven is the chest down to the belt line.

Ches Hedderson said, Take a picture of his chest. I want a picture of a scratch. Charles Stamp said, It's not a scratch, but a crease.

Just above the belt line. Across the abdomen there is probably three or four of them.

It is a crease from sitting down or something, Charles Stamp said.

Sheldon was subdued, very quiet.

Their department has installed a video image booking system. It is done through a video camera and is saved on a computer screen and put on a hard drive inside the computer. It enables them to take a picture off very quickly. This is a computer-processed photograph. Charles asked the computer to give him fifteen copies, so that accounts for the slight blurriness in the eye area.

The colour appears to be not true flesh tone. It depends on the way the light hits the person. They have three halogen lamps that are lowered from the ceiling and pointed at the person. And it depends on how the skin tone reacts under the light and sometimes they are not true colour as you would see in a 35 mm photograph. Sheldon was there for ten minutes, just long enough to take the photographs. He then left the room with Ches Hedderson. Sheldon was very quiet and he maintained that expression throughout the photographs. Charles talked to Sheldon Troke and borrowed three cigarettes from Sheldon and he told Sheldon that he had quit smoking and Sheldon said I'm glad to hear that.

SHELDON TROKE

Sheldon stayed home. Upstairs in his room crying. He was devastated. It was two in the morning. He didnt even turn the lights off. Sunday he got up and phoned the Whalens.

Donna's parents, her aunt Edie, Donna's brother Clifford, come by the door. Edie Guzzwell told Sheldon that Mrs Whalen wanted him and he went out and Edie got in the back seat and Sheldon got in the driver's side. Mrs Whalen was quite upset. She passed Donna's house and was roaring out to Donna. Sheldon gave her a hug. She gave him a cheque. Clifford told him that he was after having a few beers. He said if I thought you done this, I'd blow your fucking head off. Edie was in the back staring in Sheldon's face.

He phoned the Vivians. He asked for the son, but he was talking to Pat. Tom was over to the police station. Sheldon asked Pat if he heard anything and all he heard was when him and Donna were leaving. He was talking to Ruth Vivian. He told Ruth if you hear anything, tell it to the police.

He went to Cathy Furneaux's and then back home. Constable Bemister called to ask a few more questions. So he went to headquarters. He was there for two and a half hours, then the police drove him home. Sunday night he was crying. Monday he got up and went in town trying to find out what was on the go. He was told not to call Donna's house no more. He brought a suit to the dry cleaners. He went to Cathy Furneaux's to see if there was any suits there belonged to Raymond. His brother Paul was there. He had a jacket belonged to him so Sheldon asked him could he have the jacket back because he wanted to wear it. It's a black leather one, a dress jacket. The police have it now.

He asked Paul would he go to the wake. It was supposed to be that night and Paul said yes. When they were leaving to go home Paul asked for a run over to the 301 Club. His father drove him over there. After they dropped Paul off, they were on their way home. Sheldon asked his father to drop into Neville's to get some flowers. They went home and Sheldon went upstairs. He had pictures of Donna and the youngsters. He laid down on the bed and he was crying. He ended up getting about an hour's sleep. There was a knock at the door and he heard his mother talking. It was Gary Bemister and Ches Hedderson.

He was coming down over the steps and they said, Sheldon, we got some bad news for you. There's a parole warrant out for you. They were armed. Sheldon looked at them. Sheldon's after being arrested four times for a parole warrant. Not once did the Homicide Section come to arrest him for a parole warrant. Sheldon went back upstairs and tried to contact Jim Lythgoe. He wanted to wash his face and brush his teeth. Hedderson come up with him. Then back down. Walking out through the door, Sheldon seen an unmarked unit a couple of doors down from the house and there was another police car just driving up the hill.

They took him to the lock-up. He knows Bemister and Hedderson were armed because youre not allowed in the lock-up downstairs with handguns and they opened the trunk of their car and put their guns in the trunk.

Everything he handed over. Hedderson asked him what these keys are belonged to and Sheldon told him. He was put in cell number 9, then he was transferred to Her Majesty's Penitentiary. He was out in the yard at recreation time. There was an inmate there. He come over with a newspaper and he asked was there anyone locked up for this murder. Sheldon said I dont know, why? and he handed Sheldon the newspaper and the statement in that paper for the public not to worry because the person who did this is in jail.

GARY BEMISTER

Gary Bemister and Inspector Hedderson executed the parole warrant and they were going through Sheldon's belongings at the lock-up downstairs and these keys were a part of his possessions.

Gary tried the keys at the crime scene. They had street patrol personnel guarding the scene with deadbolt locks put on the front and back doors and the keys were given to him. The original lock sets were also on the door. He tried the knob several times and the door would not open unless you had to physically kick the door. Short of doing that the door would not open without the use of the key.

A black purse. It's the purse that partially covered the face of Donna Whalen. Gary interviewed Kim Parrott at police headquarters. He searched this purse and seized a tape player as well as a cassette tape that was in the tape player.

The tape quality was very poor. Gary started making a transcript from the tape and he requested the tape be enhanced. He sat down and played the tape, wrote out as much as he could, went back over portions that were not clear and he found the more you listened to the tape the more your ear got attuned to the voices and with each playing he picked out more of the conversation. When the digital tape came back he borrowed the cassette player and it was the same process. He heard that tape possibly ninety or a hundred times over the past nineteen months.

The tape is incoherent. The subject matter of the conversation is all over the place. There's a song you can't pick out. On a couple of places on the tape you hear a background noise, a radio or a stereo. There's one occasion where the tape appears to have been stopped.

SHELDON TROKE AND DONNA WHALEN ON TAPE RECORDER

Sheldon: What are you laughing at?

Donna: I'm laughing at you.

Donna look I'll show you what I'm going to burn all right this is called a match.

What are you doing?

What's Kim saying.

I dont know Sheldon. She dont have a phone I havent been talking to her. You dont want me—

You've got no friends Donna. Your friends are—wait now—why dont you answer me.

I was frightened to death.

I would never hurt you, never. First time in my fucking life that I cried, I never ever cried in my life Donna I never did.

DONALD SAUNDERS

In Special Handling a person is less mobile. The unit is smaller, five prisoners, and there are many searches. Someone charged with murder more than likely ends up in the Special Handling Unit, but of course there are other categories of people that end up there. The person in Special Handling has the same rights as a prisoner in any other part of the prison. For visits they are assigned a private room and a staff member is right there in that room within hearing distance. The length of the visits and the frequency are the same.

Rule number one is that all inmates entering or exiting the SHU are stripped and searched. Youre given a fresh issue of clothing when he comes out of the unit and your other clothing taken and searched during the visit. The search of visitors varies from a routine frisk to a complete exploratory frisk.

There are times when they do shakedowns. They take an area and go in and do a more detailed security search. There was an inmate in Special Handling caught with bullets.

Prisoners in Special Handling have no contact with other inmates. Food is brought to the unit and the way the building is designed each unit has a lobby area and off that area are the cells and it is in this lobby that all inmates eat their meals. The lobby is locked and sealed. There are guards in a control centre who have total vision of the unit. The cells in those units are monitored through closed circuit television, so if a person is in the lobby he's seen through a window and that's what they call actual vision. If he is in his cell he is seen on a TV screen.

The cells run around one side of that lobby. The lobby is inside the SHU. They have two entrances to the lobby and they come off a corridor, they are electronically controlled and can be manually operated.

Concerning letters, prisoners can name three people with whom they are going to correspond. They do limit the number of letters that they'll pay for and beyond that an inmate has to pay the postage. On incoming mail there is no limit. You can receive letters from anyone and in any quantity but they are subjected to a screening by staff.

There is privileged correspondence that an inmate can write in a sealed letter, that would include people like a judge, his lawyer, a minister of the Crown, Human Rights or to him, Donald Saunders. However, all routine correspondence gets sent out unsealed or sent at least to the control room unsealed. The letter is scanned, it is recorded and then it is mailed.

If you were in the SHU, the correctional officer reads the letter. A letter that makes reference to other inmates or staff or security matters is returned to the inmate and told it's unsuitable for mailing. However, once an inmate becomes known to the staff, and they have a common core of staff assigned to each unit, the degree of screening is lessened.

Donald Saunders has a photocopy of Sheldon Troke's correspondence card which keeps the record of all incoming and outgoing mail written by Mr Troke. There was no correspondence written by Sheldon Troke, just a number of items received.

Prisoners only leave the unit for recreation or a visit. The doctor's office is on the same floor, just a short distance up the corridor. A person in Special Handling is taken in when there are no other inmates there and he's under supervision for the duration of that medical visit.

There are two accesses to this basement floor, stairway and elevator. Staff use the elevator and it's used for bringing meals and escorting prisoners. However, the stairwell is also used for general population inmates who are going to see a doctor. There is a slight curvature in the corridor so when you get off the elevator or the stairwell you can't see down that corridor. When the doctor's clinic is in progress the correctional officer in charge of Special Handling moves into that corridor so that an inmate can't come down to Special Handling.

They have recreation by themselves. It's done on a schedule even though quite frequently Special Handling inmates dont request it. It lasts an hour.

The inmate submits a list of three names of people with whom he wishes to have visits. He can change that list from time to time. The visiting card is a record of all visits. The visits take place in that waiting area next to the doctor's office. Occasionally they use the doctor's office. Space is not something they have an abundance of, so sometimes they go to a different area of the prison and use an interview room that a lawyer or a parole officer entering the prison would have to use.

Inmates have an advantage over staff, they are there twenty-four hours a day and the staff are only on forty hours a week. Special Handling requires a little bit more experience and ingenuity than in the general population. Even with the best intentions it's very difficult to prevent things coming into the penitentiary and things going out. You sort of patch a hole and another one opens. Escape prisoners are an example of that. Escapes occur. Strip searches are not searches of cavities in the body parts. They are not permitted to do that, just a visual skin search. The use of different cavities is something that prisoners routinely use in terms of getting things in and out of prison.

It's very difficult to get a medical person to agree to do a cavity search. It's not worth the effort to pursue it. Inmates know this. Inmates tend to be up on the regulations.

The prison culture is pretty standard nationwide and once a person has testified against another prisoner, they usually fit in on a very low strata of inmate subculture. They are rats and you find that the majority of prisoners will, as part of their day-to-day routine, attempt to cause that person trouble and inconvenience and harm. They try to intimidate them prior to testifying. Any prisoner who has been in jail for any time will know this. There is an understanding of what they should and should not do now that they are prisoners. There is coaching between the more senior person and the newcomer. One of those areas of coaching is if you think you hear something or see something and are thinking about repeating it, it might cost your life.

PAUL TROKE

Paul spoke to Sergeant Hedderson just downstairs in this building in the lock-up. He's not doing a line-up unless his lawyer tells him. You know the blond-hair fellow, Paul said, you put him and me in a line-up you won't tell us apart. The blond-hair fellow he saw that night was Jacob Parrott. Paul knows people in the area. He's been in a line-up, they remember a face. Tom Vivian downstairs knows him. The lady next door, Mabel Edicott, Paul wasnt in her house and she was never in Donna's but he was at Donna's more than six or seven times and a couple of times he waited out in the car up in front for Sheldon. He's not going in a line-up, that lady might recognize him.

Paul was stopped by the police on Patrick Street in a stolen car. They took him to the lock-up and he saw two correctional officers. Gary Bemister asked him what he was arrested for and Paul said impaired driving and murder. That's what Gary says he heard. But what happened was he wanted to have Paul's ring, and Paul said, What do you want that for, murder? The police were following where he went and they asked him to get in line-ups. They were more or less coming out saying he was involved with it. Gary Bemister said there's witnesses saw you looking into the window, and it wouldnt have surprised Paul if they did grab him and arrest him. He was drunk. When they asked for his ring they had him in the car, what more evidence do they need, what did they want his ring for? So that's why Paul said why do you want that for, it's something to do with the murder. They were harassing Paul everywhere he went. They even question his girlfriend Trisha Hickman.

GARY BEMISTER

He picked Mabel Edicott up on Empire and conveyed her to headquarters to show her eight photographs on a card. The person I saw at the back was good looking, she said. He wasnt like anyone on the card. There was one target in the photographs: Jacob Parrott. Paul Troke was not on the card.

Gary turned her over to Percy Morgan and Percy sat her down and asked her to think back and describe what shape nose, what shape eyes. Think hairstyle, he said, think chin, if he had a moustache, shape of lips. Percy Morgan had an identikit. The chin area was a little bit longer, Mabel Edicott said, it was definitely more round. And the hairstyle is not bad, cut on the sides right close, but his hair was really blond. He didnt have grey hair, he had blond.

This man, she said, he did not talk as if he was drinking. When Mabel said next door she turned like that and looked down and she thought in this hand here he had a white cigarette. She never seen the filter part, the hand was down like this.

He had on a heavy grey jacket. The collar was up around his neck. When Percy put the moustache on him the face looked more familiar than without it. He never had no gloves on.

Mabel's kitchen light was on in the back hall. You come up the back stairs and you dont know the building you wouldnt know where her apartment was or Donna's apartment. From the front you would.

The identikit that Percy Morgan used has since been discontinued by the force and sent back to the States because they were paying quite a high rental on it. Percy does have an older type kit, this kit is about twenty years old. You'd start with a hairstyle and then go with the chin line. What Mabel Edicott felt was the best set of eyes. Some eyebrows. A set of lips, the nose and also a moustache. All this is joined together and held against the white background. Does this look like the person youre trying to describe to me?

Percy photocopied it with all the different numbers of the sheets so that if you ever wanted to recreate the composite you can do it by looking at the numbers. Then he cuts around it to clean it up a bit to get the numbers out of it, so you can put it on a poster or a bulletin.

Mabel Edicott said the moustache wasnt thick enough, so he used a pencil and thickened the moustache. That was the only change that was made to the composite. There's a date down by the neck. Later on she told him the nose was too broad. He tried a sketch. He asked Mabel Edicott to describe the scene. She had heard a knock and she opened the door. So the light showed the person standing in the doorway. The background was dark in the hallway. What she saw was a perfectly lit person with no light from the top or side.

Percy asked Mabel Edicott how she saw him. What was the general shape of the head and the shoulders. And from the hairline he worked down to the eyes and nose and mouth. That gave him a face. One has to come up with a face. It's no point in making a drawing from somebody's description if you dont come up with a face. He showed the face to Mrs Edicott and worked with her on that. Were the shoulders wide or narrow. That gives a better idea of the bulk of the body. Maybe the nose is too long or too short, he made the correction. The drawing is based entirely on her verbal description. This conversation took place at the constabulary office at ten in the morning for about three hours. They stopped for a cup of coffee.

After he completed the drawing he asked for a group of young blond men, blue-eyed and white. He looked at ten mug shots and picked out one that was very much like the person that Mabel Edicott was trying to describe.

He wanted to get a feeling. It was instinctive. There was no other reason. He thought it might help if he could see somebody of that age and colouring.

He altered the sketch slightly. It was around the ears. It would have been moving a line or two. Maybe the hairline, there was too much hair around the ears so he moved that away. Mabel Edicott was there while he made the alterations.

If you look closely you can see where he uses a pencil and an eraser. The colouring came later on.

She described a person with light hair, and a slight hairline on the upper lip. Percy Morgan could tell from his general colouring what colour his hair would be and the colour of his skin. Were there any scars? No, she said.

He was a very good-looking man. And his hair was light. So that allowed Percy to believe that his skin would be the same.

LOUISE MOTTY

Louise drove the Edicotts to the police parking garage on the fourth floor of Atlantic Place. She knew Paul Troke was in a holding cell and that he would be in courtroom 7, but she never identified Paul Troke to the Edicotts.

They walked through the main doors of the courtroom and waited until the prisoners came out. There was about eight prisoners. They were handcuffed in twos. They were about five feet away. The court was crowded that day. There was a man being brought out and there was camera crews, several people with TV, and family belonging to this guy. There were officers and lawyers and a lot of spectators, more than you would see down there on a normal day.

When the prisoners came up Mabel Edicott grabbed hold to Louise's arm. She said that guy there looks almost exactly like the man at my door. The only thing different was the hair on top of his head was fuller. He's the same build, the same height, the same hair colour. Now the young fellow that came to the back door had a jacket on, and this fellow doesnt have a jacket on, so I wouldnt be able to tell you about the size. But they could be brothers.

This was Paul Troke.

There was one other person coming out of the courtroom with blond hair. Jacob Parrott. Mrs Edicott did not react to him in any way.

Paul Troke had been in custody for perhaps two days. His hair, it gave the appearance of being gelled or spiked. He was very clean cut, he wore a black dinner type jacket with black pants on, almost like the suit the accused has on, but it was black, and his hair was gelled on top. Louise wrote notes in her 16-24s. She didnt make them right at the time. She made them after she dropped off the Edicotts and went back to Fort Townshend.

She drove the Edicotts home and then interviewed Sharon Whalen down in a room in the bottom of Presentation House. Sharon drew pictures and talked. Louise drew with her. Sharon said that she felt that the voice she heard that night was Sheldon Troke's, but it could have been Jacob Parrott. Her nanny said that Sheldon loved Donna and would not hurt her. Someone must have come into her house while her mother was downstairs at Tom Vivian's. The person may have hid in the bathroom until her mother returned and then stabbed her. Louise Motty sat on the floor with Sharon at a little table and they drew pictures until Inspector Hedderson arrived. He told Sharon that Jacob Parrott was no longer a suspect. Sharon told him her mother called out to her that night. Inspector Hedderson said, You mean your mother called out to you to help her and you didnt go?

Sharon said no.

What would your mother say if she knew you knew who did this to her and you didnt tell?

Sharon was holding a doll in her hands and was wrenching it. She was obviously upset. Louise, too, was upset by Ches Hedderson's approach to the child.

PAUL TROKE

Paul Troke's been charged and convicted of stealing cars before. He's in custody now for stealing cars. He stole that one at the Avalon Mall. The keys were in it and he sat in it and listened to the radio and then decided to take it for a ride. So while he dont have access to a car he's quite capable of taking one. He's at Renous, which is a maximum security penitentiary. Paul was originally sentenced to Springhill because of that armed robbery. It was at the CIBC on Water Street with a person by the name of Joey Yetman. Paul had a pair of orange coveralls on and a sawed-off shotgun. He pointed the shotgun at one of the clerks who was trying to get the money for Joey out of the cash register. Paul was stood up there with the gun and he was giving orders. Paul didnt say a word. The clerk says he saw Paul Troke hold the gun with two hands. It had a long barrel. Then Paul Troke said, Open the register motherfucker or I will blow your brains out.

Paul wanted to plead guilty right at the beginning of it but like there was some stories going around that he gave statements on the other people that were involved, so he wanted the preliminary to come out and who said what so when all the evidence was presented Paul changed his plea to guilty. But they charged him with uttering threats. Paul didnt utter no threats but he wasnt about to blame it on somebody else, so he pled guilty to all the charges that was read out. He didnt want to turn around and say, it wasnt me who said them words it was Joey Yetman. Paul was willing to deal with the consequences the judge was going to sentence him to. A lot better than ratting on Joey and having to put up with the things that happens to rats in prison.

Paul was afraid the police were going to come and shoot him. They were looking for him with sidearms. He told the police he didnt even know a person by the name of Joey Yetman. He said that on the date of the robbery he was at the Dunns' on Field Street, drinking in the back yard all day, so he could not possibly had been at the CIBC committing this armed robbery. He demanded that they conduct a line-up so that he could show them he was innocent. A customer at the bank picked him out of the line-up.

Paul did not lie in court. He took the blame for that armed robbery. It's not like he told the judge a lie. The judge asked Paul a question and he said yes that's what happened, but he was taking the blame, it's not like he got up on the stand and lied.

Gary Bemister: Look, up until this murder you were never charged with anything.

Paul: No.

Since this happened youre charged with impaired driving and car theft. Now youre charged with armed robbery. Youre looking at eight to ten years and we figure youre under a lot of pressure.

I'm under no pressure.

From what I understand, Paul, guilt is only a matter of time.

SHELDON TROKE AND
TRISHA HICKMAN WIRETAP

Sheldon: When me and Donna had our arguments and I threw a glass it hit me—Sheldon you got to stop this. And nothing would continue. We had our shouts and it would stop. For me to turn around and beat Donna, no.

Trisha: Do you know what the cop said to me? Did Paul ever beat the shit out of me. I said are you off your head. Just like that. Paul would never think about doing that to me.

Sheldon: I got to laugh because Donna's cracked see, God bless her soul. The cops when they were trying to charge me with that armed robbery. They went to Donna. Gary Bemister come back to me and he said that's some girl you got there. I said why? He said I asked her did you ever abuse her and she said yes. It happened two nights ago, and she hauled her turtleneck down. There was a big hickey on her neck. She said I enjoyed every minute of it. I cracked up.

Trisha: I would have died laughing.

She said it right serious to him. God bless her soul. Trisha her father and her mother are always talking about God and heaven.

Religious.

And I know Donna was a bit into shoplifting. And I got a bible there by her picture. And I ask myself God please forgive her let her go to heaven.

She's in heaven.

I hope so.

CATHY FURNEAUX

She was coming up Freshwater Road one day and outside her house a police car was hauled in on the side of the road just about a door down from where she lives. They asked her could she get in the back. The driver was Ches Hedderson. He turned around and said, Cathy you knows and I knows who killed Donna. Cathy said, I swear on my mother I do not know who killed Donna, but I wish you'd catch the maniac that did kill the poor girl.

He started roaring in her face and said Sheldon Troke killed her, and Paul Troke helped him clean up the mess and then they came back to your place and you helped them clean up. By this time Hedderson was eating the head off her. That Cathy was lying. And he kept roaring at her. The Trokes never scared her—he was the one that was scaring her. She said youre fucking nuts. And she got out of the car. Paul Troke was outside the car, walking back and forth, looking in the police car, but she never took notice. Paul was at her house just about every day.

LOUISE MOTTY

She was on duty in the downtown area that Friday night. She was riding second on the van. They were driving across George Street when Paul Troke came out of a nightclub called Sam Shades. He was with a woman. He was walking west with her on his arm towards the Sundance. It was just before one oclock. He was wearing a little suit jacket but it was short like a bellhop type and he had no shirt on underneath and a lot of gold chains on his neck.

The clubs close at two a.m. It was a nice night. There was another woman standing in the laneway between two buildings that leads into Sam Shades and she was calling out to Paul. That was Trisha Hickman.

GARY BEMISTER

They were working out of the Major Crimes office which is fairly small. There are seven investigators and it was getting cramped so they made use of a lecture theatre. They had a desk in front and several chairs for an audience. Every morning they had a briefing session. The analysts have their lists and a priority basis of what they want done. Ches Hedderson detailed the teams and gave them their duties and at the end of the day they had a debriefing. Everyone said what they did that day, any concerns, and the investigative team talked about the file and where they were going with it. They decided what could be made public and Gary Bemister was in charge of issuing press releases and applying for warrants. There was a great deal of alarm just after this murder. So Gary wanted to calm people down. He suggested that while no arrests have been made the assailant is in custody, and people need not fear him being loose. Sheldon Troke was in custody and this was mentioned in the warrant application to search his mother's house. Any time a search warrant is filed in the Provincial Court the media have access to it and unless there's an order specifically sealing the warrant the media can go down and look at it and report what the police put in the warrant and this is what happened here. Not having it sealed, it was an oversight on Gary's part that day.

THE VIVIANS WIRETAP

Pat: They gave the news about her.

Ruth: Shit I missed it.

They gave out they got two suspects.

Ruth: Two?

It's him and his brother. They says one of the children saw what went on.

They knows who done it then.

Sure I knows who fucking done it.

Him and his brother.

They got the car now and everything. She was stabbed thirty-one times.

My Jesus that's terrible.

Her shorts were wrapped around her throat.

That's brutal see. Theyre fucking nuts. Somebody should kill them. They should be executed. No that would be too good for them.

Fucking bastards.

Tom: They had it on the news.

Your mother was just telling me.

Ruth: They got one. Sure I knew that because Donna, what breath she had in her told Sharon not to come out.

Pat: Now the child is after seeing it.

Ruth: As long as I'm here I'll always think on her at the foot of the bed.

He dug the dirt and he piled it on all of us. He had that all planned. What in Jesus can we do about it. We just lived down underneath them.

JIM LYTHGOE

Could you see a possible danger if down the road someone decided to make up a story about Sheldon Troke? He would now have information that the police believed two suspects were involved, one committing the murder, the second an accessory after the fact by aiding and the disposal of evidence? That the daughter placed a 911 call and there were thirty-one knife wounds and a pair of underpants twisted around her neck? Did you have any concerns when that material came out with regards to aiding people who say well Sheldon told me this, that suddenly a lot of information is made public? And what is this from Ruth Vivian about Donna telling Sharon not to come out? That is the first we've heard of that.

CATHY FURNEAUX AND
BERTHA TROKE WIRETAP

Cathy: I was talking to Agnes Whalen this morning. She had a call right after the news last night that Donna was out to a car Friday morning talking to the driver. If that was Paul he'd be in talking with Sheldon. Paul never had the car Friday. The day Donna got buried after they left somebody came in and put a load of flowers on the grave and Agnes got a phone call saying Paul came in a white car and threw a load of flowers on Donna's grave. Now I said Agnes for one thing Paul dont have a white car and Paul got no time for graveyards because he never even went to Raymond's service he waited till eleven oclock that night and got a taxi in and got in over the fence.

Bertha: Agnes was telling me the little one who knocked around with Sharon said that Sharon used to tell her everything about Sheldon, that he fought with her mom, and the police came and asked Sharon did she tell Ashley this and Sharon said no. So you better watch who youre talking to because you could be talking to someone and he's real nice to your face and theyre the very ones that are going to tell stories to the police. I mean I knows myself that Donna was one for going out and fighting with other women.

Cathy: She had the strength in her.

If you knows that youre going to die, youre going to reach out and try to shove somebody away, I mean you got to scrob or kick or do something.

Cathy: If she wanted to, sure she could fight if she wanted to. Donna was a big girl.

JIM LYTHGOE

The beige doily was partly under the coffee table. It was folded up and bagged. How big is that thing? Let's unfold it. There appears to be a cigarette embedded into the doily. There is no reference to that cigarette in Gary Bemister's notes. He doesnt recall having seen it. There's a cigarette stuck onto this doily and the doily was under the coffee table where the deceased died. It's a Player's Light with some burgundy red material on the cigarette. There is no sign of lipstick on any of the other cigarettes. This cigarette was missed by forensics but if you look at the red colour there, it's not on the end of the cigarette. This is burned right on. It might be blood or lipstick or carpet fibre. That cigarette burned into the doily and melted the material.

It's a different brand of cigarette from the others. Donna Whalen may have been smoking this cigarette. It could have been left in the ashtray to burn or she could have been smoking it.

The cigarette now has finally come loose from where it was burned into the doily. The cigarette has fallen onto the courtroom floor.

CHES HEDDERSON

There was security put on the crime scene and street patrol officers knocked on doors and met people to see if they had any information. Crime Stoppers were brought in and there was broadcasts and posters made for tipsters.

When Gary Bemister went to the house of Bertha Troke, he was allowed into the house quite readily. She didnt wish to see the warrant. Gary searched and she said you can search the car too and gave him the keys to her red Corsica.

JIM LYTHGOE

Inspector Hedderson also went by the house without a warrant and questioned Bertha as to what clothes Sheldon had been wearing the night before. She voluntarily gave him all of the clothes that Sheldon had been wearing. A T-shirt at the Troke home had a bloody substance on it. That shirt was tested and found that the material was not blood. If Sheldon Troke or family members were going to remove things from their house that were suspicious they would have certainly removed a T-shirt with blood on it.

EDIE GUZZWELL

She was upset and she came into Fort Townshend to speak to Louise Motty. It was the day Constable Motty was bringing Sharon to her mom's wake. Edie said that Sheldon punched Rod Tessier out into a cold junk because he was interested in Donna. Everybody's chatting and Sharon is exposed to these conversations, Aunt Edie said. Sharon was at Presentation House. It is a safe house, a house that is designed for children who've been taken away from their parents. It's run by the Sisters. They are dressed in religious uniforms and civilian.

Sharon told Edie it was Sheldon's voice. Donna's mother told Sharon it couldnt have been Sheldon's voice because he was home in bed.

Edie was concerned because Donna didnt look the same in the coffin and she wondered how Sharon would react.

AGNES WHALEN AND
RUTH VIVIAN WIRETAP

Agnes: I'm tormented, I can't rest. If the murderer were brought to justice I know I'd be able to content myself.

Ruth: I dont think youre going to have to worry about him much longer. I can tell you something but youre not allowed really to know.

No I know.

They warned me but I heard what went on and I told Gary Bemister. They took a tape of me because I can't go to court where I'm laid up. And that night I heard them about quarter after one going up over the stairs. Donna kicked off her pumps and she was singing out, dont do that any more Sheldon, and she repeated it. So he's not to get out of prison.

I'm not worrying about him getting out of prison because if I thought that he killed her, I'd kill him myself.

So would I to be honest.

I didnt think he done it because Donna told me she was driving him home. But now after I heard he got out again and his mother covered up for him then I knows he done it.

Unless there's a couple of Sheldons going around but she definitely called his name. I could hear the shoes coming off and she got a fashion when she gets up over the stairs and then her voice started to get lower.

Sharon says she said, No no leave me alone leave me alone. But she dont know if she was dreaming or not.

Mabel next door she's after telling the same as I did but not the same words.

Well Donna saw a shadow out by the door and she rang me so Pat and Tom went around but never seen no one. I was still talking to her on the phone when she said, Mom listen there's somebody coming and here Sheldon came up over the stairs. Now she made a tape of him that night.

That was Thursday night. He broke the front door in.

Did he break the front door in because he had a key.

According to Tom he did because he was there. Well that night, little did I think there was anyone up there murdering her.

If only you had phoned the police. She told me all along she was going to be killed. If I dont be killed now I'll be killed when I comes back from the mainland. I said Donna what are you holding, and her father said are you frightened and she said yes Dad I am. He said something you can't get out of? She said yes but she wouldnt tell us what it was. He knew she was going to the mainland.

You can rest assured he done it.

He'll pay for it. He's a con artist. He had me fooled.

He's not getting out no more.

I thought we were after getting through to him after Abery gave him the job in the cemetery.

Theyre a tribe.

Theyre different. I said to Sharon I dont think that Sheldon done that. Then they took the children and put them in Presentation House. They might have got more out of Sharon because she's afraid now theyre going to take her again. She's clammed up and anybody says they'd take her even for a holiday she'll come and link up with me and say Nanny I dont want to go.

Donna used to come down and sit on the foot of my bed and talk to me.

She used to say Ruth Vivian is a sweetheart.

She told me all about you.

When I goes into stores and I comes out I gets all flustered. I dont get half what I wanted and I see Sharon walking out through the door with me. I thought the child would take it away a bit but I'm more of a strength to her.

She was out there that morning on the step screeching.

I said to your Pat if there's anything to make the case stronger. I'm not afraid of them. The Trokes called me up. Telling me how Sheldon missed her and was praying for her.

Dont ever give out any information to them. The Trokes asked me did I know anybody with light hair she was going out with.

I'll tell you where that's coming from. She went and had her fortune told. Madeline Ryall said she was going to leave Sheldon and go with a light-hair man. But she never had no men in her apartment.

The only one she had in there was Paul Troke. Used to go looking for his brother.

Well sure Paul got light hair. He was the fellow just had the armed robbery.

If he gets ten years.

They all should be put away. When theyre put away we'll be safe. But Ruth here is something that torments me. Did she kick up much of a fuss?

No just ahh.

Sheldon Troke.

I never heard. I never heard no voice of a man. It is like he had it planned.

My sister Edie she can't rest. She helped me rear Donna up when I went out to work because I got no support for her. Donna used to tell me everything but not what was bothering her. She was a sweet youngster all her lifetime. I thought I had him under control with her.

She told me stories. She even showed me the marks.

She carried them marks up to the hospital and showed them to me. I said keep clear of him. Now he told me he was off the drugs, he was off the beer and he said it's not worth it. And then he told me I'm not going out with Donna no more unless Donna wants me and wants to change.

He never changed.

I said Sheldon keep clear of her. Wait till she makes the first approach. He said I'm not going out with her no more and here that night he was out to the show with her where there was dancing and I said my God Donna are you getting off your head. She was either afraid to give him up or she was stuck on him.

She was afraid to give him up.

I would have got him arrested right quick. You can go to these crime places. There was one girl she talked to and the way she put it, if he done this and if he done that. She didnt say he done it.

No.

I can't believe she's gone. I has to pass along by the house every time I'm out. Sometimes I stop the car and looks at the window and sees if she's there. I dont take Sharon out there any more on account of her.

My Lord no.

But now she's having these nightmares and Edie was in from Grand Falls. She said Sharon now come out with me for a few days, we got a swimming pool. Sharon went on and she told me she loves it out there.

I guess she do.

She rang me dinnertime and said I'm in the pool and everything.

Poor little child. She knows all right but she thinks she tells anybody that—

Theyre going to take her from me again. If I say to her Constable Motty is coming down to talk to you she'll link up with me. She's in fear. She lost her mother and I'm the next one she loves in the world next to her mother.

Sure she dialed the 911.

She told me. I said you were a good little girl to do that. I said you take Cory and bring him down and go into the Vivians' and stay there till Nanny gets there.

That's what she did.

And it's a sin because Donna used to go out and leave her.

But Donna must have told her if anything happened dial 911.

And to get Pat downstairs. Pat will come up through the back way.

The last time I seen her was that night. About twenty after nine. She went in the room and was talking to Pat.

She used to tell your Tom when she was going. She was going to give Sheldon a run home and I said who is looking after the children. And she said Tom. Donna was gone about a half-hour and I rang. Sharon answered the phone and I said your mommy is not home yet.

I didnt let on I knew where her mother was to. I said Sharon dont you think you should be in bed. She said Mommy lets me stay up. I said no love all little girls are in bed this hour. Turn off the television because I knows what you are looking at on television. Not fit to look at.

No that's true.

Because he used to have the horror movies on. She said okay Nanny. I said now you go on to bed. When Mommy comes Mommy is going to ring me. I never heard tell of Donna no more.

Youre after losing your daughter.

And I tells your Pat I says help out the police and get him caught.

Yes.

And I wonders did she suffer too much. Did he tantalize her or brutalize her.

She was thirty-one stab wounds.

But did she feel them. Did she go off unconscious.

She went pretty low, her voice. You know they had it planned.

Right.

So I wants you to promise sweetheart you won't tell a soul.

I won't.

Especially the police.

You got nothing to worry about. Because you didnt tell me anything that you didnt tell the police.

Theyre worried about us talking. It's the Trokes worrying me.

I told Sheldon when he rang from the pen, until the murderer is caught I'd rather for them not to talk to me.

He's not getting out, Agnes. He could get out but just outside so far and then they'll charge him.

If he gets out in twenty-five years I'll be well gone.

Yes me too.

LOUISE MOTTY

Sharon told her aunt Edie that when her mom came home Friday night Tom Vivian came up with her for a little while. He was there for about an hour and she is not sure he left, but a short time later, a knock came on the door. Then Sharon heard Tom talking to Sheldon. She was sure of Sheldon's voice because it was low and rough. She said Sheldon never whispered in his life. She heard them talking and then a door at the top of the stairs opened and someone went down over the stairs. She heard her mother say, Stop, Sheldon, leave me alone. Her mother said Sheldon's name. Louise Motty asked Sharon if there was anything else that she could recall. She saw an arm go up. She saw this through the reflection in the mirror. This arm was covered by a red or brown sleeve. Sharon could not recall seeing a person. She only heard voices. These voices were the voices of her mother and Sheldon Troke.

Sharon was not the type of child that had to be prompted. She had all these questions she'd throw at you. She heard the coffee table tipping over. Her mother calling to her and a man's voice telling her mother to be quiet. The television was on. The lamps flickered and she saw part of the big chair, but she did not see any people. Sharon was able to see all this because of the location of the two mirror dressers. One was in her room and one halfway in her room.

Now Gary Bemister spent a good portion of the morning attempting to align the mirrors so he could see out in the living room as Sharon claimed. It was impossible for him to do so.

Sharon has never been back to the house. Louise Motty was the one that went back and got all of her clothes and Cory's things and toys and dolls and whatever else she could find.

They went into the room, the chapel, where Donna was waking. Sharon looked at her mom and said Constable Louise, do I have to stay here any more? This doesnt look like my mom.

Sharon stood with the Whalens and then they went out to the chesterfield area and she was talking most with her uncle Clifford. Iris Troke was there but Louise didnt see Sharon with her. She kept a pretty solid eye on Sharon while she was there. Louise kind of stood off but she was in the room.

JIM LYTHGOE

When Sharon was first interviewed by the police she did not tell them that she heard Sheldon Troke's name. She didnt hear his voice either. In fact, in relation to the voice, she was very clear in saying just the opposite, that she did not know who it was. What she did hear, in Louise Motty's original notes, is her mother saying No, Sharon, no.

Louise Motty told her that Sheldon Troke killed her mother, that he was in jail and couldnt come after Sharon. The police led Sharon into suggesting she heard her mother say Sheldon's name. Instead of no Sharon no she must have heard no Sheldon no.

ROBERT ASH

Her grandmother said not to mention Sheldon Troke's name because Sheldon did not do it. This was the very day that her mother was found dead. So Sharon does not mention Sheldon. But she says to her aunt Edie she did hear Sheldon's voice.

JOEY YETMAN

A couple of days before she died, it was on a Wednesday, Joey seen her. He was in the Avalon Mall up by the Sony Store and when he walked out Donna Whalen was coming out of a store. It's upstairs just down from the eating place. There was a fellow waiting for her. They started walking up towards the food court and she was talking to him. Joey seen just the back of him. He was turned back on. He had blondish white hair, shoulder length, and a white shirt and white pants on. His hair was messed up and his clothes was dirty. He was a little bit taller than Donna.

Joey contacted the police on the Sunday night after she died. Over the phone. Like somebody never washed. He dont know Tom Vivian.

CHES HEDDERSON

He gave an interview on camera that Sunday. People were afraid and they wished the police would arrest someone. The release stated that although no one has been charged there is no need for the public to be concerned that the assailant is still at large. That remark was given in response to a question by the media should people be alarmed and Hedderson's remark was passed on to Gary Bemister and he made that release over the telephone.

Ches Hedderson doesnt think he's indicating to the public that the person who murdered Donna Whalen is presently in custody. That certainly wasnt his intention. It's there but he can't say that they were his words or if they were the reporter's words. This release was given over the telephone. It wasnt a typed release that was faxed out or released by other means. If he'd heard the news release he would have called the media to advise them they were misinterpreting what he'd said. But he did not call any media. It wasnt brought to his attention that there was any problem with that release.

PAUL TROKE AND
TRISHA HICKMAN WIRETAP

Paul: Fuck things are bad enough. My head is fucked up enough and you got to be saying things like that to me.

Trisha: I dont think it came out like that.

Yes it did come out like that. I won't have got pissed off if it never.

I dont know boy, I dont know about you at all. Youre wild. That's all I can say is youre wild.

I should ask them now to fucking put me in the SHU for the night. Why?

Because I got too much going through my head and I'm going to fucking freak out. That way I won't get in no trouble.

As long as you dont get in any more trouble Paul than what youre already in my son.

I got to go.

If you have to Paul.

Trisha I got a lot of things on my mind and nobody fucking understands right.

Talk to me.

Ye all thinks it's so fucking easy down here for me.

No not at all. I dont.

Ye dont even know where to start to understand.

Were you talking to Cathy?

No.

Were you talking to anyone?

No.

Did anything happen today?

No.

Is the guards giving you a hard time?

No.

Try to relax.

Try to relax Trisha?

Youre going to court tomorrow arent you?

Was Iris out there running around for Eugene now is she? The whole works of them can go now and fucking crawl up my arse.

You dont mean that.

I do mean it. When I goes, none of them are going to hear from me again because I'm not coming back here and I fucking mean that. They can all go to fuck. As far as I'm concerned I got no family.

You do Paul.

Where is it?

Your mother and father.

That's why theyre always down to court when I goes. That's why theyre always down to visit me right. Only one person went down to see me and that was you. So you tell me where my family is?

Paul there's a lot on the go boy.

Cathy is five minutes up from the fucking courthouse. A five-minute fucking walk. Do you know how that makes me feel walking in there and nobody there? You think that makes me feel wanted?

I know it mustn't feel very good Paul.

It dont make much difference to me any more now Trisha. Everything is fucked up.

You probably needs a bit of time for yourself and I do understand it.

I know Trisha but the things that's on my mind I dont want to tell you because it's only going to scare and I dont want that. I got so much hate built up inside of me you won't believe it. I'm not talking about you or Mom or Dad but I got no time left for no one any more.

Why?

You dont see anybody doing fuck all for me. I should have learnt that a long time ago.

All you needs is a break Paul.

Trisha there's no break for me. I never got a fucking break in my
life. What fucking life I got.

RUTH VIVIAN WIRETAP

She looks some fucking old. Oh, I met her fucking once. I met her one
night when Sheldon was going right cracked upstairs. She's fucking
worse than the youngsters. Bertha would fucking knife you as quick
as she'd look at you. Her daughter is as worse again. Iris would stab
you as quick as Bertha would. Raymond and Paul too. But Sheldon
Troke frightened me when I was out there on the side of the house
and he turned around and if I ever sees you talking to Donna again,
I'll punch your fucking face in. I was going to tell Pat about it, but I
said I'd better not because Pat would go after them cocksuckers. He
was drunk and the two of them fighting and she sat on the door and
I said fuck that.

Sheldon Troke's got me on the phone and I hung up on him and
all day Sunday my phone is ringing off the fucking wall. They'd
wait till I pick it up and then hang up and it went on the whole
fucking night. One is in jail for bank robbery and one is on trial
now, but it was Sheldon fucking threatened. He said to me look,
he said, you tell the cops I left Donna at quarter to ten and dont
fucking forget it. He frightened the shit right out of me. Every
fucking bit of blood in my body just drained. If you know anything
else, tell the cops, he said. But he said this to make sure I didnt tell
the cops anything. It was sarcastic and threatening and I shouldnt
tell the police anything

I didnt like what they showed yesterday, the way they showed her
headstone.

JIM LYTHGOE

One of the television reports showed the headstone of Donna Whalen. There's no doubt that Ruth Vivian is referring to that in this wiretap.

PAT VIVIAN

That Friday was a fine morning. Pat went out to clean the doorstep and he said good morning to Donna. She said good morning back. She went up beside her car and another guy came down, blew the horn—Donna went over and talked to this man. It was a friendly conversation. Pat didnt see nothing wrong with it. She was leaning on the roof of the car with her hand.

He was a blocky young fellow. His hair it wasnt a blond. It wasnt dark. It was in between, a dishwater blond. His hair was well cut. He had on a baseball hat and a red T-shirt and the rest of him Pat couldnt see, only his shoulders up.

The car was a dark grey. The headrests of the car were up sort of high. The centre of the headrests were like a wire mesh type. It was a foreign car, smaller than a Tempo. Not like a Chev or a Dodge. An expensive car. She talked to him for five to eight minutes.

There was a show on TV which showed a car in relation to this case. Pat got quite excited as it was the car he'd seen. He doesnt know when he talked to the police. He doesnt have a photographic memory. He cannot remember everything that youre talking about right now.

Pat told the police he seen the car on TV. They approached the car lot from the fire hall side. On the left-hand side locked up in a cage Pat Vivian picked out the car. It was a grey four-door, a heavy car, no question about it. Pat dont know where this small car is coming into it. That's the car he picked out. It was a big heavy domestic car. He knows nothing about cars.

They visited the Edicotts quite often but after Donna's death not very often, very scarce. They discussed the Sheldon Troke matter. Such as what should happen to Sheldon. Manys a time. Pat thinks the death penalty should be brought back.

RUTH VIVIAN

Ruth doesnt want to sit, she's fine. She has her thing with her. She doesnt want to take a break. Look, it's been twenty-one months of hell, she wants to get it over with. You can put the paper in front of her, she cannot read a damn paper. She doesnt know how many times she's got to tell you that. She didnt watch anything on TV about this. She doesnt watch the news. Is it just a coincidence the only time she mentioned details about people in a vehicle was when it was in the paper? You can have your opinion. She's got hers. What happened upstairs, her nerves are shot and she got to get out of here. Even if she did have to wait a while to get in by the Village or New Pennywell Road. She dont get out. She's in the house. It's just as well to say youre shut in. So if she had a place with a garden she'd be able to go out at least because where she got the arthritis. If she stays here she'd have a transfer because she'll be in the mental. There was a woman murdered. Ruth dont mix with the people down here. The only place she's been in is Mabel Edicott's. People dont bother her.

AGNES WHALEN AND
PAT VIVIAN WIRETAP

Agnes: I said to Ches Hedderson I said Pat knows that car was up there.

Pat: That was Friday morning.

The car was there and Donna was down talking to Paul Troke.

I picked out the car. They give me a mug shot book. And I had my finger laid on the thing and he said Mr Vivian are you going to look for the person and I said there it is right there and I picked out Paul.

If you were a good friend to Donna you'd want her murderer caught. I know I do. I'll find out. I'll keep on until I goes down in my grave.

And Missus I'll give you a hand to do that my love. I thought the world of her.

They knows that some of the evidence they got. They can't nail him if they dont get anybody to help them. And I said to him well Pat Vivian was telling us about the car.

SHELDON TROKE

That Friday Donna got the youngsters ready for school because the kids had to be in school at nine. Sheldon was on the chesterfield lying down. Donna's mom come and they were in the kitchen having a conversation. She left around eleven. The point Sheldon's making, what Pat Vivian says about Donna going out by the door in the morning is a lie. Donna wasnt out of the house. She didnt go out until after her mother left. Donna was talking to Kim Parrott on the phone and she was on the way to her house.

When Sheldon seen this car on the news, it's all he seen was the front of it and he got a glimpse of the side of it. Pat Vivian saw a small foreign car and this car is a big dark Chevy.

RUTH VIVIAN

She is bound as a mother, she doesnt want to say nothing. She never told it to her husband. She's been holding it inside since it happened.

It is all right for you—it is all right everybody else to say it, but she's the one.

Sheldon shouted and yelled at her. He was either drunk—like he wasnt the Sheldon that she knew. He seemed like he was pretty mad. Ruth dont know who he was mad with, if he was mad with her, she dont know. But she did get the feeling that she shouldnt say anything.

He told her to mind her own fucking business and keep your mouth shut and go in the house, like he was just raving on and Ruth was afraid he was going to hurt her or hurt her boy. Tom was going to jail shortly after that and Ruth was afraid he was going to be hurt. But it is the way he said it. Ruth dont know how to explain the feeling. She got really afraid. She never mentioned it to a soul. She's been back and forth to the doctor, she finds it hard to sleep. She can't understand what she's feeling. She doesnt want to make matters worse.

It's been eating away at her. She did not tell the police because she didnt want to get involved in to it. She went past Mabel Edicott's and said hello. It had to be around suppertime. The way it was, they ate whenever they were hungry so she didnt have no time limit. No one had to go to work, no one had to do anything, they just ate when they were hungry so Ruth never paid no mind to the time.

SHELDON TROKE

Ruth is getting her information from going back and forth to her husband and to Mabel Edicott. You look at the Vivian family. Pat Vivian asks the police to come to his house. Charles Stamp goes down and takes a statement concerning a small grey foreign car. Then he's watching the news and he's talking to Gary Bemister and the whole description changes. Now the car he seen is this big brown Chev.

What he first described was a motorboat. When he sees something on TV it's a submarine, the next time it come on the news, Paul's name is given and Sheldon's name is given and Tom Vivian is charged and then the next day Ruth gives this new statement of Sheldon threatening her.

BERTHA TROKE WIRETAP

I dont give a fuck what anybody says, if she was brutally murdered she had to kick up a fight. When Donna and Sheldon fought he put holes in the wall. That Sunday Sheldon phoned and was talking to Pat Vivian. And I heard exactly the words Sheldon said to Pat. He said Mr Vivian look, you remembers lots of times youre after hearing me and Donna fighting and I was wondering did you hear something and you werent saying nothing because you thought it was me. Mr Vivian, whatever you heard, I'd like you to tell the police to help them out because Donna drove me home that night, I had nothing to do with this and anything that you can tell the police can help them.

CHES HEDDERSON AND
THE VIVIANS WIRETAP

Ches: You can hear the cars go up the street. It's not so quiet here is it.

Pat: When youre in bed you can't hear them. There could be a accident down the road and I be in bed asleep I dont know.

You won't see too many in uniform around here now. The officer upstairs is gone so if you hear anything.

I can give you a call.

How is Mrs Vivian?

She's not well. Gone to a psychiatrist.

How's Tom doing?

Pretty good boy.

Big loss.

She used to ask Tom to go over to the supermarket in the car.

Is that right.

I suppose youre handy to it all clued up now.

We're at the final stages. We're going through the statements and picking them out.

It must be hard with the little girl.

Brave soul of the lot, isnt she. She is not afraid to tell her story.

They got charges laid against him.

New charges laid—people charged for giving a false alibi.

IRIS TROKE AND
SHELDON TROKE WIRETAP

Iris: Mom and Dad are locked up.

Sheldon: What? At the lock-up?

At the lock-up.

Holy fucking Jesus Christ.

But Sheldon you knows what theyre doing dont you.

Iris they can't fucking lock Mother up Iris.

Theyre trying to pressure now Sheldon. I mean it's not right.

But they can't apply pressure, we didnt do nothing.

Sheldon dont go getting on like that boy. Take it easy because I mean this is just blown out of proportion.

We're talking about Mom, Iris. She can't fucking handle being locked up.

I know Sheldon, we're going down.

Well go down and get her the fuck out of there.

We can't get her out of there.

Even if you get her out in the visiting room and talk to her. I'm going to get Jim Lythgoe on the go.

I phoned down Sheldon. They took her from the holding cell. I went mad with Gary Bemister. I told him about locking her up, she got claustrophobic.

They can't do this. No one fucking never done nothing.

I'm getting out of the bath. I'm going to phone down and ask the matron dont go putting her in the lock-up.

Let her go in and sit in the fucking little office. Let her sit where the phone is at.

That's what theyre doing Sheldon. They won't lock her up.

Her nerves are gone. She hasnt been through nothing like this before.

I know buy. I dont know what they can do. How can they charge someone to accessory after the fact—

If no one is charged.

If they havent got the person who did it.

It's a trumped-up fucking charge.

Well you'll hear it all two oclock anyway Sheldon. Which I'll be down to hear. Dont go worrying about it because—

I'm not worried about it Iris. I knows we're fucking innocent but I'm worried about Mom. She's down in the fucking lock-up. She can't fucking be down there.

I'd say she's out there now with the matron. Clayton was in the holding cell.

I know Clayton can handle a couple of fucking hours or couple of weeks being locked up if they fucking want to push it that long. But Iris, fucking Mom, Iris. Because Mom is fucking taking a heart attack.

I dont say she's locked up Sheldon. Holiest to God boy. Wait now just hold on now. I told the matron if they brings her down, dont go putting her in the holding cells. She said no honest to God Iris I'll do with her what I done with you that time and that was put her in the little hallway.

She can't fucking take too much more.

But how can they be charged with accessory after the fact.

Theyre charged with obstructing justice.

By saying theyre lying and you left the house that night.

How much more can Mom take.

They got nothing and theyre going to come down heavy on everyone.

I dont mind them coming down heavy I can handle that but fucking Mother can't.

I know Sheldon.

She's going to have a heart attack next. Cocksucking bastards.

She'll be all right.

Are they ever going to leave us alone? Do they think we're that fucking cruel that I went up and did something like this? And now my mother's hiding it for me?

I know.

I'd like to go one on one with them. In a fucking fist fight. I hope theyre listening too the cocksuckers.

I told Gary, give her another polygraph.

If they wants bail for Mom, I dont give a fuck whatever everybody got in the family put it up.

Mom won't spend not one fucking night in that lock-up.

BERTHA TROKE AND
PAUL TROKE WIRETAP

Bertha: When they charged me and Clayton they probably thought they were going to shake Sheldon up and say I can't have Mom being charged and I got to come forward but I mean the young fellow can't come forward and admit to something that he didn't do.

Paul: Well this is all right, as soon as me and Sheldon gets in the clear it'll be too fucking late then.

They've been looking in the wrong direction ever since it started.

Buddy's out still on the fucking loose whoever the fuck it is. Some fucking nut.

I guarantee you I tried to cooperate with them.

I did too Mother.

That morning I went out and took that polygraph test, me washing I dropped everything and I was out there all day and what do I get, fucking abuse.

Same here.

They want you to turn around and say what they got in their mind.

I done everything I could to fucking help them. That's all I got is fucking sand kicked in my face for it.

Ches Hedderson flipped out. He went right off his head at me. He was trying to scare me. If they mind to get out and look around other places.

CATHY FURNEAUX AND
PAUL TROKE WIRETAP

Cathy: I was over there for five hours. I took the polygraph test. I said I got nothing to fucking lie about. He came in and said Cathy it's a few things on it you lied about. I said listen here, I can swear on my mother's grave may she roll over a thousand times that I never lied and I knows I never lied. He said they can get me and the youngsters away from all the fucking Trokes. Afraid of the Trokes. I said I'm not afraid of the Trokes. I got no reason to be afraid. They never done nothing to harm me.

Paul: Fucking dirtbags.

I told them the whole fucking truth and that's all I can tell them.

It's gone too far now Cathy, arresting Mom and Dad.

THE VIVIANS WIRETAP

Tom: I just told them I'm getting poisoned with this. It's harassment I say.

Ruth: Theyre seeing what you'll say. You said around three oclock they kicked in the door and I told them I heard it all at quarter after one.

Tom: They thinks I'm lying. That I'm holding something back from them.

Pat: Son this is what he'll do. He'll hook up a few wires. And he got a thing there on the phone like that. Then he'll deal up a deck of cards and ask you to pick a card. It's only fifteen cards. You look at one and he'll ask you was it a five? and if you says no he'll say was it nine? and you says no. You says no to everything first time. Then the second time he asks was it five, you got to say no to all of them again. And say you picked out number three like I did. I picked up number three again, second time. He knew it he said you picked card number three.

CHES HEDDERSON AND
THE VIVIANS WIRETAP

Pat: You know what happened there. Sheldon might have been there and killed her and left and got Paul to come back and give him a hand with it.

Ches: We know two people came and went in there that night and there's cars used. If you know anything about it, who came and went.

Pat: He was seen in the back hall the night before it happened. I was moving furniture with her and it happened one oclock in the morning. Trying to look around her window. So his alibi didnt hold up for him. His mother caught lying.

Just because youre caught lying, doesnt mean the person you lied about committed the offence.

That's true there.

Do you know what you did see?

I could have told you I saw him up there, him and his brother. No boy I can't put a man in jail until I have something to say for sure right. If I had to see him up there I would have told you. Different from taking off and turning your back away on what he done.

Well that's it, you would like to prevent it from happening again.

They left in a car. He had the dark shirt right. Down there, you cannot see a car from here.

You were talking to Mrs Edicott yesterday.

She heard a bit of the news. I told her it showed Donna's picture on TV and that Sharon saw whoever killed Donna.

They never said it that way, Pat.

The old woman is having a hard time of it. Ruth was saying to me I wish it was all over and settled. The words come out of her mouth, she told me that he did it. That's what Ruth told me.

She told you.

She told me not to talk to no one about it.

Not to talk to us about it?

Not you.

That would be obstruction.

Yes that's all I need.

I suppose if Sheldon was arrested things might get a little more relaxed too.

Yes it would.

Once the charge is laid.

Hope no one bothers me is all.

Would you feel more comfortable if you knew he was already charged with it?

I dont know.

Would that help your memory a little bit?

JIM LYTHGOE

Here's a police officer telling witnesses that Bertha Troke is lying about her alibi. Just look at what is settling in the minds of these people. The police are fully aware that the Vivians and the Edicotts are conversing back and forth. Between Tom, his mother Ruth, his father Pat, all prospective witnesses, and theyre talking about what the police had to say to them. Pat Vivian is gaining an awful lot of information somewhere along the way. The tapes show as to where it's coming from—directly from the police.

THE VIVIANS WIRETAP

Ruth: Those bastards theyre trying to get me to say that I seen Sheldon with her the night I never seen him. I dont know if she was coming home or if she was going out or what she was doing. All I know is she was on the step and she do walk heavy in those pumps.

Pat: Did you hear, he said would I be comfortable if I knew what Sheldon was charged with? It's only a couple of more and they'll have the whole family down there.

Tom: She's getting away with it. She might have said he was in bed and he sneaked out through the door in that hall. It could have happened couldnt it Dad.

Well how would you prove it?

Tom: I can't see how she'd get hooked for that.

Pat: She took the lie detector and failed it. I bet you the fuck he went home that night and came back out. Sure enough they got her for obstruction.

Ruth: She put the icing right on the cake for him.

Tom: Saying he was home when he wasnt.

Pat: She'll get everything though out of court, he'll make a deal for her.

Tom: If she's still alive. Sheldon make a deal, ha ha. They got all the evidence they wants on him anyway.

Pat: Like he said Bertha's after turning state's evidence. She dont want to go to jail for a long time.

Tom: She's turned state's evidence?

Ruth: Oh yes, she's testifying against him.

Dont repeat that for Jesus sake, dont.

No, no, I dont tell no one.

That's how they got him right. She got herself a lawyer and her lawyer advised her to come clean if not she's going to jail for a long time.

JIM LYTHGOE

It's obvious that the police knew as there was a wiretap in the Vivian home and the Edicotts were frequent visitors there. We have Ruth Vivian coming in and she gave a whole series of statements. Every few weeks she had something new to add about Sheldon. You will recall her evidence that she did not talk about this with anyone. To put it mildly I seriously doubt that because the words are right here.

Look at the effect of this information coming out about Bertha Troke and Clayton Troke being charged, look at the way these witnesses dealt with it.

HOWARD STRONG

Ruth Vivian saw things that other people couldnt see. She saw scorpions on the wall and her skin was infected with scorpions. She heard voices and she visited heaven from time to time. She saw the holy water in a vase change colour. That meant she was a saint. She displayed a lack of interest in her usual activities. She had been neglecting her personal care. She was communicating on a regular basis with angels. She had been seeing her dead parents and having conversations with them. She was going to be in heaven again on Christmas and would see her parents again.

Mrs Vivian is a pleasant lady older than her stated age. She was admitted for pain control—she has a very bad arthritic condition. She has a dementing illness in the front of her brain and the cause of it Dr Strong doesnt know. She was very ladylike and proper when he first saw her. But then her personality coarsened, she became disinhibited. She swore on occasion. She has a grade ten formal education. She had difficulty with school work and had to repeat grade nine. After leaving school, she worked as a cleaner. She married

Patrick Vivian at age nineteen and was not employed outside of the home thereafter.

A number of doctors, including her family doctor, have no explanation why all the pain that she had been suffering—which was close to a crippling pain—suddenly disappeared. She felt that this was a miracle. She had been taking ten to fifteen Atasol 30s a day for fifteen years.

Chloral hydrate is an old sleeping medication. It is the first sleeping preparation ever discovered and it is not used frequently except for older people. She has, in Dr Strong's opinion, a frontal lobe dementia. The difference between delirium and dementia, if you have a TV set and the screen goes fuzzy, either a tube is gone or the fine tuning is off. A dementia is when some of the material is missing. A delirium is when the brain is not functioning properly as a result of some tuning problem. For example, medication or a small stroke.

The medication that Ruth was taking produced an acute confusional episode. There was an underlying dementing process starting. So her brain was vulnerable to begin with. This frontal lobe dementia was building up then reached a stage where people noticed it. It could take years or it could take weeks or months.

The holy water turning colour, the colour was blue.

IV

THE JAILHOUSE INFORMANT

Leander was sent to Her Majesty's Penitentiary on a parole suspension—
he had a sign of alcohol on him. This was where he met Sheldon
Troke, they were in custody together. They got along on the unit at
HMP. There's anywhere from twenty-five to thirty inmates housed in
a unit and there's a common recreation area and some people have
their own cell, some are double bunked. A unit is a cell block.

One evening there was a letter addressed on CBC by a reporter.
The letter was from Sheldon's attorney, Jim Lythgoe. Lythgoe was not
impressed with a remark that Ches Hedderson had made concerning
his client's involvement in the Donna Whalen homicide.

This report upset Sheldon and he asked Leander that night would he
write a letter to Mr Lythgoe for him. The letter said that Lythgoe's report
would force Ches Hedderson into laying a charge. They were more or
less backed against the wall and this would force them. Leander didnt
have much problem in doing anything for Sheldon. It was not unusual
for one prisoner to write a letter for another. They went to Sheldon's cell
that night and Sheldon placed a towel over the door. Sheldon
was sitting on the bed, Leander was on a bucket by the desk.
Sheldon explained what he wanted on the letter and Leander wrote it
down in point form. Sheldon was quite emotional. He had done some
valium that had come into the penitentiary that day. Sheldon asked

Leander to pass him the picture he had of Donna Whalen on the wall with a verse of the Our Father written under it. As he passed him the picture, Sheldon grabbed Leander by the wrist—Sheldon referred to him by a nickname known as Dolly. Dolly, do you think I murdered Donna?

Leander said he had no reason to think such a thing, even though his suspicions were building. Leander looked at him and Sheldon was sobbing. It was at that point that Sheldon said, I murdered her because I loved her.

Leander wrote the letter with Sheldon's return address. The letter was done very business-like and there was probably one paragraph on the first page and a few lines on the next page.

It was four to six days later that Sheldon was charged with the murder of Donna Whalen.

SHELDON TROKE

He's lying. It's all lies.

LEANDER DOLLYMONT

Sheldon treated him nice, he was charming and attractive. When he went down to rec, Sheldon talked to him and Leander looked upon him as a pretty decent person. It didnt seem to bother Sheldon that Leander was a homosexual. Homosexuality in prison does take place. You will meet people who will treat you with disrespect, but within the prison system it is accepted.

A relationship started between them and it was kept very secret from inmates at the penitentiary. It was kept secret to the point that there was nobody going to say anything to Sheldon. He more or less put it out in a joking manner. It began by Leander being really good to Sheldon. Being homosexual, he does not deny that he was attracted to him.

Leander helped him out with canteen. He spent a lot of time talking to him, playing cards—it was during that summer Sheldon learned him to play crib. They spent a lot of time together. Leander was helping him through a bad experience. They became affectionate with touching and kissing and it led to oral sex. This took place in Sheldon's cell. Sheldon was Leander's top-notch man down in the pen. The penitentiary was no help to Leander, it was more harm than health.

Sheldon was well known, people looked upon him as heavy. He was one of the rulers of HMP.

SHELDON TROKE

Dolly used to be down to the pen chasing everybody around. Oh, this one's cute, that one's cute, look at the arse on that one. Sheldon never had nothing to do with him. When Sheldon first met him he was coming out of jail. It was like a woman talking and Sheldon was talking to some friends down in the bottom flat and somebody yelled out and said Trokie and he turned around. Dolly come over and said are you Paul's brother? Sheldon said why? and he turned right red and he said I knows Paul and that same day Sheldon went up to Unit 4 and Paul was up on Unit 4 and Dolly come up and Sheldon said to Paul who's your friend? and Dolly blushed.

LEANDER DOLLYMONT

You've heard of valium brought into inmates in packages, thrown in over the walls and given during field day. Sheldon had been really sick for three days and then one night he done a lot of valium. The guards had known about that and Leander was the one going to the kitchen to get Sheldon his juices. Sheldon had a shower and a few more valium. It was more nerves with Sheldon than the flu. The penitentiary was like the flu. He wasnt eating and he was sweating to the point where you could take his bedclothes and wring the water out of them. Sheldon had difficulty with getting out of bed to associate on the unit. The pressure of it all. The night Sheldon asked Leander to bring a pen and paper to Sheldon's cell, Leander knew he was going to write something. He brought a writing tablet that he had in his cell. There was a verse of the Our Father underneath the pictures. They had designed it on a piece of cardboard. Sheldon took the picture on his knee, Leander remembers him taking his wrist, he did not grab it or physically hurt him or anything, he just took his wrist and he said, Dolly do you think I murdered Donna? Leander said Sheldon listen I think you loved her too much for that and Sheldon closed the cell door and told Leander a story. Leander had a can of pop, Sheldon had a coffee.

Sheldon was in quite an emotional state. He asked Leander that night did he like him as a person. When Leander said that I'm not the type of person who likes everybody, Sheldon kept repeating but do you like me in a different way. Leander thinks he meant could he be emotionally close, could he relate to him on a personal basis. He said yes because Leander more or less feared to upset Sheldon—he needed to talk to someone because he was upset and crying. When Leander said yes, he stopped.

Sheldon just wanted reassurance that Leander wouldnt betray him. Leander assured him that whatever he said or discussed would be kept in confidence. Sheldon asked him to take Donna's picture from the wall and Leander gave it to him. Looking at her picture, he said that he never loved anybody this much, he had been planning on starting a family with this woman and she was his only reason for staying out of trouble. Sheldon told him first that he found out that

Donna Whalen was having an affair with Jacob Parrott and because of that he stabbed him.

SHELDON TROKE

Jacob Parrott was never stabbed. Go ask him.

LEANDER DOLLYMONT

That Friday night Donna Whalen dropped Sheldon off and told him the relationship was over and she didnt want to see him any more. Sheldon went into his mother's house. His mother noted him being emotional. He went upstairs to the washroom and shot up. He felt dizzy. He sat on the bathtub to regain balance. He came downstairs, called his brother Paul at Cathy Furneaux's house. He told Paul that he was going to act on the discussion he had in the park on the previous day.

Sheldon asked his mother to return him to Donna's. His mother obliged, but Donna was not home. Leander doesnt know how Sheldon gained entry. When Donna returned home she had a male companion with her. Sheldon said that he hid in Cory's room, until the man left.

Sheldon confronted Donna and she threatened to charge him with break and entry. Sheldon was on parole at the time. Sheldon said they had a heated argument in the kitchen. She grabbed a knife from the drawer. He was sobbing. He said Dolly I wrestled with her I didnt know what I wanted to do. He got the knife and stabbed her continually. He said I dont remember anything else till Paul was standing there, Paul came in and moved the body into the living room. Then Paul took him to Iris's house and he returned to clean up the murder scene. Paul moved the body into the living room. He did this alone.

BERTHA TROKE

She doesnt know Leander Dollymont, but she did hear tell of a Dolly. One time Dolly phoned the house looking for Paul. At the time Bertha did not know who it was, and she gave Paul a smack and told him it was an old woman on the phone about sixty-five years old and could he do any better than that. She left the bathroom door open to hear the conversation because she really thought it was a woman and she did hit him and he hit the wall because he was mad. She sounds like she's drunk, she said, sixty-five years old phoning you.

Bertha did not drive Sheldon from her house down to Donna's house that night. If Sheldon had to want a run anywhere Clayton would be the one that drove because Bertha doesnt like night driving. Her car wasnt out of the driveway that night. Sheldon didnt ask for a run. If there was something like that going on Sheldon wouldnt have come home in the first place.

LEANDER DOLLYMONT

Leander asked him, Are the police going to get anything? Sheldon said they can never get anything, Dolly, the clothes and the weapon theyre with Donna. Sheldon worked in a graveyard with Donna's father. He done repairs to graves, so he assumed Sheldon buried the clothes and the weapon.

After Sheldon cleaned up he returned to the murder scene. Paul met him on the steps and didnt allow him inside. Everything had been taken care of and it was time to be getting out of there. The next day Sheldon went to work at the graveyard and waited for the news of her death.

PAUL TROKE

Paul doesnt know Leander Dollymont. He does know a Dolly. He knows him from jail. Dolly doesnt have any reason to lie about him. Paul's never done anything to him.

His hair in June was blond. It's no different than the way it looks now. In summer the sun lightens it a bit. Paul's not the only guy who goes downtown with blond hair. He'd have it shaved on the sides very close to his head.

One of these assaults involved Eugene Driscoll. Paul hit Eugene in the face with a beer bottle three or four times. Eugene come in the house after Paul's girlfriend Trisha. Eugene was giving Cathy Furneaux a hard time too. Paul was asleep on the couch when they got home and when he went down Eugene was inside the house. Paul asked him what he was doing there and he started getting saucy and wouldnt leave and Paul flicked a beer bottle at him. He never held on to it, he hit him with it.

GARY BEMISTER

This was the graveyard where Sheldon Troke worked. That graveyard is on Blackmarsh Road. Gary Bemister cut and rolled up some sods and dug in the ground. They didnt do the entire cemetery. The police disturbed about twenty graves. It took about six hours. There were no exhibits taken.

LEANDER DOLLYMONT

Leander grew up with money, he didnt do fraud for money. He could be like his brother today, he could be home with a sportscar. He wasnt the type for suicide and that's all he will say on it.

Leander would not betray Sheldon Troke for money, but if there's something through Corrections Canada to help him get on his feet when he gets out, he's willing to accept it.

They became very close. Leander helped Sheldon many times with canteen. Private things too, such as what he signed for Jim Lythgoe or conversations he had with his mom. Leander cared for Sheldon Troke a lot.

At first Sheldon portrayed an image of how much he loved Donna Whalen and to see the person that committed such a horrible crime brought to justice. But on the night that he told Leander that he murdered her Sheldon said that Donna had been having an affair and that she was going to leave him for Jacob Parrott. He couldnt handle losing her. At a party there was an argument. Sheldon and Donna and Jacob Parrott. Donna went to the washroom. When she came back Sheldon took her on his knee. Jacob made a gesture towards him in hauling her off. Sheldon went to stand up, Jacob pushed him back into the chair. Sheldon came to his feet again and Jacob pushed him into a glass cabinet. The glass door broke and Sheldon went right through the glass door. He got an antique knife from the cabinet and struck Jacob once in the head and twice in the stomach. Jacob was brought into the hospital and never named Sheldon or pressed charges. That's when Jacob started talking about moving to Toronto. It was just a short period of time before Donna's death. Sheldon was experiencing quite a high when he told Leander this.

Donna was going to Toronto to share a relationship with Jacob Parrott there. He couldnt deal with the fact she was going to leave him.

SHELDON TROKE

This never happened.

LEANDER DOLLYMONT

One evening on the news the police had impounded a car found near Glovertown. This car was owned by Paul Troke. Sheldon walked across the unit and said that fucking car had fucking nothing to do with Donna's death. The inmates like to watch *Here and Now*, it keeps you intact with society and what's going on in the court system. Who is coming to the penitentiary. The first question that arose in Leander's mind was if you had nothing to do with Donna's death, how do you know that car had nothing to do with it.

SHELDON TROKE

The first time the car come on TV Sheldon said it's about time. He made a phone call to his mother after the news and he learned that the car was his brother's. Sheldon said, What the fuck are these people doing? It come on again. This car is owned by Paul Troke, Sheldon's brother, and then Ches Hedderson was on talking about him.

When that car first come on, Sheldon had no idea who owned the car. If that car come on again five days later, he may have shouted then. Leander Dollymont was on the range. He heard the rumours going around. People down there would ask questions. If Sheldon could, he would have answered their questions.

LEANDER DOLLYMONT

On the night that he shared with Leander what he had done to Donna Whalen, Sheldon needed a shoulder to lean on. A towel over the door is a sign of privacy—if other inmates see a towel over your door they know they're not supposed to enter, they should knock or it's a sign of privacy, it's a sign that you're doing something that other inmates should not be involved in. No one else entered Sheldon's cell that night.

DONALD SAUNDERS

A private conversation is fairly easy in a unit like 4A. The prisoners have ways of sending messages to each other—internal messages that are quite opposite to the rules. If an inmate puts a towel over his door, this is a sign that the inmate wants some privacy.

Prescription drugs in the prison is impossible to prevent. They hoard medication and then use it all at once. The lack of cavity searches is one of the main reasons for that.

Quite a number of inmates are functionally illiterate and can't write. Those inmates get a friend to write a letter for them. Also, an inmate might be able to write but simply requests somebody else to write it for him in terms of style or content. Unit 4A it might be easier to get correspondence out without there being any record of it than it would be in the SHU.

Letters to lawyers, to ministers, to different government officials, they are just sent in the mail. That's privilege mail and nothing happens other than it's mailed as quickly as possible. There is a booklet that's given to inmates with a full list of those people. There is no way that you can check who that letter is actually going to. We have to go by the name of the person which it's being written to.

There's a dry cell at the penitentiary. If they have reason to believe that an inmate has drugs concealed in a body cavity they place that person in a dry cell and leave him there until theyre satisfied there is no drug or contraband item concealed or until it's found. The duration is usually seventy-two hours. A dry cell has got no plumbing and when a person wishes to use the washroom there is no toilet so he's given a bucket. The bowel movement is checked for drugs. The common way of concealing drugs is ingesting a condom or a balloon and the other way is insertion through the anus.

He is issued a towel. There are no hooks to hang up towels. Sometimes the towel is hung on a door and they try to stop that. It is against the regulations to hang a towel on a door and the reason is it's a security one. A towel hung on a prison door will cause damage to the hinge and locking mechanism if the door is closed because the towel forms a wedge and when the door is pushed to it sprains the hinges and throws the locking mechanism out of proper position. It's a constant battle, you dont permit inmates to do that.

A correctional officer can see the lobby. There's no blind spots unless doors are wide open. However, when a person goes in the cell you cannot see in there unless you go into this lobby area and look into the doorway. Correctional officers are expected to do that, go in and actually remove the towel.

LEANDER DOLLYMONT

Sheldon was taken out to the graveyard by the corrections officers at Her Majesty's Penitentiary, to Donna Whalen's grave. It was raining. When he came back from the grave he said that Donna's family had been there waiting for him and he sobbed in the room and sat and stared at her picture again for a while. Sheldon couldnt stand losing Donna, especially to Jacob Parrott.

When Leander was released it was Thanksgiving. He went up to the Southern Shore for about ten days. He did not acquaint his parole officer of his whereabouts. He was on the run and drinking and cashing bad cheques. He was at a bar called Harold Hayden's Lounge. That's in Calvert. He had some money on him. The RCMP of Ferryland came to arrest a man who had a verbal argument with his wife. When they arrested him, they took Leander because he had been at the house. Then they discovered who Leander was and that there was a warrant out, so he was held in custody. Leander had spent time alone with this man, Eugene Driscoll. It was not a sexual relationship. Leander was drunk at the time. He wasnt falling around but if he was given a breathalyzer he'd be considered drunk. They placed him in the Ferryland lock-up. Leander knew that he was going back to HMP. The guard on duty questioned him on why he was emotional and he took Leander out to his office to have a talk. Leander told him, Constable Kelly, about his childhood and getting involved in crime. He did not want to go back to the penitentiary. Some very negative things occurred there, he said. Kelly asked Leander in relation to what. A bank robbery and a murder, he said. Are you referring to the Troke case? Leander told him yes.

They had a discussion about Sheldon Troke, that he had murdered Donna Whalen, but Leander did not say that he'd had a relationship with Sheldon Troke. Leander's family was deeply hurt by his going out and doing fraud, so he could very well imagine how much it would hurt their pride to know that he had a relationship with Sheldon Troke. It's true that from the age of eighteen he had proclaimed to his family that he was a homosexual, but that dont mean you have a relationship with someone of less your character. So he lied about the relationship between himself and Sheldon Troke. He said they were just friends. He's aware that there's a lot of mixed feelings towards homosexual activity. Leander wanted to clear his conscience of what he knew about the death of Donna Whalen without causing any damage to his own character.

That first statement to Kelly he refused to sign because he knew he had lied. He was intelligent enough to know what that meant if it was later discovered. He didnt sign it because he wanted all his conditions met. He asked for two things. To receive federal time in a western Canadian penitentiary—federal time is two years plus. Second, that he receive counselling for being a child sexual abuse victim.

He did not want to spend time in a closed environment such as an RCMP lock-up. He was experiencing a lot of emotional things and didnt see it as being a very healthy environment. There is no access to counselling or getting out of the cell for exercise.

He wanted closed court for his testimony and his identity not made public. He looked at it as being something damaging to his family's character. He has a brother and a sister whom he loves and cares about. They would be deeply hurt by all of this. He's deeply hurt himself.

He'd been taken to supper by Constable Kelly. When he left supper that evening he tried to escape his custody. Leander was running towards the Village Mall. He was dressed in a winter coat and jeans. Constable Kelly apprehended him within three minutes and he escorted Leander back to the car where they had a chat, phoned in for instructions on what to do, and they continued on to the lock-up. He did not struggle at all with Constable Kelly, he started crying.

He wanted to get away, he didnt know where he was going or what his intentions were—it was more of an impulsive action than anything. He has made no other attempts to escape custody.

LEANDER DOLLYMONT
LETTER TO EUGENE DRISCOLL

Hi Eugene. I guess you've heard the details of my escapade. Well my philosophy is you can only stick out your neck so much for people. I thought I loved him but from the way his lawyer attacked me in court he used me. The final questions involved everything from being a male slut to my being of an aggressive nature. I feel I left Jim Lythgoe with short straws to pull at. If Sheldon wants to play hardball I'm willing. I never asked for this and when testifying against Sheldon I could have cried every time I looked at him. Despite everything I still want to be friends with you. I miss you and I want you to write me. Tell me what kind of a dance Bertha Troke is doing now that her son is out of the closet. I'm going to tell your mom where I am to. You are my sweetheart Eugene but I'm never coming back, this was the big break for me. Love Dolly.

LEANDER DOLLYMONT
POSTCARD TO SHELDON TROKE

Quick think of a number between one and ten you lose take off your clothes. Sheldon, this is a little reminder of the night you pissed on the floor. I should have left it on my slipper. I dont think I would be like him in the cartoon picture and say Rats. More like can I have it. I think about you all the time and hope you are doing okay. I have no doubt that youre innocent. I was out with Kim Parrott the other night and I told her there were two things you were not capable of, your charge and being my boyfriend. She laughed for nearly an hour. Call me on Monday at four oclock. Dolly.

SHELDON TROKE

The card with the strange-looking cat on the front. You got an iron sink and the toilet is all built in together and you got two buttons there for pushing the water and the water comes up this way. You have a lot of trouble with the water. You push it and sometimes it squirts right up on the floor. Now if that's after happening and someone walks in the cell and walks in it and says what's that? You say that's piss.

Dolly thought Paul Troke was gorgeous. Then a couple of days later, he was going around saying he thought Paul was gorgeous until he seen Sheldon. Sheldon was on the range and there was a guy on remand getting moved and Dolly was saying I hope he gets moved over here.

Dolly used to make gestures towards Sheldon and to other inmates. No one really paid no attention to him. There was times you'd be sot down watching TV and Dolly'd come over and he'd put his hands on your shoulders and start rubbing your shoulders and you'd tell him to get away from you. One time Sheldon was sick—he was sot at the table saying to the inmates that he havent even got enough energy to get a shower or a shave and Dolly said if you were mine, you would never have to do that, and Sheldon had to call him aside and tell him a joke is a joke, but dont go getting carried away.

Sheldon got a good few years in a federal institution and everything you do goes on your record. You'll find a lot of stuff on his record that's after happening, but you will not find any homosexual activity.

Dolly wrote this: There are two things you are not capable of. Your charge and being my boyfriend. That is correct. There's lots of occasions Sheldon asked inmates how to spell a word and he got four dictionaries in his cell down there and a thesaurus.

He was in the SHU and a guard called him over to the bubble and handed him a piece of paper and said this is your lawyer's secretary. Give her a call and call collect. Sheldon didnt recognize the number, but he phoned it and a woman answered the phone. The way this phone works, you give your name to a machine and the machine cuts in and asks the party would they accept the call and sometimes you got to wait for a second and then you push a number and there's people that would swear on the operator of the machine and this woman did swear and Sheldon couldnt see Jim Lythgoe's secretary getting on like this and then he knew it was Dolly. Dolly was drinking. He was after talking to Eugene Driscoll. That's when he got this postcard. He was up in the country with Eugene Driscoll. Witless Bay.

EUGENE DRISCOLL

Eugene met Leander at HMP. Eugene was coming out from Unit 2 when he heard a woman talking and he looked to see who it was and it was Leander. He did not like Leander Dollymont, as he was an obvious homosexual. But after a time he accepted him for what he was. They had to go to a federal institution. They went on a plane from St John's to New Brunswick, to the Atlantic Institute in Renous. They were at Renous for about a week when Leander was transferred to Springhill. Eugene wasnt in Springhill very long. He was there for about three days and got in some trouble and had to be shipped back to the Atlantic Institute.

He saw Leander again when he was released from Renous and returned to St John's. For the three days they were first at Springhill there were some guys from Halifax who were on Leander's back. Eugene didnt like guys from Newfoundland getting threatened by guys from Halifax. Eugene said to Leander once walking to lunch to stay close to him and dont mind these guys from Halifax. So he became his protector. Eugene, outside of prison, met Leander at the Capitol Lounge. Leander frequented the bar quite a bit.

LEANDER DOLLYMONT

Leander dropped in to the Capitol Lounge every second day. There's an early curfew on Emmanuel House. He had to be in at eleven. Sometimes he drank at the Capitol Lounge. Sometimes he didnt have money and didnt drink. He wouldnt term them a rough crowd, it was a quiet bar. He met Joey Yetman down there. Joey asked him where he was getting the money, did he have a cheque machine. He said he had family sending money on a regular basis, that he was also receiving Social Services.

Joey thought, due to all the fraud Leander had done, he must have a cheque machine and he wanted access to it so as to make a series of cheques which would have been filled out and Joey could go into stores and cash them himself. Joey questioned him a bit to say come on now give me that cheque machine. Leander said that a friend had the cheque machine and that friend was gone to Halifax. He was stalling him. Leander never received any money for prostitution. If he told that to Joey, it was in a joke. Leander often left Capitol Lounge and came back. He was very good friends with the bartender, he probably darted back five and six times a day, but it was never for prostitution. Yes he left the bar with men he'd met at the bar. He even had one-night stands, but he never received any money for sexual activity. On a couple of occasions when they laughed about the activity at the Capitol Lounge Leander made a joke about turning tricks, but Leander never performed an act of prostitution. Joey drew the wrong conclusion.

LEANDER DOLLYMONT
LETTER TO SHELDON TROKE

Hi Sheldon, sitting here sipping on a beer. I guess you heard I went on the hop from parole. The fuck with them. All they wants is a rope on you and keep pulling on it so I said fuck ye pull on this and I packed my clothes and took off. But I said I would keep in contact and I will. Every thirty days fucking parole officers shoving you back in jail so I'm not saying I won't finish the time but I'm having a ball first. I hope you are doing fine, there is a guy here with me that knows you but I can't put any names on this letter. I'm a fugitive, but the Labatt's Blue tastes good and the hell with parole. I was speaking with a good friend of mine the other day who is a priest. I told him to remember you in his prayers, but knowing all them priests he might only imagine having you in the sack. In the next month I guess you will be having your preliminary. I hope it goes well. I never knew you were called slicker. When I was told that I said he's a slicker alright in more ways than one. Remember the night you had me spelling the words for you, you burnt out fucker. I was going with this guy for a couple of weeks, a moose hunter. Lord fuck, I spent two weeks out in his camper, parole and girlfriends going nuts, not that it's any Jesus odds to me. I hope you are taking care of yourself, always remember Dolly is thinking about you. You are one person I see a lot of good in. Tell Joey I said hi. I see his dad all the time. Tell him me and his dad came from Gander one morning, walked in on his wife seven in the morning, his dad called me a tramp, anyway take care, and fuck off and let me go drink, kiss, hug, Dolly.

JOHN NOFTALL

Leander moved to Riverbend in April. There's six inmates to each housing unit. This is minimum security. When you first move to Riverbend, you enter the dormitory. Then you move to a section called day parole—it's an overflow for the housing unit. Then youre into a unit where youre assigned a job. They have microwave ovens, washer, dryer, central vac, wall to wall carpeting. You cook in your own house, like they bring the food materials to your house and a couple of inmates will cook a meal.

One evening Leander was by the dorm and John asked him was he interested in moving into their house. They had an inmate leaving. Leander told him he didnt have any problem where he moved so John asked Leander to make a request to staff that he be placed in the house. John also went and seen the house man, Royce Opel.

Inmates in the house had a meeting before Leander moved in, which was very natural to do, and made a decision on him moving in. Riverbend Institution is very much like society, it's based on inmate input and inmate requests are looked at, but Leander did make the request.

Leander didnt deny his homosexuality to anybody while he was at Riverbend.

John Noftall was moved out of Riverbend Institution for coming into Leander's room late at night in just his underwear. It was about three oclock in the morning. There had been problems ever since Leander moved into the house. John Noftall had been imposing on Leander, and the staff at Riverbend were very concerned for Leander's welfare. Mr Noftall was a sexual offender who had denied all forms of treatment.

Well, that's Leander's story. But John Noftall is living common-law and has a child of his own. When his wife and son were visiting at Riverbend the warden took the boy out to the farm to see the animals. The visits were relaxed and wide open. You pick up a pay phone and call for Chinese food or pizza and spend lots of time with your family. Leander will say that John Noftall's wife had left him and gone to BC because John had been looking into windows of neighbourhood women while they dressed. That's Leander's story.

Leander made a formal complaint to the prison of sexual harassment. The prison acted upon the complaint and placed John in medium security. But the truth is Leander ended up in John Noftall's room. Walking by a picnic table where John was with some other inmates, Leander was called over and there was a discussion about Leander being in his room.

Every night Leander and John spent time together in his room before bed because there was six bedrooms to a house and sometimes Leander went in Florentine Patia's room and talked to Florentine, sometimes he went in John Noftall's and talked to John.

Leander shared knowledge with John Noftall about the case of Sheldon Troke. He didnt tell John Noftall he was an informant. He gathered it when Leander came back to testify, that is one of the reasons that Leander's scared of ever returning to eastern Canada.

LEANDER DOLLYMONT

There was an inmate at Riverbend, Donny Thole, who was from St John's. Leander was very scared of something leaking out about Sheldon Troke. John Noftall had been giving Leander a hard time on why he was in western Canada, so he devised a story to tell him to cover his ground: Leander left the Eastern Prison section because Sheldon Troke had a conversation in Leander's cell about a murder. The cell was bugged but Leander was denying to police having known anything and he didnt want to testify. So they separated him and Sheldon by putting Sheldon in the eastern section and Leander in western Canada but he was never going to testify. That was Leander's story.

JOHN NOFTALL

John robbed two pharmacies to obtain prescription drugs and there was a convenience store next door to one of the drug stores and he robbed the convenience store and one of the customers in the store. He had a drug habit. There was three of them doing the robbery and John stole the drugs and the other two guys were convicted of robbing the tellers in the store.

While in prison he was having a confrontation with an inmate by the name of Bear Melaney and John was stabbed in the thigh. He pulled the knife out of his leg and stabbed Bear in the chest. This was Christmas Day. He proceeded to go to his cell, fix his leg and then he didnt talk about what happened until a year and a half later. He spoke with his attorney. He gave him the circumstances. He didnt have any intentions of killing this man.

Two others were charged with the offence and the judge dismissed the charges on them. They said these two people were acting as a lookout so John could kill this gentleman—that was a theory that the prosecution had. But that's not what happened. John was sentenced to six years concurrent with the four years he was already serving.

He was released on day parole. He went to Vancouver. Him and a friend robbed a man on the street. Two years for that.

He has given evidence against individuals and undergone a name change. His wife of seven years and his son and himself are in the witness protection program. He's living now in Riverbend, which is minimum security. There are no fences or guns. If anybody wanted to walk away they could. It's pretty well known as the elite prison institution in Canada.

It was common knowledge at Riverbend that Leander Dollymont was a prison informant. He had written statements against inmates at Riverbend and had them removed. He asked John if he could close the door and close the window to the room, it's a very small window. He had something very important that he needed to get off his chest.

Leander came in and sat on the chair beside the bed and told a story about a psychologist at Springhill. Leander was in Springhill and he was transferred to Stoney Mountain because he told the psychologist that he had suspicions a man by the name of Sheldon Troke was involved in the killing of his wife. So they moved him to Stony Mountain, which is a medium security prison in Manitoba.

John asked if Sheldon had been charged and Leander responded no I dont think so. Sheldon Troke was having a relationship with him on the street in St John's, they were lovers, but they had a falling-out because Sheldon Troke was spending more time with his common-law wife and their children than he was with Dolly. John asked him, Do you really think that Sheldon Troke killed his wife? and Dolly said no I know he did not kill his wife but I want to put the son of a bitch away forever.

John said dont you think youre going to get yourself in some kind of trouble if you take the stand under oath and you perjure yourself? Dolly said he didnt have any concerns about that—Sheldon was a piece of shit. He described some scenes of the murder. A car abandoned on a dead-end street and some clothes with blood in the car. It was the victim's vehicle. No blood matched Sheldon Troke's blood. There were no witnesses against Sheldon Troke on the murder charge. Dolly was the only one who knew Sheldon's whereabouts on the day of the murder.

If you go to court and testify under oath you can end up doing seven years. Dolly says well it's my word against his and I'll go into that courtroom and I'll tell it my way. John said well Dolly you could end up in jail for a long time. Leander settled down then and said well then I'm not going to go and testify at all. That's all John can recall from that night. The officers told Leander to go to his own room. Eight hours later John was removed from the institute because Leander accused him of assault. John was moved to a medium security prison in Prince Albert.

Leander never told John that Sheldon Troke and himself were cellmates or had even shared the same penitentiary or anything taking place in a cell and the cell being bugged.

John is in this Riverbend Institution under the witness protection program. The last thing he's going to do is try to find out if somebody else is. In Riverbend if there's even a verbal complaint made about an inmate assaulting another inmate he's removed. Sixty-seven percent of the inmates in Riverbend are sex offenders and the other thirty percent are known informants. It's not an institution where it's kind of like we're all in the same category here.

John was sent to Riverbend for a sex offender treatment program for voyeuring and looking into windows. His son was a year old and they were called in to a pediatrician's office. Their son suffers from a rare disease and he was to die within six months. John started drinking again, he was using some drugs, he was very upset and didnt share the emotions with his wife.

John Noftall's identity has been changed. They've been relocated, so to talk about things that he'd done in the past to other inmates could possibly lead to them finding out who he really was.

He took it for granted that what Leander said was true. When John went inside the wall he found out there were several allegations made against him by Leander Dollymont. Then he saw Dolly getting a suit for court. He was going to court in the next couple of days. John was concerned and he talked with his attorney in Prince Albert. John told him he had some information about a murder trial in Newfoundland,

the accused's name was Sheldon Troke, and that Leander Dollymont
was going to falsely testify in court.

There was a hundred-thousand-dollar contract put out on John's
wife and his son and himself in Vancouver and John has serious
concerns about being here today, not knowing whether there's a ban
on his testimony. But when a man comes to you and tells you he's
going to testify on another man and get him convicted of a crime
he didnt commit and possibly spend the rest of his life in jail, that's
something that concerned John very much and he felt that he had to
do the right thing there.

John doesnt have a vendetta against Leander Dollymont. John
asked his attorney to phone the courthouse in St John's and find out
who was representing a man named Sheldon Troke. The courthouse
told him to phone Jim Lythgoe.

LEANDER DOLLYMONT

There was a guy in the house who was a prison informant. John
Noftall put plant fertilizer in his coffee. One night in the weight pit
an inmate was being beaten to death by a weight bar almost. This
inmate spent ninety days in hospital. Leander didnt want something
like that to happen to him. He was very scared of John Noftall so
he figured he had to do something to cover his own back. John
said they couldnt force you to move from one prison to another
because he refused to testify. Leander told him there was a woman
psychologist in Springhill who was aware of Leander's connection
with Sheldon Troke and that she had turned over information to
the police. It was a story Leander devised. He told John Noftall
that's how it came out and they bugged the cell—because he
asked Leander why would they bug your cell—Leander told him

that's how it came about. He talked to the psychologist and she turned over information. Leander refused to testify, they wouldnt keep him and Sheldon Troke in the one prison. He didnt tell John Noftall he was a prison informant. He portrayed a different image. Leander said that Sheldon Troke was also at Springhill. He told a story that John Noftall would believe. Leander said his mother was taking action against this psychologist because she had released confidential information to the RCMP. John Noftall asked well why arent you subpoenaed. Leander said it had to do with a psychologist turning over confidential information to the police and there's an act there that can keep this evidence from being released and his mom's working on it. Leander told him a story that John would believe. Why wasnt there a charge ever laid? Leander said, There was no other incriminating evidence found.

Leander got his attention. John told Leander he'd done the right thing by not testifying, your year will go quick up here and you done the right thing and if they ever do lay a charge you dont have to say anything. He made remarks like that, so that told Leander he had John's confidence. Leander had won.

TELEVISION

Plainclothes police officers are carrying concealed weapons in Supreme Court. They are protecting a fellow police officer who is facing charges of dangerous driving. Each day the armed officers are seated right outside the door leading in the courtroom, but protecting him from whom? Nobody in connection with his trial. This is what it's all about—the theft of two handguns and a rifle from the trunk of a police car. Police officers speculated the guns might be used to free Sheldon Troke. Troke is on trial in Supreme Court for murder.

So what's that got to do with this trial? The trials are happening at the same time. The officer, police suggest, might be used as a hostage to free Sheldon Troke.

JUDGE RICHARD ADAMS

Some of you might have heard on television last evening and on the radio broadcast this morning, something about a matter which is taking place in another courtroom in this courthouse and involves the suggestion that, somehow, a hostage might be taken and that hostage exchanged for Sheldon Troke. I dont know if any of you heard it. It is absolutely necessary that a person comes before the court presumed to be innocent unless and until he is convicted after a fair trial. The suggestion that something like that might happen is detrimental to the presumption of innocence. The other thing is I wouldnt want you to feel that there was something happening which we knew about and you knew nothing about. So, I'm raising it with you now. On the break this morning I spoke to the director of Court Security and my question to him was a very simple one: to your knowledge, is there any foundation, in fact, to the suggestion? And his reply was equally simple: I've made enquiries and there is no foundation for the suggestion. So youre in the know now and can put it out of your minds and we will carry on with the trial in the normal way.

LEANDER DOLLYMONT

Leander was down by the clothes room one day and Sheldon was there, hiding his valium. You often come across inmates, they have a hand down their pants inserting a package into their anus. Inmates internally package pills and other drugs and when they need them it takes a bathroom issue to get them out.

Sheldon was down by the clothes room hiding the valium on himself, shifting them from pocket to pocket, separating them to sell. There was other inmates there too. It's kind of a little hallway and there's three or four showers for people who live on the wings and Sheldon went joking around with Leander and said with those white teeth I could french kiss you.

That led to oral sex, in the last shower room down. There was inmates over by the clothes room. There's about a distance from here to that window over there. It was in a pretty shaded area but they probably all noticed.

There was a lot of comments made but it was always in a joking way. There was nobody in that penitentiary going to look at Sheldon Troke and refer to him as a faggot.

SHELDON TROKE

Dolly says they had sex. You'd think he'd remember that.

LEANDER DOLLYMONT

Sheldon said the car had been purchased from Billy Bennett. Leander is related to Billy Bennett. Billy Bennett, at the Cottage Tavern, told Leander that the Trokes had purchased a car from him but there was some type of technicality where the car wasnt paid for till a couple days after Donna's death. Billy said Paul Troke had access to the car whenever he wanted it.

SHELDON TROKE

Sheldon told Dolly that car wasnt abandoned. That car was broke down and given to George Bennett. Now Dolly dont know George Bennett, but he know a Billy Bennett. Billy Bennett is after spending time in jail down there so he turns around and says oh Paul Troke used to have a loan of that car off Billy Bennett. Billy Bennett never owned that car. Someone else owned that car. When Paul bought that car, it was radiator trouble. The car broke down and he gave the car to George Bennett.

BILLY BENNETT

Billy Bennett has owned two cars. The first one was a Ford Fairmont. She was black with red interior. He scrapped that and sold it to a certain taxi driver at Super Ace Taxi who wanted to buy it. He also owned a Pontiac Bonneville. He broke a pole off with her. She was impounded then after to Collision Clinic where she stays as far as he knows. She wasnt fit to put on the road. Well they had to use the jaws of life on him, had to cut the four doors off her. The drive shaft was in the back seat and the motor was partly in the front seat. She was a light blue.

Billy Bennett has a criminal record. Everything except that assault sixteen months, that's definitely wrong. His mother's maiden name is Dollymont. She's from Placentia. He knows of a Leander Dollymont, also known as Dolly. He's heard tell of him within the penitentiary as a bit tipsy, but he's never met him. He's not a cousin. He could be where he's from Placentia. There's a few Dollymonts out around Placentia. Whoever he is he's full of it.

Billy Bennett lives off Freshwater Road, lived there all his life. That's close to the Cottage Tavern. He dont go there much now. This car he had he was ready to get it done up, Paul Troke never had access to it. Billy has a drinking problem, he was in hospital there not too long ago. He got pancreatitis again so he tries to stay away from it now. He's been trying since he got out of hospital. Not trying, he's been staying off it because he has four cysts on the pancreas.

He done his time for it last year and got picked up for it the year before that. He never got charged for eight months after and he started his time in March last year. The accident itself was the year before that. It took eight months for them to get the blood where they had to send away to see how much his blood reading was. He's had accidents in between that and after that. They found him in his apartment dead twice. Not dead drunk, *dead* dead. They had to pull him back to life. This was drugs related, diet pills, yellow jackets. He's taken a lot of medication but he's been cutting back. It was alcohol and prescription drugs. Somebody would come up to him and say Billy I saw you downtown last night and he'd say sorry I can't even remember.

The Cottage Tavern, he was barred from there. He still got in but if they called the cops he drank at his own residence.

CATHY FURNEAUX AND
EUGENE DRISCOLL WIRETAP

Cathy: They should have brought someone in from away that knows what they're fucking at. They got me harassed to death. I even swore on my mother's grave and Hedderson turned around and looked me in the face and said you're a liar. I was ripping then. I said I'm the only one got keys to my house which I do but they be's threw in the drawer but they never asked me where they's be to. He said there was a taxi came to your door that night. And I said when? And they said did Sheldon come to your house that night? Sheldon did not come to my house because the way my door opens up and closes, Eugene, you got to push in on it because the door is right tight. And I was asleep on the chesterfield. I let them search this house three times looking and then the fourth time they ransacked it. They tore it apart. They actually tore the fucking house apart. So that was four times and then not counting the twenty times theyre after getting statements. Then he's saying to me your son was up. Your son can go down for accessory after the fact because he's lying too. I said listen here he's only sixteen years old. Robert's not lying. He said youre in with the Trokes tight. I said I went out with one Troke, one Troke only and that was Raymond and he was never in jail the whole four years I was with him and he wasnt either.

SHELDON TROKE

If Sheldon was working, every night he was home. The latest time he can recall Donna coming home is the night her and Iris were out to a club, but he do remember one morning waking up six-thirty and Cory was crying and Sheldon got out of the bed and was going out to let Cory out of his room. At the same time, Donna was coming in from the living room and Donna had her shoes on and Sheldon said to Donna this is an awful hour to be coming home and she said what are you talking about? I'm home since three. Now he dont know if she was home three or not.

JIM LYTHGOE

Leander Dollymont says well how am I going to know this stuff. It's kind of obvious how he knew, it's on news reports. We have to

answer extremely serious allegations that have been made by Leander
Dollymont and by Ruth Vivian. In fact, it would be fair to say that
they are the two key witnesses about what Sheldon would have said
in one case, being Leander Dollymont, and what Sheldon did and
said for Ruth Vivian. Kim Parrott she's more or less talking about
what Donna may have told her or some other little tidbits, but that's
the case in effect. There's no evidence whatsoever from any of the
forensics. As a matter of fact, the evidence so far is that the forensics
were botched. We're in a situation where we have got to be able to deal
with these allegations, these are not collateral matters. Did witnesses
make up their minds as to guilt. We've had numerous witnesses from
the Crown stand up and for no valid reason say oh I was afraid of the
Trokes. You ask them were you threatened, no I wasnt threatened but
I was afraid of the Trokes. The image of the Trokes is out there like
a dark shadow hanging over this whole proceeding ready to jump on
anyone who is going to say anything that they dont particularly like.

LEANDER DOLLYMONT
AND SHELDON TROKE

Leander came forward to testify because what Sheldon Troke told him
was bothering him. It wasnt something that he wanted a part of. To
go around for the rest of his life knowing that there was a little girl
and a little boy out there who lost their mom, who was murdered and
somebody had confessed to him that they committed the murder.

Sheldon Troke: Look at me.

Jim Lythgoe: Sheldon.

Sheldon Troke: That wasnt said.

Richard Adams: Mr Troke, any more outbursts and you will be
removed.

Robert Ash: Mr Dollymont, youre not going to be intimidated in this court, all right?

Jim Lythgoe: He's not trying to intimidate him.

Robert Ash: Did you ever see that type of anger before?

Leander: Yes I did.

Sheldon Troke: It's hurt.

Robert Ash: Mr Dollymont you dont have to stare at him, if he stares at you, just ignore him, all right?

Okay Mr Ash.

SHELDON TROKE

He says to Robert Ash that he cannot go around and have it on his conscience about two youngsters. Them youngsters are the farthest thing from his mind. The things that he got up here and said were not said. He's trying to use two youngsters to save hisself from going to jail. The first thing he asked was that he'd get a year. What do you do out of a year in a federal institution? Two months. He was out on parole for fraud. Two years, they go federal. While he's out on parole he gets picked up again. What's he looking at this time? Three, five years. So he turns around: I got these stories.

They were on the same range for five weeks. You got a range there that's thirty foot wide, seventy feet long. They got cells going down both sides and at the bottom of the back of the wall you got three cells. A TV in the middle of the floor. You got sixteen cells. Sometimes there's inmates has their doors open and their radios going. There could be three people in one cell talking. Two in another cell talking. There could be five in another cell talking. Two out watching TV, three out in the kitchen.

Leander Dollymont wrote him. He sent two cards and a letter. Now

Leander Dollymont goes around in the pen and he's very feminine. All the inmates see this. They dont pay no attention to that. Theyre not biased, at least Sheldon's not anyway. The guy's a homosexual, he sent letters. It means nothing to Sheldon what he wrote.

DONALD SAUNDERS

Sometimes mail is dropped off at the gate or at the Administration building and it's sent down by the Guard Room to the inmates and it do not go to the correspondence office to be searched. Sometimes staff reads it and passes it on themselves. It's a practice to remove all stamps that come into the penitentiary. Sometimes liquid hashish is underneath the stamp and it's just a precaution they take. They destroy the stamps.

Mail that's accepted at the gate after hours will be brought to the Guard Room. This is done to help out an inmate—he knows his mail is after being dropped off at the gate and he might say look Mother dropped me off a letter, can you get it for me.

The two letters that you have there they should have been recorded but they werent.

Towels on the doors are not supposed to be there but sometimes they do be there. It's up to the staff members to take them down. The cell doors are just ordinary doors with a little opening, ten by ten, for Corrections Officer to see in through. And sometimes, whether it's going to the bathroom or just an inmate wants to be just left alone, a towel will be passed over the glass. They could have a little cardboard sign put in the window, just to block out the view.

If a guard comes onto the unit that message is spread around so all of the inmates know a guard is in their area.

If an inmate got a letter that was smuggled it would make sense that you'd tear off the stamp so that anybody casually seeing it will assume it had gone through the proper system. All mail received coming in and out of the penitentiary is supposed to be stamped as Censored.

This havent been done. It is supposed to be done. A few years ago inmates complained, they'd be sending their mother a card in the Mercy Home, and all of a sudden they got a card in for their mother with a big stamp on it Censored H.M. Penitentiary. So that was stopped, we didnt censor cards going out. From then on it seems like it has fallen off that these letters are not censored. I've checked with the man in Admissions and he is not stamping them as he is supposed to.

That's mail going out. And coming in, both of them are supposed to be censored. That if he went down to the unit as a warden and seen that letter in anyone's cell, without this mark, Censored, then it got in without the right way.

Two staff members are supposed to open the mail in case there's any money, you have proof that two guys read it. That's placed in the inmate's fund and he is given a form of how much money was in his letter.

SHELDON TROKE

Sheldon is in this courtroom, he's here and theyre saying that he's going to kidnap a cop. Sheldon's father comes in and they tries to ridicule him saying he's home and he's watching the news or watching the clock. Can you blame him? Every time his children goes out, theyre in this courtroom. Theyre going to kidnap cops. That shows that your cops lie. They get caught right at the quarter line. Sheldon done everything in his power to help these police officers and they turn around and do nothing but accuse him. Not once did Sheldon say to them, you can't have this or you can't have that. It's all he says, you dont need a warrant. Whatever you wants, you can have it. They phones him up one night and asks him to go with them and do something, he does it. He passes everything with flying colours. He's fucking crucified. Excuse the language. Is there anything else you want him to do? You can sit there. You can twist everything around. No matter what you do, Sheldon Troke still did not kill Donna Whalen.

Leander is an out-and-out liar. How could Sheldon confess to him that he killed Donna when he didnt kill Donna? Sheldon asked his lawyer Jim Lythgoe to launch a complaint and that complaint was drawn up and it was brought down to him to sign and Sheldon read it before he signed it. He knew what was coming on TV. The night it was supposed to come on TV, it did not because it was handed in too late. It come on the following night after.

Sheldon was upset when Hedderson was on the news. They put a car on the news then five days later they say Paul Troke owns the car and this is Sheldon's brother. Then he gets on TV saying, yes we're after Sheldon. We're going after Sheldon. They gives a statement from Ruth Vivian. Nine days later, she gives another one. The next day they comes and charges him.

If it's a hundred inmates there, a hundred of them put towels over their door. There's no place down there to hang a towel. You come out of the shower and you got a soaken wet towel, where do you hang it? You hang it over your door. It doesnt matter if there's anything up to the window or not. You still knock on someone's door. This guy, Dolly, he's out with the RCMP he's giving them a story of a bank robbery and then a murder. They hands him over to the constabulary and one of them says come on Leander, Sheldon wouldnt say these things to you. Oh he would, I'm his lover.

ROBERT ASH

When youre asking yourself the question in terms of who killed
Donna Whalen, perhaps one way to think about it is who else other
than the accused had a reason or a motive to kill her? The evidence
indicates that there is no such person, that person does not exist. The
evidence points to the accused, and not to some strange blond who
went to Donna's apartment out of the blue. The police were unable
to find any evidence of anyone else threatening Donna other than the
accused.

JIM LYTHGOE

This is unfair. This suggests an obligation on the accused to identify
some other perpetrator, contrary to the presumption of innocence.
You can accept this evidence, or you can accept this conspiracy theory.
Throughout this so-called investigation, Sheldon Troke cooperated
with the police fully and he didnt have to. He did a DNA test and
a polygraph test. He was even willing to submit to hypnosis. Why?
Because he did not murder Donna Whalen. The Crown's chief
witnesses are Leander Dollymont and Ruth Vivian. If you look closely
at some of the things they told the police, it was just not so. Even after
Leander failed the polygraph test, Inspector Hedderson said that he
would be a good witness. There was but one significant thing that
Leander Dollymont said: did he guess it or was it a rumour? That was
whether the body was moved. Leander said that wherever he went, this
was the main topic concerning Sheldon Troke.

　　Mabel Edicott said that Paul Troke looked similar to the person
who knocked at her door that early morning. Mabel Edicott viewed
a photo album. It had five pictures of Paul Troke in it. She said that
the person who was at her door was not in this photo album. This was

done because Paul Troke is Sheldon's brother. She didnt identify Paul Troke.

Live probes and telephone interceptors were placed in the Vivian household. Their conversation was taped. Tom heard the door kick. They think the murder weapon was buried up in the graveyard. Pat said she was probably killed in the bedroom and brought out.

This was said two months before Leander Dollymont gave a statement to the police. This is very important evidence and the jury was not allowed to hear it. Yet the jury were told how important Leander's evidence was because Leander said Sheldon told him that the body was moved, and the evidence shows this.

Ruth Vivian was asked by Inspector Hedderson when was the last time she heard an argument coming from Donna's before Friday night. She said about two or three weeks ago. She didnt say Thursday night. Ruth Vivian heard the name Sheldon mentioned Thursday night and not Friday night. She said nothing of a loud argument on Thursday night because she has her days mixed up. Tom Vivian kept in close contact with Donna's family. What was said to the Whalens by Tom Vivian about what his mother said she heard? How much of this was repeated in the presence of Sharon, and what of Sharon's first statements? Sharon says she heard someone say be quiet, Sharon. The voice was unfamiliar. It was much later when Sharon says she heard the name Sheldon. Edie Guzzwell is asked if she told Sharon that she didnt have to worry because the person who murdered her mother was in jail. Same with Constable Louise Motty. She gave Sharon the reassurance she was obviously seeking. Sharon herself said that Constable Motty told her that Sheldon is the one that murdered her mother.

Ruth Vivian never mentioned seeing Sheldon until two months after the murder, right after the news release of Paul Troke and a car.

Ruth Vivian said she never watched the news, never spoke with anyone and never gossiped about this matter because it was not her topic. The wiretaps clearly show she watched the news, talked to people and gossiped about anyone and anything.

Gary Bemister said his clean-up theory was based on Leander Dollymont's statement, but the police had this clean-up theory on the news two months before Leander gave a statement to the police.

Sheldon has read the victim impact statements and he agrees with most of what they say. He feels for Donna's family more than they know. He only has a faint idea of what they must have gone through. He is also a victim of a savage crime, although people dont want to believe this and, in their minds, they have justice served. Sheldon has no answers to his questions and can only perceive this case one way and he goes to bed and he wakes up: that Donna went out with Sheldon Troke and because of this there is no need for an investigation. No need for justice for Donna.

DONNA WHALEN
LETTER TO SHELDON TROKE

I never wanted you like that, Sheldon. I didnt like the arguing and I didnt like the fighting and the violence and everything else, the way you used to get on with me. Jesus, I was frightened to death to say something to you and I didnt know if a table was going to tip over or what. Sheldon, I promise to love you in the good times and in bad with all I have to give and all I feel inside and the only way I know how, completely and forever. Wishing you were here, love, always.

SHELDON TROKE

Since Donna's death Sheldon's been left with disbelief and bewilderment. There is not a day that goes by that he doesnt think of Donna and her children. Who would have done something like this and why? Sheldon doesnt know of any enemies that Donna had. She was a wonderful person and a loving mother. There's no words to express his sorrow and loss. There is just contemplation. He loved Donna and he still loves her and he has wonderful memories of the things they shared and he will cherish them. One day he will find out who murdered Donna and until that day he will not rest and neither will Donna. Nobody won at this trial. We all lost. Society gained, society gained a murderer. Thank you, my lord.

TRISHA HICKMAN AND
PAUL TROKE WIRETAP

Trisha: I wants to confront you with something now and I wants you to tell me if you can remember it or not because I dont know if you were whacked out of it but I knows you were after having a few beer that night and the two of us were lying down in bed. We were talking and then we had sex and then we're lying down afterwards having a cigarette and you told me something that happened a while ago and it startled me. About you and Donna. See that's wild, you think I would have fucking known right there and then but still I never broke it off with you and if anyone would even I mean that's like something you'd fucking hear in a horror film right. You know, you'd be on the news or something right. Burnt boy.

Paul: All I'm saying is you should not freak out and go off your head if anything ever happened to me.

I will be.

Because the chances for me.

I will go off my head and I will be hurt and I will flip out if anything ever do happen to you and dont you ever doubt it. I'll go off my head. No matter what, I will fucking go nuts and it's bad enough being down there and knowing the charges that youre coming up on for robbery and knowing the time that you'd be spending away. That's all bad enough but if I ever found out that something happened to you, that'd be enough, that'd be enough for me. My heart is probably broke right now.

Paul: I can't change your feelings or nothing but what I'm trying to say is, I dont know. Some fucking wild boy. It dont even seem like reality to me any more. This seems like a big fucking bad dream.

Trisha: I know what you mean. I can relate to that. I'm not thinking on reality yet because like when I'm talking to you and youre down there and I can see you and write you letters and I got your pictures and your cards, every night before I goes to bed. It just seems like it'll be another few months. That's all it seems right now but deep down I knows it's longer but when I'm thinking about it, it's like no way, there's something going to happen and youre not going to do the time. Is that fucked up?

No.

I dont know what to think. I dont know if that's fucked up or not.

V

EPILOGUE

Robert Ash, the Crown prosecutor, had this to say about the death of Donna Whalen: there are many ways to kill a person. In this case, it is difficult to find a word that adequately describes the manner in which Donna Whalen was murdered. One can use the word *brutal*, one can use the word *vicious*. But then you consider the way she was killed, she had a pair of underwear wrapped around her throat so tightly they did not loosen during the transfer of the body from the apartment to the morgue (Dr Abery was under the impression that they had been tied there—it was only when he cut the underwear off that he realized they were twisted into place). There were a number of minor wounds—a series of pricks in the area of the chest. Sadistic is an accurate description of these wounds. The last few moments of Donna Whalen's life must have been horrific for her, as she was stabbed repeatedly in her own house, knowing her children are in the house and are open to danger as well.

The jury returned a verdict of guilty of second-degree murder.

Before sentencing, the judge heard evidence of an incident, four years before the murder, which was inadmissible for this trial. Sheldon Troke was making fun of a man, saying that his brother Paul Troke had gone out with the man's girlfriend. This man, lying on a loveseat, laughed back at Sheldon. That laugh appears to have been too much for Sheldon Troke to take. In his frustration and anger—

no doubt liquor was a factor—he went to the kitchen, got a knife and returned to the living room. Sheldon Troke recalls stabbing the man once in the thigh, but the evidence shows there to be two stabs to the side of the chest and stabs to the thigh and the leg. There's no doubt a knife was used, and used in a vigorous manner. The stabbing with the knife was excessive and out of all proportion to the events of that night. It was irrational and atrocious behaviour. That the man survived is pure luck.

Other factors that weighed into Judge Adams's sentencing included Sheldon Troke's intimidation of a key witness, Ruth Vivian, his lack of remorse and his attempt to concoct a false alibi. There was a history of violence towards the victim—this was not an isolated incident. The numerous wounds, any of which could have killed Donna Whalen, suggested an abnormal possessiveness—this was not the type of murder where someone is stabbed in the chest once and then the attacker stops. This was an overkill, a refusal to accept that Donna Whalen wanted to break up with him. There was an attempt to cover up the murder. Sheldon took steps to have his brother Paul come to the house and help move the body from the kitchen to the living room—this is not someone so intoxicated he does not know what he's doing. There's an awareness here of his circumstances. The body of the deceased was left in the living room with the knowledge that Sharon Whalen would find her mother dead in a pool of blood the next morning, a horrific scene for a young child.

Jim Lythgoe, for the defence, responded by discussing the prior stabbing. There was a willing and enthusiastic group looking for entertainment and action that night. A good supply of hash, lots of beer, bottles of vodka and whiskey, music and dancing. The victim's conduct and behaviour that night was offensive, annoying to almost everyone. He pestered the women and irritated the men. He was very drunk. He propositioned certain women. He did his best to taunt and intimidate the men—he challenged them to arm wrestles. He bragged about his strength. He made himself obnoxious and, to put it mildly, was a real pain. Sheldon's action appears to have been sudden, but he had gotten into the hard liquor and was quite drunk. If you compare these incidents, Sheldon Troke was not into drugs or alcohol on the night of Donna Whalen's murder. While the police decided to hold him until well into the afternoon before they attempted to get any blood samples, there was no indication that he was impaired. So, it's a different situation.

In terms of prior assault, Sheldon Troke, on the one occasion that he admitted to striking Donna Whalen, reported it to his parole officer, knowing he would be arrested. He turned himself in and spent a number of months in jail. Then he went to anger management programs.

With regards to remorse, Lythgoe said, Sheldon Troke has deep remorse for the family, but he staunchly maintains his innocence. That will never change.

The Crown suggested he intimidated Ruth Vivian. But Sheldon Troke advised her to tell what she knew to the police. All other witnesses who had dealings with Sheldon Troke said that he was polite and courteous and asked them to cooperate with the police. It was unfortunate that Ruth Vivian took Sheldon's tone to be threatening when he meant to be encouraging.

The false alibi as an aggravating factor. It wasn't false, it was the truth—Sheldon Troke spent that night at his mother's house.

Sheldon did not dispute what has been said with regards to this being a vicious, senseless killing. Sheldon was sorry for this, Jim Lythgoe concluded, but he was not the one who did it.

With all this in mind, and having listened to over five months of testimony, Judge Richard Adams sentenced Sheldon Troke to life imprisonment with no eligibility for parole for fourteen years.

Sheldon Troke was an obvious "person of interest" for the police to question after the death of Donna Whalen. He was on parole for this prior stabbing offence and had a lengthy criminal record. A few months before the murder, he'd been convicted of assaulting Donna Whalen. The neighbours and Donna's daughter all testified to seeing or hearing arguments between Donna and Sheldon. Sheldon himself agreed that their arguments were so loud people on the street could hear them. He had once dug a knife into the kitchen table. He admitted to being at Donna's for the last few days of her life, and testified that she drove him home only a few hours before her murder. He was one of the last people to see her alive.

Very early in the investigation the police had drawn up a theory that Sheldon, after being dropped off at his parents' house by Donna, had found a means to return to Empire Avenue that night. He had waited for Donna to come home, knocked on her front door, been invited in and then murdered her. His brother Paul was called and he arrived at the back door, but knocked at the Edicott residence by mistake. Paul then cleaned up the murder scene and the brothers left soon after, ending up down at Cathy Furneaux's apartment.

However, the evidence compiled was not fitting this picture. For example, both Keith Edicott and Tom Vivian heard the noise of the coffee table tipping over soon after Paul Troke knocked on the Edicotts' back door. This was close to three oclock in the morning. This noise, which woke Sharon up, failed to coincide with the time when Ruth Vivian heard Donna screaming out "No Sheldon stop it," which was roughly one a.m. No one, besides Ruth Vivian, heard Donna call out at that time of the night. Donna did yell out "No Sheldon stop it" the evening before (it was recorded on the audiotape hidden in her purse). Once these inconsistencies in the evidence became apparent, the police should have revisited their premise to see if it was flawed, to see if in fact Ruth Vivian might be confusing events from the two nights. No one on the police team was thinking of alternative scenarios. Instead they spent a lot of time forcing the contradictory evidence to fit, distorting it by reinterviewing witnesses and suggesting they change their story, or ignoring the evidence altogether.

The police believed that Sheldon's parents knew their son left their residence that Friday night and were deliberately providing him with an alibi. They were arrested and charged with obstruction of justice. While Bertha and Clayton Troke were in police custody, a surveillance device was planted in their home. There was much publicity over the false alibi charge, which cast a shadow over Sheldon Troke's defence. Even though the charges against his parents were eventually stayed, members of the jury would know that they had been arrested for lying about Sheldon's whereabouts.

The police used wiretaps on other key witnesses, and what these wiretaps reveal is that neighbours and friends were talking to each other, following media reports and generally reframing their evidence to the wishes of police. In one case, Tom Vivian, the son of Ruth and Pat Vivian, was arrested as a possible suspect and then, immediately after that, his parents were once again interviewed to see if they wished to add any further details to their stories. Of course they changed their stories. Ruth Vivian quickly assured officers that, after bingo, she had seen Sheldon Troke in and around Donna Whalen's residence. That she had bumped into him and "every drop of blood in her veins froze." Her husband, Pat Vivian, had described, early on, a car that had been parked outside Empire Avenue the night of the murder. Months later, he was watching the local television news and saw a car the police had impounded and was convinced this was the car he'd seen that night. The car was completely different from the one he'd originally described.

There were many attempts by police to gently coerce witnesses into making statements that fit the police theory of the murder. Ches Hedderson's bullying of Sharon Whalen, suggesting she did not do enough to halt her mother's killer, is a chilling indictment of the inspector's methods. Sharon was removed from the custody of her maternal grandparents because the police were concerned that Agnes Whalen, who early on asserted Sheldon Troke's innocence, might convince Sharon that Sheldon did not kill her mother. This removal and placement of a nine-year-old child into protective custody, far from the loving care of relatives, only served to punish Sharon and make her feel she wasn't giving the police what they desired. The fact that her testimony remained largely unchanged is remarkable. The ambulance driver, Jim Pike, said that at the scene that morning, Sharon Whalen said she heard her mother calling out "No Sharon no" sometime during the night. She sat up and never heard anything else, thought she dreamed it, and went back to sleep. It was police investigator Louise Motty who suggested to her that what she heard that night was not "No Sharon no" but "No Sheldon no." Exhausted and confused, Sharon agreed with their leading questions. And yet, later on, when she was on the courtroom stand, she still had enough doubt to say she wasn't sure what she heard, or who said it, only it was a man's voice, a man she wasn't familiar with. That this voice was low and quiet, unlike Sheldon's loud and argumentative voice, did not seem to matter to the police. Louis Motty inadvertently reinforced in Sharon the notion that Sheldon was the murderer by reassuring her that her mother's killer could not hurt her because he was in jail. Sharon knew that Sheldon was in police custody.

Finally, the Crown called a jailhouse informant to testify. Leander Dollymont had an extensive record of fraud convictions and, when he initially approached the police with his evidence, failed a polygraph test. Despite this, he was a crucial Crown witness and his story became the Crown's theory even though police investigators found no evidence to support it. It has been said that jailhouse informants rush to testify like vultures to rotting flesh. They constitute the most deceitful and deceptive group of witnesses known to frequent the courts. The more notorious the case, the greater the number of prospective informants. They are smooth and convincing liars.

Leander Dollymont was interviewed a second time and allowed to testify. Leander said the murder took place in the kitchen, that the clothes Sheldon wore were buried in the graveyard, that Donna Whalen returned home at midnight with another man who left before the murder occurred, that Donna Whalen was wearing her clothes at the time of the murder, that Sheldon Troke went to his sister's house to clean up after the murder, that Paul Troke was driving a car he bought from Billy Bennett, that Sheldon used taxicabs when travelling to and from Donna Whalen's residence, that he shot up three times after being upset with Donna, and that he stabbed Jacob Parrott in a fight over Donna a few weeks prior to the murder. All of this testimony was found, in the end, to be false and, when asked about it, Leander said that he of course did not witness any of these events, but was told about them by Sheldon Troke. Why Sheldon Troke would confess to murdering Donna Whalen but then give Leander Dollymont false information about *how* the murder was conducted was never questioned. Leander Dollymont later recanted his testimony, saying the police harassed him into making a false statement. He said there's a man in jail doing life that he doesnt know if he's guilty. Leander doesnt think he is guilty. He then confessed to making up the story of Sheldon Troke's confession, and suggested the police not only knew about it, they forced him to say it. Sheldon Troke, hearing that Leander had recanted, said this: The police done no investigation. They said Troke's got a record, he's got a past, and he's violent, he done it. Leander Dollymont was sentenced to five years in prison in connection with his false testimony in the Troke case.

Gary Bemister said, after the trial, that Ches Hedderson did not always take notes and he did not share information readily. Throughout the investigation Inspector Hedderson often visited witnesses by himself. Ches Hedderson is a big man. His presence can be intimidating. What evidence there is of his manner suggests he was aggressive and confrontational. His method of coordinating the investigation was telling his team what to do and when he wanted it done.

The police visited the Vivian residence dozens of times. Ruth Vivian was interviewed on the promise that she would not have to take the stand. She gave six written statements to the police. Most of these statements were inconsistent or revealed new details she had never mentioned previously. Her testimony became so unreliable that a doctor agreed she was delusional, that she believed angels were visiting her. Still, her testimony stood, and the fact that she bumped into Sheldon Troke around eleven p.m. Friday night helped the Crown's case that he returned to Donna Whalen's after being dropped off at his parents' home.

There was an assumption by the police that witnesses were afraid to come forward with evidence—the incident of the hostage scenario at the courthouse is almost farcical but illustrates the paranoia surrounding the Troke family at the time. The phone calls Clifford Whalen received at his hotel, while disregarded by the judge, were still heard by the jury and made them wonder about the extent of the

Troke clan's power to intimidate. This was the atmosphere in which Sheldon Troke was tried. The police felt they needed to put pressure on witnesses to get them to reveal what they knew. There was also a belief that witnesses needed time to remember all of the details, rather than an understanding that what someone says soon after an incident is usually the most reliable version of events. Subsequent interviews only confuse or tamper with a witness's testimony, as people learn things in the news, talk to each other and reshape their memories to fit into the picture they think authorities want to hear. The pattern of reinterviewing key witnesses was established very early in this investigation. Ches Hedderson drove his officers to collect evidence that fit the theory in place. No one on the case was involved in what is called contrarian thinking.

Sheldon Troke knew how the police operated and had never, in the past, volunteered information while being questioned by the police. He was wily and street-smart and understood that if you were charged with a criminal activity, you should not speak to police without a lawyer present. Instead, this time he helped the police throughout their investigation, a reversal in behaviour, which should have been considered curious if he was in fact the culprit.

The forensic team failed to notice a cigarette butt wrapped in a doily under the coffee table. When the doily was removed from an exhibit bag at Sheldon Troke's trial, the butt fell out. There was a red stain on the cigarette, which the court assumed was lipstick belonging to Donna Whalen. Years later, a society for the wrongly convicted had the cigarette tested at Ontario's Centre of Forensic Sciences. The red stain was melted carpet from Donna Whalen's living room, and the DNA on the cigarette belonged not to Sheldon Troke but to his brother, Paul. The doily was under the coffee table, and so Paul Troke had to have been there before it was tipped over. The tipping of the table occurred immediately before the murder (Sharon woke up and heard the table knocked over and her mother calling out her name).

On the day of this announcement, Paul Troke was found dead in his home of a drug overdose. He had been trying to turn his life around after his release from prison the year before, following a seven-year term for armed robbery. After Paul's death, Cathy Furneaux came forward with information about the night of the murder. Cathy said she found out Paul had left her home after she went to bed and that knives were missing from her home. Also that night Paul had washed his own clothes for the first time ever and a taxi driver delivered a bottle of rum to Paul very early that Saturday morning. Inspector Ches Hedderson also said he learned that Paul Troke and Donna Whalen might have been sexually involved, and that Donna had information that implicated Paul Troke in the bank robbery.

From the outset, though, the police did not ever consider that Paul Troke acted independently and murdered Donna Whalen with no assistance from his brother Sheldon. Paul Troke had a criminal record as extensive as Sheldon's and, as it turned out, was better acquainted with Donna Whalen than he'd let on. The police understood that Paul Troke had been the person who knocked on Mabel Edicott's door late that night, but their scenario had him arriving merely to help Sheldon clean up. Forensic evidence suggests that there was, in fact, no clean-up.

Sheldon Troke's lawyer, Jim Lythgoe, spent considerable time trying to reject the idea that Paul Troke was at the scene at all. If the defence had taken a different tack and agreed that it was Paul who knocked on the Edicotts' back door, and that perhaps Paul was the one who killed Donna, then it may have been a scenario the jury could agree with. It is unknown whether Sheldon Troke had instructed his attorney not to develop this approach.

Those who knew Paul Troke said he acted like he was being eaten away by guilt after the murder. In his investigation Inspector Hedderson found no new evidence that pointed to Sheldon Troke, but key evidence against Sheldon Troke at trial was found to be unreliable, including Ruth Vivian's testimony, which destroyed his alibi. Sheldon Troke and Jim Lythgoe did not help matters by suggesting that many witnesses were lying, including Ruth Vivian. The fact is, Ruth had problems with her memory, and while what she saw and heard was probably accurate, the dates on which she experienced these events were often confused. She did hear Sheldon Troke late at night up at Donna's, but this was on the Thursday night after he visited the Chinese takeout, not the Friday night of the murder. She did hear pumps, but that too was on the Thursday night when Donna went to answer the door for Sheldon. The police found sneakers at the top of the stairs, the last thing Donna wore Friday night, and Sheldon confirmed that they both wore sneakers that night. Gary Bemister's response was that it didnt matter what Donna wore, as only the toe of the shoe hits the stairs. So even though Ruth Vivian heard pumps, the police were fine with finding the sneakers. Sheldon Troke and Jim Lythgoe also took exception to police testimony, to Pat Vivian's description of the car and to Sharon Whalen's own testimony. Sheldon Troke said that Sharon wasn't intentionally lying about what she heard and saw, but that the police were suggesting a lot to her, and youngsters are very impressionable. The Crown prosecutor took this to mean that Sheldon Troke was indeed saying Sharon was lying in her testimony, a fact that the jury found hard to believe.

Six years after Sheldon Troke's conviction, following an application to admit fresh evidence, the Newfoundland Court of Appeal overturned his conviction and ordered a new trial. Two police investigations into the murder concluded that Paul Troke, if alive, would have been charged with the murder of Donna Whalen and that there exists no credible evidence upon which to charge Sheldon Troke. The Crown entered a stay of proceedings and, a year later, this stay expired. No further charges were laid against anyone in the death of Donna Whalen and, nine years after her death, Sheldon Troke commenced civil proceedings against the provincial government alleging police negligence and malicious prosecution.

The public housing unit Donna Whalen was living in has since been torn down, though several other duplexes still exist alongside hers on Empire Avenue. If you walk up from St John's harbour you will take the stairs beside the courthouse where Sheldon Troke was tried and convicted. You will pass Cathy Furneaux's row house where Paul Troke lived. If you keep walking you will cross Merrymeeting Road. From here to your left is the area of Buckmaster Circle and below you, to the north, the field where Donna Whalen lived. Beyond this field are the university and the provincial House of Assembly where the lawyers and judge and police officers received their education and their instruction. To the east is Quidi Vidi pond and Her Majesty's Penitentiary and the wide open sea. The city has prospered since the murder of Donna Whalen. Sheldon Troke is still living here, cycling in and out of prison on misdemeanour charges. While in prison, Sheldon got addicted to a painkiller for cancer patients. He was also wired into morphine. Oxycontins, he's said, do nothing for him—that's how high the drug was he was doing in jail. His lawyer, Jim Lythgoe, still represents him. He says the drugs offered Sheldon a crutch. That Sheldon was ashamed that people thought he was Donna's killer. He was insecure and drugs are a way to escape the world. There are times Sheldon has asked the court to put him in jail to get him off his drug problem.

The court and the government recently awarded Sheldon Troke two million dollars and an apology for the wrongful murder conviction.

Some members of Sheldon's family have thought all along that Paul Troke was involved in Donna's death. There was a sense that Paul was trying to shift the blame. And the whole process tore the Troke family apart. It came out that Sheldon's older brother, Raymond—now deceased—was a police informant. Paul Troke, in fact, may have killed Raymond, and he certainly killed himself upon hearing about the DNA evidence pinning him to the Donna Whalen crime scene. Iris Troke doesnt speak to her mother or father any more, there was a stabbing incident between Iris and her father, Clayton, and there was an arrest after several members of the family accosted each other after a radio open-line show discussed who might be to blame for the deaths of Donna Whalen, Raymond Troke and Paul Troke.

These days people dont think Sheldon will make it to next week. He says that's enough for him right there to prove them all wrong. He's far from killing himself, but he does have to keep a check on it. Years ago he could go on a tear for three days and wake up with no money and be forced to sober up. But now, with the settlement from the government, there's no limit to his excess. He has to be careful. Some days are better than others. But don't get him wrong—he's not walking around whacked out of it all the time. Since being released, he has talked about his brother's involvement in Donna Whalen's death. He has visited Paul Troke's grave. He finds it hard to forgive the brother he had loyally defended. He wonders if he's in hell.

APPENDIX

Donna Whalen was the murder victim. She had two children, Sharon and Cory. Donna's mother and father were Agnes and Aubrey Whalen. Her aunt is Edie Guzzwell. Her brother is Clifford Whalen.

Sheldon Troke, the murder suspect, has two brothers, Paul and Raymond, and a sister, Iris. His mother and father are Bertha and Clayton.

NEIGHBOURS

Donna Whalen's downstairs neighbours were the Vivians: Ruth, Pat and their son, Tom. Next door were the Edicotts: Mabel and her son, Keith.

FRIENDS

Cathy Furneaux went out with Raymond Troke. She has a son, Robert Furneaux. Trisha Hickman was Paul Troke's girlfriend. Kim Parrott was Donna's best friend. Kim's ex-husband was Jacob Parrott. They have a son, Nicholas. Kim's boyfriend was Rod Tessier. Eugene Driscoll, Joey Yetman and Vicki Pinhorn were friends of Sheldon's. Albert Canning was a former boyfriend of Donna's.

POLICE AND DOCTORS

Inspector Ches Hedderson and Constables Gary Bemister, Charles Stamp and Louise Motty investigated this murder. Percy Morgan was the sketch artist. Jim Pike drove the ambulance. The doctors who testified were forensic pathologist Philip Abery, family doctors Norman Seviour and Hubert Galgay, and psychiatrist Howard Strong.

LEGAL

Jim Lythgoe was Sheldon Troke's defence counsel. The Crown prosecutor was Robert Ash. The Supreme Court judge was Richard Adams.

OTHERS

Douglas Saunders, director of Her Majesty's Penitentiary

Leander Dollymont, police informant

John Noftall, witness for the defence

Tang Man, Chinese takeout operator

Michael Porter, taxi driver

Scott Locke, bouncer at the Sundance Saloon

ACKNOWLEDGMENTS

This novel is based on court transcripts from a murder trial in St John's, Newfoundland, transcripts that are in the public domain. I've changed the names and conflated some characters and turned most of the testimony into a third-person narrative. The epilogue is a reworking of selected statements made by the Right Honourable Antonio Lamer in his public inquiry into how the criminal justice system dealt with three discredited murder convictions in Newfoundland. Some of the prepared summations made at sentencing by the defence counsel, Crown prosecutor and the judge have also been paraphrased. The quote concerning the reliability of jailhouse informants is from Justice Peter Cory's *Sophonow Inquiry Report*, which dealt with the wrongful conviction of Thomas Sophonow. I've mixed in several newspaper reports updating Sheldon Troke's situation, as well as a few personal comments about the location of Donna Whalen's home on Empire Avenue.

I must thank my editor, Nicole Winstanley, and my readers, Larry Mathews, Lisa Moore, Lynn Moore, Anne McDermid and Christine Pountney, for helping me shape this story.